Larry,

Thanks a lot for taking time for me, and helping me with my efforts to sell my books.

After all this time, I've had a lot of fun talking to some of the people in the Chicago Branch of Keane. When looking back, I realized what a tremendous collection of all-star players that through happenstance found themselves together. I'm sure you'd agree with me when I say that that Branch without corporate interference could have become, by far, the best in the company!

I was happy to hear you describe some of your accomplishments, and not in the least bit surprise at the success you've achieved.

Best of success during the rest of your retirement,

Praise for John Santone

"John is one of my true heroes...an exceptional person...a remarkable philosopher. In reading his story, I'm struck by the common intersections in our two lives. So many of the truths he learned are things that I also experienced although would not have been so eloquent or insightful in their learning or telling. While we grew up literally worlds apart, the basic lessons remain similar. Hearing John relate those truths has brought them back to me as once again fresh. He is a unique individual with a real talent for storytelling. The ability to tell a story well is one of the most ancient of human traditions, and those who could do it well were always honored and respected for their talents and the contributions they made to the tribe. It was the way we learned in the era before the written word. To include John in that number is no mistake. He is a wise man with a story to tell."
—Walter R. Brewer, M.D.

"I am so impressed by John's creation...He is an amazing person who has led an exceptional life. Documenting that life is just the logical next step, and many will learn about living a full, rich life from his labors."
—Tom Ackerman, Owner, Context Financial, Lexington, Kentucky

"The first chapters of this compelling book take a young boy through the growing pains of adolescence into adulthood in a witty, delightful, and insightful manner. John Santone was the boy who grew to success in the business world by using street smarts and always trusting the courage or his own instincts and convictions. The story is ageless, just as relevant to everyone now as it was to those of us who had the opportunity to have met John on his journey."
—Jan Donovan, Corporate IT Director, Boulder, Colorado

Journey of NORTH DENVER JOHNNIE

Using Street Smarts to Add Value to Your Career

JOHN SANTONE

Copyright © 2017 John D. Santone
All rights reserved.

No part of this book may be reproduced in any manner without the written consent of the publisher except for brief excerpts in critical reviews or articles.

ISBN: 978-1-61244-590-8
Library of Congress Control Number: 2017915325

Printed in the United States of America

Halo Publishing International
1100 NW Loop 410
Suite 700 - 176
San Antonio, Texas 78213
Toll Free 1-877-705-9647
www.halopublishing.com
E-mail: contact@halopublishing.com

I dedicate my book to Jill Tisdale Deem. She worked for me on the Fiberglass Project in 1978, and she worked for me again in 1982, which will be discussed in Part 2 of *Journey of North Denver Johnnie*. As I predicted in this book, Jill had incredible potential and in later years became a valuable key employee at Johns Manville, AMS Consulting, Petro Lewis, and the National Renewable Energy Laboratory (NREL), moving up the ranks to become the Chief Information Officer. She held this position for more than nineteen years and retired in 2015.

In 2016, when I won a major poker championship, I sent her a picture of me with the trophy. I also wrote a short story about why I was so proud of my accomplishment. Jill congratulated me and complimented me on the story. She told me I should write a book! At that point in time, I had produced a little less than fifty percent of *Journey*, but Jill had no idea that I'd started writing it.

Next, I sent her and another dear friend, Jan Donovan, about half of my incomplete manuscript. In less than three days, I received super reviews from both of them. I honestly don't think I would have ever finished my manuscript without their encouragement. Even though both of these outstanding women were friends, the comments they provided made me believe they were sincere in their critiques.

Jill's efforts to support me went well beyond encouragement. She invited me to come to Colorado to stay with her and her husband, Scott, a published author, at their home in Conifer. This visit was the major reason I was able to continue writing; I was able to reconnect with my friends in North Denver and make a return visit to the pool hall that gave me my nickname and the street smarts I've used throughout my entire life in both business and my personal life.

Leading up to my stay at Jill's home, she and I were able to reconnect at a level we enjoyed when we worked together long ago. She told me that my visit to her home was her way of saying thank you for being a good boss and great mentor. Jill stated that I was one of the reasons she felt her own career was so successful, reaching the highest levels in the information technology (IT) profession.

In her own words, Jill said, "John had an uncanny way of making me believe I could achieve anything. His stretch assignments made me take a hard look in the mirror each day knowing there was no room for self-doubt. While some people believe IT is IT, John taught me that to be successful, you need to embrace the mission of your company and truly understand it." Jill's words literally caused me to cry out of joy and happiness.

It is so easy for me to thank Jill for letting me continue to be in her life and honor with this dedication.

—John Santone

Contents

Prologue		15
Chapter 1:	North Denver Johnnie, or Johnnie Dane	19
Chapter 2:	Smarter or Dumber	25
Chapter 3:	Johnnie Dane Meets *Grease*	27
Chapter 4:	High School Memories: Sophomore Year *First Fight*	31
Chapter 5:	High School Memories: Sophomore Year *Survival, Girls & Cars*	39
Chapter 6:	High School Memories: Junior Year *Here's Johnnie*	44
Chapter 7:	High School Memories: Junior Year *Early Pool Hall Years*	50
Chapter 8:	High School Memories: Junior Year *Learning Italian*	57
Chapter 9:	High School Memories: Junior Year *Two Down, One to Go*	63
Chapter 10:	High School Memories: Senior Year *What Happens When You Become Obsolete?* *& Why Won't Things Stop Changing?*	82
Chapter 11:	High School Memories: Senior Year *Meet Doberman*	85
Chapter 12:	High School Memories: Senior Year *Izadore*	91

Chapter 13: High School Memories: Senior Year
Introduction to the Family Fun Center   95

Chapter 14: High School Doesn't Last Forever
Introduction to the Real World   101

Chapter 15: Navy Career Sinks   117

Chapter 16: Remember Faye?   128

Chapter 17: My Career Begins   133

Chapter 18: Colorado Sid and North Denver Johnnie   163

Chapter 19: Public Service Company of Colorado
Clerk   179

Chapter 20: Public Service Company of Colorado
Transmission Engineering Department   204

Chapter 21: Public Service Company of Colorado
Information Systems Department   219

Chapter 22: Public Service Company of Colorado
Information Systems Department:
Junior Programmer Training Class   227

Chapter 23: Public Service Company of Colorado
In-House Training Class:
Section 1—Decision Logic Tables
Section 2—Computer Programming Design   234

Chapter 24: Public Service Company of Colorado
In-House Training Class:
Section 3—Assembler Language Programming
Section 4—CICS Telecommunications Peaches   238

Chapter 25: Public Service Company of Colorado
In-House Training Class:
Sections 5—7 and Beyond   245

Chapter 26: Goodbye to Public Service
Company of Colorado 260

Chapter 27: The Big 3-0, a Key Life Event
for North Denver Johnnie 265

Chapter 28: Information Handling Service
IBM 370 VM1 270

Chapter 29: Information Handling Service
NDJ and Dale Carnegie 276

Chapter 30: Information Handling Service
IBM 370 VM1 Sys Gen 285

Chapter 31: Information Handling Service
Dale Carnegie Training 295

Chapter 32: Information Handling Service
Fred #1 out, Fred #2 in, NDJ on his way out 307

Chapter 33: Johns Manville Corporation
Welcome to the Big Leagues 317

Chapter 34: Johns Manville Corporation
NDJ Expands Leadership Skills 328

Chapter 35: Johns Manville Corporation
The Fiberglass Project 339

Chapter 36: Johns Manville Corporation
Go West Young Man 363

Epilogue 371

Appendix 1: North Denver Johnnie's Job Choices
and Motives for Leaving Old Job 377

Cast of Characters: (In order of appearance) 379

Acknowledgements 387

About the Author 389

JOURNEY OF NORTH DENVER JOHNNIE: PART 1

Using Street Smarts to Add Value to Your Career

Prologue

Journey of North Denver Johnnie is a self-help, motivational book intended to provide career management assistance for people in the workplace. In my book, I give suggestions for developing a plan to achieve your career goals, and I demonstrate why it is important to have a strategy to make them happen. My "street smarts" education has given me a somewhat unconventional, unorthodox point of view. Seeing things from a different perspective often results in an outside-the-box approach to solving problems or creating new products.

Did I really adapt the street smarts of this book to help me in my career? Yes. These true stories describe what I learned from those experiences. As you read example after example of street-smart logic, you may think about things differently. You may start wondering, "What do I need to do to win here?" That approach will lead you down a different path.

I began my career as an entry-level laborer in a foundry, and I advanced to an executive manager in spite of the enormous obstacles I faced. When I first entered the workforce, my one and only strategy was to work as hard as

I could to meet or exceed my boss's expectations. That's it. No more to say about it. Most people would say that at that point, as a blue-collar factory worker I didn't actually have a career to manage. But that's not the way I saw it.

This book illustrates that the bar is much, much higher than one might expect. Many employees become discouraged and sabotage themselves by adopting a poor attitude about their company or management, gossiping about coworkers, absenteeism, or a lack of punctuality. Certainly we all have seen people like this, and if you are honest with yourself, you may actually be just this type of employee. But I seriously doubt it. Why? Because you are reading this book. There is an outside chance that someone who loves you gave you this book, someone who remembers you when you were at your best—a happy and energized go-getter. That person loves you a lot.

There are people that have acquired a great deal of debt, having taken out loans to pay for college or whatnot. And then, voilà! You landed your first good job. Congratulations! Applying knowledge is obvious, but you also need a strategy to get ahead. Commit to meeting or exceeding your boss's expectations. Put in the effort to make sure you understand what their expectations are, and find out what they believe are the most important things to do to exceed them.

Using this strategy, most employees assume that if there is an end-date associated with the deliverable, then get it done sooner. They think that getting something done early is preferred and that they will undoubtedly exceed their boss's expectations, right? Perhaps, but maybe not. What if the person who is going to use the early-arriving deliverable is not available to use it because they are performing unrelated work? Look forward. Once your task is completed with precision—albeit early—please have your boss's expectation defined for you. In this way, you may become a more valuable member to the team. Communicating with your boss may even help them identify forward-looking goals just in the case things go smoothly in your project.

I am excited about my book and the possibility that it will represent me in a manner that—at its core—is based on a very strong, blue-collar work ethic that my father taught me. My dad was a housepainter and the foreman of his paint crew. He also had a talent for producing an exceptionally high-quality product, and because of this, was able to earn the respect of his workers. He was also a loyal company man who showed respect for his managers and appreciation for the work they found for him and the equipment they provided to do it. These precious traits that I inherited from my dad are the basis of my work ethic. They have helped me enormously, and I hope I have made my father proud.

Now I hope to assist my readers by empowering them to believe in themselves and achieve some of the best things that life has to offer—not only for themselves, but also for their families. I've been very fortunate. I have had some significant achievements. However, in the end, it is the respect I've earned from the people I have worked for, worked with, and my trusted customers that I value so much in my life.

Thank you for buying this book. I hope you enjoy it.

John Santone
a.k.a. North Denver Johnnie

Chapter 1

North Denver Johnnie, or Johnnie Dane

I really only had two choices: become Johnnie Dane or become North Denver Johnnie. Johnnie Dane was a wimp, and North Denver Johnnie was a tournament-level pool player/poker player and an executive for a large computer consulting company.

There are defining moments in everyone's life. For me, one of the most important was when I was thirteen years old in eighth grade at St. Catherine's parochial school. I walked up the stairs from the school cafeteria onto the playground. Waiting for me was Peter Schavinski. Peter was a German immigrant with a strong accent, thick glasses, and the awkwardness of a still-blossoming nerd.

Peter walked directly toward me. As he approached, I said, "Peter, what's up?" He did not answer, and when he blocked my progress, he punched me in the stomach as hard as he could. The punch was totally unexpected and knocked me to the ground. I had just eaten lunch, and I was really hurting from the impact of this surprise attack.

Peter started screaming at me. "Don't call me a Nazi! Don't call me a Nazi!" He told me he would knock me down if I got up. He was delirious.

I was the smallest boy in our class. I had attended St. Catherine's for eight years and was academically ranked number two overall, second only to Elizabeth Zarlingo, who was much smarter than me. But I was the best male student and on track to receive a scholarship to Regis High School for Boys, the top Catholic high school in Denver. Regis was a school that I couldn't afford to attend without the benefit of a scholarship.

I found myself sitting on the asphalt playground with Peter looming over my fellow classmates and me, waiting to see what would happen. Peter was four or five inches taller than me, and at that very moment, I felt that he was stronger, faster, meaner, and whatever other "er" you'd want to use. At the same time, I knew I could not remain seated on the asphalt my entire life…or until the bell rang. The longer I sat there, the more humiliating it became.

To add to the tale of the tape, I was a bigger nerd than Peter. My glasses were thicker. I had virtually no social skills, no friends, a cowlick that people stared at, buckteeth, and as I mentioned earlier, I was a midget. As grim as those traits sound, they were the building blocks of the person that would become North Denver Johnnie.

Seated on the ground, I knew I had to buy time to catch my breath, to think. I told Peter I hadn't called him a Nazi, but he did not believe me. I needed to do something because he wasn't going away. I told Peter that if he wanted to fight, we should go across the street to the park so the nuns wouldn't see us. He agreed. I got up and walked toward the park, which was about a half-block away. We crossed the playground, went up some stairs, walked to the crossing light, crossed Federal Boulevard, and walked forty more feet onto the grass.

I turned and raised my hands to defend myself. Peter walked toward me, and when he got close enough, he hit me in the mouth. Then I hit him in the face. Then he hit me in the face, and then I hit him in the face. Neither one of us knew how to fight. We didn't know how to block a punch or even think to dodge or duck to avoid being hit. It was brutal.

After Peter hit me three or four times, I wanted to quit. I wanted to start crying. The last time he hit me it jolted me to the point where tears and defeat were so close I knew I couldn't take much more. But it dawned on me in that very instant, a millisecond before I was done for, that it was my turn to hit him. Somehow, the logic that would serve North Denver Johnnie so well in the future told me that I shouldn't quit until after I hit him.

I hit him in the face, and he started to cry. At that very instant, the bell rang and it was time to get in line to return to our classroom. We walked back across Federal Boulevard and got in line to follow our nun into the school. Our nun was Mother Superior, which meant she was the boss of the other nuns. It was her first year at St. Catherine's. She was a tough, hard-looking, unhappy person who wanted to assert herself as a disciplinarian.

Sister Mary Magdalene noticed that Peter was crying. She went over to him and asked what happened. Peter explained that I called him a Nazi and that we had had a fight.

When we filed into our classroom and were seated, Sister Mary asked me to stand and face the class. She then lectured me about how cruel it was for me to call Peter a Nazi and that because he was new to our school, I should be ashamed of myself for ridiculing him in front of his classmates. Further, it was inexcusable for me to beat up on poor Peter. She was going to make sure Father Lemieux, the monsignor, was informed and that I should expect severe punishment.

I found the presumption of my guilt based totally on the fact that I had won the fight absolutely unacceptable; it was the straw that broke the camel's back. I had never talked back to a nun or priest for eight years, but that was going to change.

She told me to be seated. I said I would not be seated. I said that I had been one of the top students in the school for eight years. I had never done anything wrong and could not believe she would take the word of a person who had been here for less than two months. I told her I did not call Peter a Nazi and that other boys in the class lied to Peter and were responsible for intentionally creating this mess.

I told Sister Mary that she jumped to conclusions and should have asked me for my side of the story. I told her that I would never be able to forgive her for the way she handled this and that I was leaving the school and would never return. I walked to the coatrack, put on my jacket, and left St. Catherine's forever.

I walked three blocks down 43rd Street to our home. It was about 1:30 p.m., and my mother asked me if I was sick. I explained what happened. It was the only time I can remember when she did not assume I was lying or making excuses for something that was less than perfect. Somehow, she knew it all was true, including the part about me never going back.

I was enrolled in Skinner Junior High, a public school. Mother Superior, meanwhile, had managed to get to the truth. She quickly acknowledged her mistake and asked my mother if I would be willing to return to St. Catherine's. I said no. Recognizing that the Catholic school system had lost a pretty good student, they made an extraordinary offer. They would allow me to remain in public school to complete eighth grade and then enroll me at Regis High School on a scholarship for ninth grade. I said no.

I cannot fully understand why my parents didn't force me to accept the second offer, but they didn't. I cannot understand where I got the courage to say no twice, but I did.

Looking back, this was the first tiny glimmer of the person that some would know as North Denver Johnnie. It was the beginning of the end for Johnnie Dane, but Johnnie Dane wouldn't go quietly.

My birth certificate reads "Johnnie Dane Santone." Up until eighth grade I had been sheltered. Shielded. Protected from everything imaginable. I was later told that I didn't like the feel of grass. Even my clothes had to be handmade, mostly gabardine.

My mom thought I had cute legs so she dressed me in shorts virtually year-round. I have pictures of me at three or four years old wearing shorts outside with a snow shovel in the background and snow on the ground.

On one hand, I was pampered, protected, and kept from harm. On the other hand, my mother's expectations of me academically were extraordinarily high. I was subjected to harsh abuse and never had a carefree moment. It was impossible for me to have a balanced view of myself. I was a wimp who was able to take a lot of abuse. So did that mean I was sort of tough, that I had some strength? The verbal abuse was accompanied by corporal punishment because my mother was an addicted gambler, and as with most gamblers, lost most of the time.

Johnnie Dane had thirteen years of wimp training, representing a sizable lead over North Denver Johnnie, who was born in a park on Federal Boulevard.

NDJ Life Lesson:

Never give up, especially when it's your turn.

Chapter 2

Smarter or Dumber

Attending public school expanded my horizons in ways I could not imagine. My parochial school education placed me in the upper echelon of students at Skinner Junior High. I was ahead of most when it came to English, math, spelling, history, and geography, but the hundreds of hours spent on catechism and other religious teachings during the past eight years put me at a major disadvantage in many areas of learning.

I did not know how to play sports. Many of my fellow students at Skinner spoke more than one language, knew how to type, knew how to do woodworking, knew more about science, they could dance, and in general, had a more well-rounded education.

I had to decide whether I was smarter or dumber than most. At my old school, it was always important for me to be ranked highly in my class because I was chasing the Regis scholarship. In my new school, there wasn't a way for me to establish a similar goal, and there wasn't any easy way for me to compare myself to the other students. At St. Catherine's, I had a simple and direct method to get feedback that told me I was a top performer. Being accepted at Regis reflected that status and indirectly, at least in my mind, made me think my life was on the right path to success and safety.

After sizing things up for a few months, I decided I was dumber than most. I came to this conclusion because I believed it would motivate me to try to catch up and that ultimately it would help me fit in and be accepted by others. I realized later in life that I would always be a little—and sometimes a great deal—out of step with most people, but if you think about it, how could I become North Denver Johnnie and be like everyone else?

Deciding that I was dumber than most was nothing more than an unsophisticated way of saying that I would never underestimate my opponent. At this point in *Journey*, it is probably clear that NDJ is goal oriented and highly competitive. For the rest of his life, North Denver would always assume the person across the desk from him was smarter or that the companies he competed with for contracts were smarter. Having this philosophy made it impossible for him to be complacent. It would serve as the replacement motivator for his mother because it was based, at its core, on the fear of failure.

NDJ Life Lesson:

Never underestimate your boss, fellow employees, the competition, or your wife.

Chapter 3

Johnnie Dane Meets *Grease*

The big day finally arrived—my first day as an inmate of North High School. North High was an imposing building constructed circa 1930. It could accommodate about 2300 students but instead housed 2300 young adults, forty percent of which were a 3-to-1 favorite to end up in jail someday. Thanks to an undermanned law enforcement department, I suspected that only fifteen percent of my fellow classmates would get caught enough times to play out their first-time offender get-out-of-jail-free card, their probation card, and actually end up in the can.

The school was a little like being in Beirut for eight or so hours per day. There were gangs, both male and female, knives, razor blades, fights, and racial hatred. The two dominant gangs were the Pack Rats and La Raza. The Pack Rats were seventy-five percent Italian and twenty-five percent anything but Mexican. La Raza was never acknowledged as the name of the other gang by the Pack Rats. To the Pack Rats, the other gang was the Mexicans, which was one hundred percent Mexican.

The Pack Rats were like the guys in the movie *Grease*—pompadour haircuts, leather jackets, switchblade knives, hot rod cars, cigarettes rolled up in their sleeves, and all the mannerisms that go with the part. They carried their books a certain way, tucked up into the pit of their arm. They walked cool and stood cool as though they were hoping to get a scholarship of sorts into another organization whose name had five letters, but not Regis—the one that starts with an M and ends in an A with "afi" in the middle.

Unlike *Grease*, this was real. If you weren't a Pack Rat or a Mexican, you fell into one of several categories. You could be a Jock, a Nerd, a Student (which was the most dangerous category), a Regular (non-descript, not smart, not dumb, not cool, not a nerd), or an honorary pack rat (note the small "p" and small "r"). The last category was preferable because you didn't have to worry about the Pack Rats jumping you, and the Mexicans would think twice before messing with you. There was a price to pay for the Pack Rat sanction, however; you had to be willing to serve when called upon.

The Mexican gang was particularly troublesome because of the relationship they had with other gangs at West High School. Many of the North High Mexicans wanted to attend West High but were just outside the school district boundary. The Mexican gang's affiliation with gangs at West High was the primary reason that the honorary pack rat membership existed. It was a matter of numbers. There were at least two instances when the Mexicans at North High joined forces with their West High counterparts to face the Pack Rats. In each case, the honorary pack rats were expected to fall in line.

To become an honorary pack rat, you had to be chosen. I am not sure how it all happened, but from the first minute you walked into that school you were evaluated. My cousin Tommy was a senior when I was a sophomore. He was affiliated with the Jocks. He wasn't on any of the teams, but all his friends were, so I guess he was a small-j guy.

Tommy's mother was my mother's sister. Tommy attended public school from the start. He was nice looking, had quite a few friends, and had figured out how to survive at North High. My initial thought was to try to follow his example. I thought that if I could demonstrate that I had an affiliation with Tommy and his friends that I might be swept along in the small-j tide.

It didn't take long for me to figure out that trying to become a Jock groupie wouldn't be easy, especially since I barely knew anything about sports. Most of my cousin's friends were either basketball players or wrestlers. Tommy's best friend, John Marvin, was the starting center on the basketball team. If I had been able to dribble better, I believe I could have dribbled at full gallop between his legs and never have to duck. It was clear to me that I wasn't going to fit into their clique.

Now, at this point I know I must have at least thought about changing my mind about Sister Mary's offer to go to Regis. I honestly can't remember. But I do know I never discussed the possibility with my parents. Why? Most likely because there were things that I liked about North High in spite of the danger. And don't forget, I was undefeated after I kicked Peter Schavinski's ass.

NDJ Life Lesson:

Most of the things you are afraid of never actually happen, unless of course you let someone know you're afraid.

Chapter 4

High School Memories: Sophomore Year
First Fight

North High School 1962 to 1964 would have been the perfect place for Frankie Valli and the Four Seasons to go to school. I say that because the song "Walk Like a Man" comes to mind every time I think about walking to school to take my chances. Oh yeah, I almost forgot that I was supposed to get an education. My most vivid memories involve fights, cars, girls, the pool hall, and becoming an Italian.

The school was a tough place to be no matter which gang or group you fell into. For me, my affiliation began to take shape in the third or fourth week in my tenth-grade biology class. As fate would have it, I sat behind Don Wagner's girlfriend, Connie Thomas. Don was a Regular. He was about three inches taller than me and weighed about forty pounds more. To me, he looked pretty strong, and I wouldn't have gone out of my way to pick a fight with him. He struck me as the type of guy who wasn't used to having a girlfriend in the first place, and he was very jealous.

For some reason, Connie liked to talk to me, and she passed notes to me during class. I didn't think anything of it other than I liked being noticed by a girl, and I was getting a little practice interacting with the opposite sex. Somehow, Don found out about our exchanging notes and was waiting to talk to me outside of biology class. He confronted me in a very loud and aggressive manner and put me on notice that he would knock the shit out of me if I kept messing around with his girlfriend.

Now, these were the kinds of events that shaped your entire future at North High School. If you backed down, you were screwed. If you didn't back down, you were committed, and there was no way to change your mind. All of it happened in an instant, as in this case, and out of the blue Don Wagner chose me out to fight if I didn't stop talking to Connie. Of course, all of this is happening in the hallway outside of biology class with a dozen or so classmates watching every move.

My response was simple, to the point, and unambiguous: "Fuck you. I'll meet you at Rocky Mountain Park after school. Four p.m."

At North, there were several commonly known fighting venues: Woodland Park, Rocky Mountain Park, and Columbus Park. Naturally, fights broke out spontaneously at any location, except Jim's Pizzeria. Everyone knew that it was totally unacceptable to fight in the pizzeria or its parking lot. In reality, there was an imaginary circle around the pizzeria about one mile in diameter that was a kind of a demilitarized zone. This concept would later be adopted by the United Nations.

Woodland Park was where real Pack Rats and honorary pack rats would fight each other or people not affiliated with

La Raza. Columbus Park was where Pack Rats would fight Mexicans. You had to really have balls just to go watch a fight at Columbus Park. I only went there once in three years to watch Frank Garcio, fifth or sixth toughest Pack Rat, fight the number-two ranked Mexican. Frank won that fight, but the most important part of that event was that the Pack Rats had arrived en masse to watch. Columbus Park was located at 38th and Tejon in the heart of the Mexicans' territory. It was the perfect place to get ambushed by a mob of Mexicans. Attending this fight and "backing up" Frank Garcio was the price you paid for being a small-p/small-r pack rat. Fortunately for me, nothing happened after the fight, and we all left the park without incident.

Rocky Mountain Park was where you went to have a fight if you were a nobody, so to speak. And you would go to a specific area of the park. All of the fight-staging protocol was learned within the first week or so when you became a student-inmate at North. If you made a protocol error, like telling Don to meet you at Woodland Park, you could expect to have a few Pack Rats make sure you paid for that error. If they didn't like Don and you were winning at Woodland Park, they would let you win then beat the shit out of you. If you were beating Don at Woodland Park and they favored him over you, one of the Pack Rats would hit you while you were fighting so that you were essentially fighting Don and any nearby Pack Rat.

So the die was cast: I would meet Don Wagner at Rocky Mountain Park at four o'clock later that day. When there was going to be a fight, word spread at lightning speed, even when it involved a couple of nobodies. It was kind of a gladiator mentality, and everyone was plugged into the fighting pipeline.

Meanwhile, I had the entire day to worry about meeting Don. I didn't have a car, so I needed someone to give me a ride. The rest of the day, people came up to me and said, "I hear you chose out Don Wagner at Rocky Mountain?"

I nodded and thought, "You know, not one of these people talked to me yesterday." I could see other people pointing at me from across the way. Choosing out someone was big at North.

Jimmy Spinelli gave me a ride to Rocky Mountain Park. He had his dad's 1959 white Buick with red interior. This was not a cool car to show up in. The car pulled onto this dirt road next to the baseball field. There were about forty people who decided to watch the fight, pretty good for unranked opponents. I got out of the car and waited. I waited for thirty to forty minutes, but Don didn't show. At North, you didn't win by virtue of a no-show. Now I had the rest of the day and night to think about my next move.

I got to school the next day about forty-five minutes before the first bell rang and went to the smoking area. In the '60s, everyone at North smoked, and there was a designated area for smoking. Within the area, the gangs had a sort of reserved section and everyone else sort of found their own spot. I had been there about fifteen minutes when I saw Don Wagner walking toward me. I felt that I would be in better shape if I began walking toward him instead of just waiting for him to arrive. Waiting made me feel that I was at a disadvantage.

He had momentum, he was moving, and thus he was the aggressor.

As I walked toward him, I tried to think of what to say. I could say, "I was at the park last night, but you didn't show up." Well, that seemed stupid; of course he knew he didn't show up. Within a few seconds, we were face to face a few feet apart.

Before I could say anything, he said, "I couldn't get a ride to the park. I'll definitely be there today after school." Now, if I would have said, "Okay," then I would have had another entire day of worrying. So instead, I hauled off and hit him in his left eye—a move I learned from Peter Schavinski. I really let him have it.

Now talk about your gladiator mentality! The smoking area was North High's version of the Roman Colosseum. It was a sunken area, about eight or ten steps below the ground level of the parking lot, and the stairs to the enter the school were twenty feet above ground level. People had a great viewing area, including the teachers.

After I hit Don, I did not make the same mistake that Peter Schavinski made with me. I remembered how debilitating Peter's surprise attack had been, so after the first punch, I followed it with a second and third and so on. Don fought back but was genuinely injured. His left eye had swollen shut, and he was unable to get his bearings and steady himself. He threw some punches, the most devastating of which was a roundhouse right that hit me squarely in the forehead. But I was in a zone that made the punch ineffective; I was going to make sure Don did not have a chance to recover.

Fights seem to last much longer if you're in the fight versus watching it. Another thing about fighting is that you don't know what event will end the fight. Peter Schavinski started to cry, and the bell rang for class. Would I have stopped hitting Peter if the bell hadn't rung? Usually, the fight ends if someone "gives in" or "gives up." At North, if you give up, you still may get one or two good smacks that are intended to let the onlookers understand that you are someone they should not mess with.

In my fight with Don, I was winning, and something unexpected happened. One of the Pack Rats decided to smack Don from the side. I don't know why, and I really didn't even know the Pack Rat that did it. But when the teachers saw that the fight was no longer one-on-one, one of them stepped in and stopped it. Don and I were taken to the office of the Dean of Boys, Don Evans. Mr. Evans was really, really tough and not the kind of guy that you could even maintain eye contact with. If he looked at you, you would definitely blink first or look away.

By the time we got into the dean's office, Don Wagner's eye had swollen to the size of a golf ball. It looked really bad, and as we were escorted to the office, the other kids got a good look at Don's face. Since most people did not do a great deal of fighting, there was no way to for them to determine how hard you had to hit someone before their eye gets totally closed and turns into a yellowish-purplish lump. Human nature being what it is, I moved way up on the list of people not to mess with insofar as the Nerds, Regulars, and small-j jocks were concerned.

A monumental consequence of my door-popping Don was that one of the Pack Rats indirectly gave me a sign of approval by smacking Don to end the fight. Looking back, I showed balls. I demonstrated that I had thought things through, that I had no recourse but to escalate the situation with Don after being stood up at Rocky Mountain Park, and that I was Italian. These were the qualities that small-p/small-r guys were made of. Actually, I had not entirely thought things through to come to the conclusion that I had to escalate things as a result of the no-show. I started the fight then and there because I didn't want to worry all day. I made the correct decision for the wrong reason.

The positive was that I knew I had figured it out after the fact. I began to see things from a street-smarts standpoint. Once I began to develop an understanding of the thought processes that made sense to the guys running North High, I gained a level of understanding of what it took to be successful in the world of business. It was not mental and physical toughness that provided common ground for the street guy and the executive; it was the ability to recognize the right move and to be decisive. The move can vary from situation to situation. Smacking Don in the smoking area after being stood up at Rocky Mountain Park was the right move because Don was a Regular. If he had been a small-p/small-r guy, it would not have been the move unless you yourself were small-p/small-r.

The move may change, but usually there is a move that is the best.

NDJ Life Lesson:

The best move is usually very simple and straightforward. If you have to struggle to understand, execute, or explain your move, it's the wrong move.

Chapter 5

High School Memories: Sophomore Year
Survival, Girls & Cars

When you are a sophomore without a clue and without a car, you are pretty much relegated to trying to survive and observe. It's a little like one of those nature programs on PBS where you see this uncoordinated newly born bird stumble around and flap its wings, but it doesn't go anywhere. But just like in nature, if you're a bird, at some point you had better figure out how to fly. At North High, you had to figure out where you wanted to be in the social hierarchy and have the skills to get there.

For me, the key drivers were survival, girls, and cars. Since North was such a violent place, most people were concerned about trying to survive. Just like the jungle, the strongest survived. They not only survived, but the strongest and toughest guys also seemed to enjoy a lot of perks, including the coolest cars and the cutest girlfriends. At St. Catherine's, the nuns and priests created an environment from the top down that valued and rewarded academic excellence. At North, values were established from the bottom up.

Since there were so many students, there were hundreds and hundreds of cute girls. But to me, many of them were way beyond cute; they were gorgeous and they were sexy. In the morning when it was cold outside, the kids would walk around the hallways. The main building was square shaped, and some kids would stand up against the walls and watch the other kids go round and round until the first bell. This parade-like atmosphere gave everyone a chance to see what Cheryl Piccoli was wearing—she was known to wear low-cut blouses, and she had a great rack—and to see if it were possible for Glenda Crumbaker to get any more perfect.

The Italian guys had gold chains around their necks with Italian horns hanging from them. Some had pinky rings and gold bracelets. They wore wing-tipped shoes, and some had taps on their heels. While it was considered cool to clack around with taps, most guys saw them as a disadvantage. You could not sneak up on someone, and you were more prone to slipping when fighting or fleeing the scene.

Because of this observation, I decided to adopt an image that I thought was cool and one that I was comfortable with. It also had to be believable. I couldn't try to dress like the toughest guys in school for obvious reasons. It wouldn't make sense for me to wear a T-shirt and roll my sleeves up to expose a puny bicep. For me, the image I wanted to create had to be almost like a trademark kind of thing. I would basically look the same every day for three years. To pull it off, I needed two pairs of wing-tipped shoes, brown and cordovan. I needed about five faded sweatshirts (gray, blue, green, black, and maroon), and I would cut the sleeves off just above the elbow. I needed five short-sleeved shirts and five long-sleeved shirts. When I wore a short-sleeved shirt, the sleeve would extend about two inches past the cut-off sleeve of the sweatshirt. I would need about four pairs of blue jeans, absolutely no white socks, and a brown leather jacket, not black. The key thing I was trying to do with this new look was to give myself the best possible chance of getting laid. At this point, the girl thing was a higher priority than the survival thing.

Besides a new image, I knew that I would need to come up with a car before the start of my second year at North. I would turn sixteen in August, and my junior year would begin in September. Without a car, Frankie Avalon would have a hard time getting laid. Besides transportation and privacy, a really cool car could move a guy's social ranking up into a very elite category, which would almost guarantee some kind of back-seat action. These were the naïve days of the '60s where it was widely believed that there were two kinds of girls: the nasty ones and the ones that you would probably be forced to marry someday.

The parking lot was behind the school and close to the smoking area. It was dirt and gravel, so there were no denoted parking spaces. But, like everything else at North, there were rules, bottom-up kind of rules. First, only the real Pack Rats could park in the first row. Those were the parking spots closest to the school and most visible to the smoking area.

Joe Fazaro, the toughest guy in school and the head of the Pack Rats, had a gold '57 Chevy four-speed with black interior and chrome reverse wheels. The gold-metal flake color on Joe's car was a custom paint job, along with the tucked and rolled black leather interior. The side panels were also tucked and rolled, and a custom headliner matched the overall "black is bad" look. The gold car could be spotted instantaneously at great distances. When you saw the gold car coming in your direction, you always looked but acted like you weren't looking, but you knew you needed to look in case Joe signaled you to pull over or something. You would never ever wave at Joe Fazaro when he drove by. He might mistake it for flipping him the finger, and he might need to work on a new "break your nose punch" and decide to try it out on the next person to wave at him. Joe was in row one, parking space one.

The rest of the parking lot was filled with cars that were spectacular. There were hot rods that included a '32 Ford 5 window coupe, a '40 Ford coupe, and a '46 Ford convertible. There were muscle cars like the 409 Chevy, 426 Ford, fuel-injected Corvette, and the Dodge Hemi. I will never forget the sound of the engines and the glasspack mufflers. I would watch the cars drive by and go into the parking lot. No one drove fast around the school. For one thing, the parking lot was dirt. Driving fast would create dust, and dust was unacceptable. Besides, you couldn't look cool and pick up girls if your car was going more than two to four miles per hour, which was the Official Standard Italian Cruising Speed (OSICS) sanctioned by the Sons of Italy.

By the end of my sophomore year, I had established the following goals: survival, girls, and cars. I prioritized my goals as follows: girls (in order to get laid), cars (in order to get laid), and survival (in order to get laid more than once). I remember I was leaning against a wall one day before class started, watching the girls walk by, and I couldn't help but reflect on the unexpected turn of events—my fight with Peter—that caused me to be at North. And in my moment of reflection, Cheryl Piccoli dropped her books, bent over to pick them up, and I said to myself, "Thank you, God! Thank you, Sister Mary, and thank you, Peter Schavinski, you big prick."

NDJ Life Lesson:

You have to continuously assess your strengths/weaknesses and develop goals to accomplish your objectives.

The key thing to remember is that if you want change, you have to change things.

Chapter 6

High School Memories: Junior Year
Here's Johnnie

September 1963. The first day of school was the unveiling of the new image—not the North Denver Johnnie image, just the Johnnie image. It would take two more years to acquire the North Denver handle.

I had my new wing-tipped shoes, faded sweatshirt, blue jeans, plaid short-sleeved shirt, gold chain with Italian horn, better-looking glasses, and a really cool car. Through the power of positive thinking, I willed my cowlick into place, and my prayers that my teeth would all be about the same size were answered.

During the summer before school started, my dad taught me how to drive and purchased a 1950 Mercury from my cousin Tommy. The 1950 Mercury was the car James Dean drove in the movie *Rebel Without a Cause*. James Dean was one of the most popular teen movie idols of that era. Having the same cherry Mercury that he drove as a teenage hero in the movie helped me be guilty by association: James is cool, his car is cool, Johnnie has his car, and thus, Johnnie is almost cool.

My Mercury was light gray on the outside with Aztec blue and white Naugahyde interior. The headliner was white with a blue leather bead covering each seam and matching the blue part of the seats. The door panels were white Naugahyde. The front part of the seat was white, seventy percent of the part you sat on and leaned against was Aztec blue, and the top part of the back of the seat was white. Blue leather beads separated the colors on the front and back seats. All of the controls for the heater and radio were white teardrop-shaped knobs. The car had a three-speed standard transmission with the shifter on the column complete with teardrop knob. The ignition switch to start the car was located on the right side of the steering wheel in the dashboard. The starter button was on the left side of the steering wheel.

The car had a flathead engine that was spotless with chrome acorn bolt covers. The entire undercarriage of the car was painted flat white, and there were two chrome Scavenger pipes hanging below the undercarriage. It had mellow glasspack mufflers and was raked back to front so that the rear end was raised six to eight inches and the front end was lowered slightly. It had 4-inch-wide whitewall tires and chrome cone hubcaps. The car was in perfect condition and would turn your head when it drove by.

In the rear window it had a red and yellow decal of a lion running. The red lion signified that you attended North High School. This was a badge of courage kind of thing. It was pretty powerful if you ran into some kids from just about any other high school, with the exception of West, East, and Manual. All of the other schools would pretty much never mess with someone from North with a cool car and a red lion.

I washed my car as often as possible so that it was perfectly clean every day that it was possible for it to be clean. I can remember bending the garden hose to break the ice so that the water would flow. When you did that, you ended up with ice cubes on the lawn that looked a little like dog turds. The gray exterior paint was thinning, so water spots would show if I didn't wax it every six to eight weeks. In those days, I used Simoniz wax, which meant that it was a two or three-step process depending on if you wanted to start with the cleaner wax. Simoniz wax was the hardest to rub off, and it was about a four-hour event to wash and wax the Merc.

On the first day of school, the new sophomore girls represented a tremendous opportunity for potential conquest. Plus, there was the outside chance that the new image and new car would create interest by one of the junior class girls who just three months earlier wouldn't have poured a bucket of water on my head if my hair was on fire. Plus, and best of all, the car made it possible for me to go back to Skinner Junior High and meet the cutest girls in ninth grade, just like the guys from North did when I was in ninth grade. It was almost impossible for a ninth-grade boy to compete with someone two years older with a cool red lion car from a bad school when you were still riding a bicycle, or at best a moped. I am pretty sure that ninth-grade girls were put on this earth to, at a minimum, give you the first hand job where your hand wasn't involved.

So, on this first day, I drove down Clay Street looking for new faces. I pulled over and asked three girls if they wanted a ride to school. They hesitated and then said yes. They were good looking and sexy, not the kind of girls that would be walking down Clay Street for very long. It was obvious that these girls would attract and be pursued by the coolest guys at North, but for now, I was acceptable, at least for the next twelve blocks. How does Bob Seger's song go? "I was using her, and she was using me. We were both using each other." Yada, yada, yada.

When I pulled up in front of the smoking area with three jam-up girls, people noticed them, my car, and me, probably in that order.

I was on a winning streak. I began my junior year with a new image, a new car, and I had driven to school with three attractive girls. Anytime two good things happen in a row, I believe that is potentially the start of a winning streak. I had just had three good things happen in a row, and with momentum on my side, it became easier to have a fourth good thing happen. I developed my philosophy on winning by watching improbable things happen when people won money at the horse races. As a result of my mother's gambling addiction, I spent a lot of time at the horse track during the summertime.

NDJ Winning Streak Philosophy:

When two good things happen in your life, you may be at the beginning of a winning streak.

In order to recognize a winning streak, you must be constantly vigilant.

By definition, winning is good. Two good things back to back put you in position to have three good things happen back to back to back.

If a third good thing happens, you are definitely on a winning streak.

Big wins are made up of winning streaks. You simply cannot ever win without the benefit of a winning streak at some point.

The key to winning big is recognizing that you are on a winning streak, making it possible to buck the odds and take more risk for as long as possible.

To take advantage of a winning streak as long as possible, you must recognize it for what it is as soon as possible.

As soon as two good things happen back to back, this occurrence is literally the birth of the life of a possible winning streak.

Believing I was on a winning streak made it easier to take the next risk, like driving around Skinner Junior High School to try to meet a cute girl. To obtain most goals, you need a plan, initiative, confidence, and perseverance. In gambling, you need to bet more when you are winning and less when you are losing. Most people bet more when they are losing and try to "double up to catch up." At this moment in time, I was winning. I was on a streak, and I believed that I would be able to win my next bet. Recognizing my good fortune made going to Skinner Junior High each afternoon after school cruising for babes the right move for the right reasons.

NDJ Life Lesson:

Always notice when good things happen to you. This will allow you to recognize the possibility of experiencing a winning streak and give you the confidence to take a bigger risk and be more aggressive.

Chapter 7

High School Memories: Junior Year
Early Pool Hall Years

When I was seven or eight years old, my parents gave me a toy pool table for Christmas. The pool table was two and a half feet wide and five feet long. The pool balls were roughly the size of half-dollar coins, and the pool cues were about three feet long. Underneath its surface, metal tracks ran the length of the table. The six pockets had holes in the cups so that once a ball entered the pocket, it would fall through the hole onto the track and run down into a collection tray at the end of the table.

I was fascinated with the colored pool balls against the backdrop of the green felt and by the challenge of trying to sink all of the balls without missing. Since I didn't have any friends, playing pool in the basement was something I could do by myself whenever I wanted. I played this game so often that after four years I had worn the felt off the table and used up all of my replacement cue tips. Even then, I would just roll the balls to see where they would end up when I banked them off a side rail or end rail. I began to visualize the angles that the ball would follow based on the angle it created on its inward path to the rail.

About a mile and a half from my house, someone converted the Wonder Bread store into a pool hall. It was totally redecorated and had twelve brand-new Brunswick pool tables, three brand-new Brunswick snooker tables, and one completely restored billiard table. The felt on the pool tables was royal blue or gold. The felt on the snooker and billiard tables was green.

A very large man by the name of Forrest Fischer owned and operated the pool hall. Mrs. Fischer worked at the snack bar, along with a couple eighteen-year-old kids who worked part-time. A guy by the name of Harry Marks worked the night shift. He was an ex-marine—crew cut, polished boots, pressed trousers, by-the-book kind of guy. Nobody wanted to mess with Harry Marks.

The pool hall was called Fischer's, and it was located one block inside of the line that bordered North Denver and the suburb of Westminster. Fischer's was on 51st and Federal Boulevard, and Westminster started after 52nd street. North Denver guys rarely went north of 50th Street where the Scotchman Drive-In restaurant was located. It was almost like another demilitarized zone existed between 50th and 52nd Streets. This meant that you could go down to Fischer's and play pool, and it was unlikely that you would run into any of the Pack Rats in that part of town.

When I walked into Fischer's for the first time, I could not believe how beautiful it was. The colored, shiny pool balls, the lighting over the tables, the sounds of balls striking each other, and the thump of a ball being cross-banked into the side pocket made me feel like I was somewhere over the rainbow.

When I first began playing, I was not very good. It was something I liked to do, but the table was so big, and my four years of pee wee pool didn't seem to help me at all. Nonetheless, I liked it and went to Fischer's at least three days a week, usually more. After a few months, one of the patrons noticed me practicing day after day, and I think he felt sorry for me. He came over to me and asked if I would mind if he gave me a tip or two to help my game. His name was Virgil Abernathy, and he was a postal worker. He was about fifty-five years old when I met him.

The first thing he taught me was how to create a good bridge with my left hand, the one that rested on the table supporting my cue stick. I had an open bridge, and he explained that it is impossible to be a good pool player without a closed bridge. A closed bridge means that your left index finger is wrapped around the cue, creating a stable platform to strike the cue ball. The other fingers would rest on the table and be lowered or heightened depending on which part of the cue ball you wanted to strike. To draw the cue ball back toward you, you would spread your fingers so that the tip of the cue would strike the southern hemisphere of the cue ball. To create follow English, or top spin, you elevated the bridge so that you would strike the cue ball somewhere north of the equator.

In Virgil's second lesson, he explained how to line up the shot. He provided me with good fundamentals that enabled me to be consistent and provide a strong foundation that would not crumble under the pressure of tournament play or a one-hundred-dollar game of one-pocket. Next, he explained how English worked and how to use it to make shots that did not appear possible. He taught me how to play shape, which is a term for being able to position the cue ball where you want it after you shoot a ball into the pocket. Shape requires strategy and good touch.

As I progressed through my lessons, it became clear that the game required good hand-eye coordination, physical stamina, a great deal of concentration, and strong mental toughness. My relentless practice—coupled with a love for the game and a strong mentor—was the key ingredient to becoming a tournament level pool player. Virgil helped me understand the not so obvious subtleties associated with the mechanics of the game and the strategies associated with winning.

So, who was Virgil Abernathy? In 1963, Virgil was the best pool player in Denver, and maybe the third, fourth, or fifth-best snooker player in America. He had beaten the 1939 Snooker World Champion in a tournament match in the mid '40s and was always the person called upon to play exhibition matches when the top celebrities came to town for the grand opening of a new pool hall or a major tournament. I saw Virgil play Willy Moscone, who was the Straight Pool World Champion, and give him a very good accounting with over one hundred onlookers watching the match.

Virgil was a soft-spoken man and had a wife and four children. As a postal worker, he didn't make a lot of money, but when you were a real player like Virgil, you didn't need money to play in the big games because someone would back you and give you a percentage of the winnings. A backer is also known as a "steak horse." Virgil knew all the backers and they knew him. The word on Virgil was that he would "drinks a bit" like Bo Jangles. And he was known to experience the high-speed wobbles for the cheese. To translate this from street slang, Virgil would choke under pressure and was not able to play for high stakes (cheese). All players had a speed limit, which represented the amount of money they were able to play for and still be at their best. Beyond that speed limit, their game would quickly erode.

In the pool hall, money was how you kept score. People would play for different amounts of money depending on the type of game being played and their speed limit. A top local player would play ten to twenty-dollar nine-ball at a minimum. No top players would ever play eight-ball unless it was on a bar table in a beer joint. A strong one-pocket player would never play for less than twenty dollars per game. Straight pool, first to one hundred, would be a minimum of fifty dollars per game. Snooker would be a twenty-five-dollar minimum. And there were times when road players came to town and play the local talent for hundreds of dollars per game. The road players were professional and would "spot" the local player to make the match more even. An example would be spotting some guy the eight-ball in a nine-ball game. This meant that the better player would win only if he made the nine-ball, but the weaker player only had to make the eight-ball. Of course, if the nine-ball fell in at some point during the game, the weaker player would also win. Aspiring players would play for less, but they had to raise their speed limit to play with the big boys.

Nobody played pool for fun, at least not the "players." The players were the studs in the pool hall who even had groupies called "sweaters." The sweaters watched the players compete and would sweat the action (street talk for worry about the outcome of a match). This means they would watch the drama unfold hour after hour until someone was busted or unscrewed their stick. Unscrewing your stick is like tipping a chess piece over to acknowledge defeat. Sweaters could take side action and bet with other sweaters on their favorite player or with one of the players against him. Whenever there was a big game, there were sweaters.

At the beginning of my junior year at North High, I took a job at a drug store so that I could have spending money. I can't remember how much I was paid, but I do remember that by the end of the school year I resigned my job at the drug store. I quit because I could make five to ten times as much money at the pool hall playing nine-ball. The drug store job was simply costing me money, and I preferred being self-employed anyway, so to speak.

My best friend was Danny Polidori. Danny's dad owned a neighborhood market that specialized in homemade Italian sausage. There was tremendous competition among the sausage makers and there was an ongoing buzz about their products between the little Italian women in the neighborhood. The Manzanillo family's market-made sausage was one of Polidori's biggest competitors. In order to stay ahead of Manzanillo, Polidori offered free delivery on Saturday. On many Saturday mornings, I rode along with Danny in his father's 1959 Ford light-green pickup truck.

One Saturday, Mr. Polidori asked me how my job at the drug store was going. Kidding around, I told him I retired in order to be a pool player. He promptly replied that I was going to grow up to be a bum. I saw Mr. Polidori about fifty more times in my life after that day, and each time he saw me, his first words were, "Bum, you're going to be a bum."

NDJ Life Lesson:

Strive to compete at the highest level. You cannot become a champion without losing, and it is losing that ultimately teaches you how to win.

Chapter 8

High School Memories: Junior Year
Learning Italian

My mother and father were Italian, and both of their parents were born in Italy. Unfortunately, many first-generation Italian-Americans felt strongly that their children should only speak English. Some Italian immigrants even changed their last name or "Americanized" it. They would do things like change Martino to Martin. My last name is Santone, but it was not changed from Santini. The Santone name is fairly common in the region of Abruzzi, Italy. In any case, I was not taught to speak Italian as a child.

At St. Catherine's elementary school, about thirty percent of the kids in my class were Italian. There were five girls: Alice Garza, Carol Galasso, Karen Botero, Elizabeth Zarlingo, and Piorina Ritola. Piorina Ritola was as pretty as her name. There were five boys: Tony Yackavetta, Johnnie DeSalvo, Joseph Vichorelli, Johnnie Pollice (paul-a-che), and me. Larry Griffith's mother was Italian, but that didn't count. The priests and nuns made sure that the kids were not Italian, German, Irish, or anything except Catholic. The pope, of course, was Italian, and they were willing to acknowledge that.

At North High School, being Italian was something that was noticed since three-quarters of the Pack Rats were Italian, including the small-p/small-r variety. In the '60s, Frank Sinatra, Dean Martin, and a few of their buddies were known as the Rat Pack. Frank Sinatra was referred to as the chairman of the board and was widely reputed to have known and socialized with members of the Mafia. At North, Joe Fazaro was the leader of the Pack Rats and the prototype of a tough, macho Italian of that era. Most of the Pack Rats did not speak Italian either and in fact disliked the Mexicans because they spoke Spanish. The Pack Rats wouldn't even acknowledge that the Mexicans spoke Spanish; instead, they disliked the idea that they spoke "Mexican."

There were several reasons that the Italians in North Denver had such great animosity toward the Mexicans. The primary one was that North Denver was seventy-five percent Italian up until the late 1940s. Then, over the next decade or so, the Italian population shrank to about forty percent, and the Mexican population grew to the same level as the Italians. As the balance of power changed, so did the neighborhood. There was more crime, more unkempt properties, more gang violence targeting Italians, more loud music, more Mexican gang members vandalizing property, and an overall reduction in property values. Italian families that had lived in the neighborhood all of their lives were afraid to sit out on the porch at night.

Growing up in an Italian household did expose me to all of the food unique to our heritage but not much else. Other than Michelangelo and Christopher Columbus, I would have been hard-pressed to come up with a famous Italian name that was not a gangster or singer.

Both of my parents gambled at the horse and dog races, and my dad liked to play dice. In Denver, like most big cities, illegal gambling was controlled by the mob. I remember the time when my dad and about twenty other guys were arrested playing bar booth (a dice game unlike craps). The incident was written up the next day in the Rocky Mountain News. The mob members, of course, were all Italian. When I was with my parents at the races, I would see my dad's Italian buddies and the guys that ran the dice games and took football bets. After a while, you could almost tell by looking at someone and hearing them say a few sentences that they were a part of the "Italian thing." Most of the people my dad grew up with and hung out with when he was a teenager were in the mob or were on the fringes. They all spoke Italian, and they liked to gamble, wear nice clothes, and fight. I'm not sure they really liked fighting, but they acted as if they did.

Joseph Vichorelli, the kid in my class at St. Catherine's, had a cousin named Eugene Smaldone. Eugene would drive his black Chrysler New Yorker to our house with his nephew to give me a ride to school when it snowed. Eugene's father, Clyde, and his uncle, Checkers, were the main Mafia guys in Denver.

Through the years, I got to see a lot of Italians. I saw how these guys dressed, heard them talk, and watched their mannerisms. So, when I saw Joe Fazaro, I knew I was looking at the real deal.

Danny Polidori and I would go to the "Sons of Italy" picnic in the summertime and learned how to play motta and bocce ball (Italian lawn bowling). Motta is a game that you play using your fingers and calling out a number from two to ten in Italian. You make a fist with your hand and gesture as if you were going to pound on a table as you faced your opponent. Both of the players, with fists clenched, pull their hands down once, then twice, and on the third pull they display one to five fingers and yell out a number. The object of the game is to call out the number that totals the fingers presented on your hand and the other person's hand. In other words, if I held out four fingers and my opponent held out four fingers, and I yelled *ochoa* (eight), I would win if the other person yelled out any other number. If the other player also yelled *ochoa*, it was a tie.

Motta was very simple game to learn, but like with most things, there was more to it than met the eye. As unbelievable as it may seem, there are good motta players and bad motta players. Motta is a strategy game in which you must manage your tendencies in order to deceive the opponent and at the same time try to learn the tendencies of the other players. In some ways, it is a war of wills. A strong player imposes his will over the other. The stronger player intimidates the other. When he yells *ochoa* for the win, he does it a little like the announcers that broadcast World Cup soccer and scream, "Goal, goal, goal, gooooooaaaaal!" When you hear this extended, embellished, and powerful pronunciation of a four-letter word, it makes you wonder if they are having some kind of vocal orgasm—a really good, long one.

Likewise, when playing motta in the tradition of World Cup soccer and you yell the winning number, you must savor it, rub it in, and sing it out. When you begin a victory yell at the very first instant that you declare yourself winner instead of embellishing your yell after you know you have won, it tells your opponent that you have him figured out, that you own him. It tells him *you* are the boss. It tells him *you* knew he was going to display four fingers before he did.

The number that your opponent yells—say in this case where he displays four fingers and yells *seta* (six)—means he thought you would display two fingers. The way you played the game earlier in the match may have led your opponent to believe you would display two fingers. Is this an accident? If you're a really good motta player, it probably isn't an accident. A possible scenario is that earlier in the match you displayed three fingers and yelled *ochoa* hoping he would display five fingers and then in the next iteration again displayed three fingers and again yelled *ochoa*. Now, the next iteration is the key. You display two fingers and yell *seta*. What you have done is create an artificial tendency that is easy for you opponent to remember. He now thinks that three fingers, followed by three fingers again, will lead to two fingers. You have set the trap for him to expect you to display two fingers and are hoping that when he recalls that sequence, he will only have time to remember that you yelled *seta* when it happened. The game is played at a very fast pace, so you don't have time to analyze this one call to the degree I have described here. When you have set a trap and it works, you can easily yell at the top of your voice, with your personal inflection and appropriate repetition, "Ochoa, ochoa, ochoa!" all the while thinking, "This is really sweet! Thank you, God, for letting me be Italian."

Unknowingly, all of these influences helped me develop a sense of what being Italian was in the '60s. It allowed me to fit into the small-p/small-r pack rats. It helped me develop an identity and feel like I was in a place where I fit, where I belonged, and where I was liked. We had Italians at North that didn't feel the same way and were not a part of the small-p/small-r thing. There were also a lot of Mexicans that were not a part of La Raza. But for the first time, I had a sense of who I was. I was growing self-confidence and had a much-improved self-esteem.

NDJ Life Lesson:

It is not where you are at any point in time but rather where you have been that defines your reality.

Chapter 9

High School Memories: Junior Year
Two Down, One to Go

I had managed to survive my junior year at North High School and, in the process, reinvent myself. I changed my appearance, became a born-again Italian, established myself as an up-and-coming pool player, and became a small-p/small-r affiliate.

Throughout the school year, there were many other memorable events worth mentioning. If I were going to rank my great moments of 1963, the Top Ten list would look like this:

10. Got Laid
9. Jim's Pizzeria
8. Scotchman Drive-In
7. Steady Girlfriend (not to be confused with number ten)
6. Joe Fazaro Fight (versus La Raza's new leader)
5. Became a small-p/small-r guy
4. Learned Italian
3. Cool Car
2. Played Pool
1. Made Friends & Set New Goals

10. Got Laid

One thing I didn't realize would happen when I got my car was that it started the official countdown to blastoff, so to speak. Guys talk about girls a lot, and at some point, you are asked if you have ever gotten laid. This is a question you cannot lie about because it is almost like being asked if you speak Chinese. If you lie and say you got laid and really didn't, your greatest fear would be that they would ask you a sex-related question that is so fundamental to the event that it would be analogous to them saying, "Who is Joe Fazaro?" in Chinese. But guess what? You don't know what they're talking about.

When you don't have a car, you aren't given a lot of slack as to why you haven't gotten laid. But once that excuse disappears, the "break your cherry" watch is on full alert. I cannot remember how many times I was asked if I got laid yet during my junior year. This was peer pressure at the max.

I ranked this event tenth and in all honesty considered leaving it off the Top Ten list altogether. For one thing, it seemed to me that for an event to make the Top Ten list, it should be something that took longer than thirty seconds to occur. And I am being kind to myself by rounding up to the nearest half-minute.

Another reason I considered leaving it off the list was because one of my buddies arranged for it to happen. I was at a party where everyone was drinking 3.2 beer and doing their best to get drunk. There was this girl whose name I cannot remember, but she a bad reputation (code for she put out). One of my friends from Skinner Junior High, Michael DeBaca, introduced me to her and made it clear to me that she was willing to put out. The party was being held at his girlfriend's house, so he directed me to a downstairs bedroom and told me that I didn't have to worry about being interrupted. Michael did everything except leave me a how-to manual.

It happened so fast that I actually decided the best thing for me to do following my coming of age moment was to talk to the girl. Believe me, I wanted to get out of that bedroom more than anything, but I needed to stall to give the appearance that we were having sex.

Michael DeBaca was the second-best-looking, just downright handsome guy at North High School. He was Spanish and French with a great smile and perfect black wavy hair, and he was well built with a happy personality. The girls loved to look at him, loved his smile and his charm. The guys liked him because he was a stand-up kind of guy, loyal to his friends, a good athlete, and friendly to both the cool guys and not-so-cool guys. He was one of the rare exceptions that could compete with the eleventh-grade guys from North with cars for the affection of any girl at Skinner when he was in the ninth grade riding a bicycle.

Since I described the second-best-looking guy at North, I at least feel compelled to mention who was number one. His name was Johnny Romola. I am not going to say that he was better looking than Brad Pitt, but I will say that he was so much better looking than the rest of us that you just might think of Johnny Romola as the Brad Pitt of North High School.

Thanks to Michael, the pressure from my peers to get laid was gone. On the other hand, I knew I had a lot to learn if

I was ever going to get someone to have sex with me more than once. And it hadn't escaped me that if not for Michael, I would still be a cherry. That's the way life is. It leaves it up to me to decide if getting laid that night was a good thing or a bad thing. In this instance, my conclusions were: 1) It was a good thing because I got my peers off my back, and 2) Michael DeBaca showed me he liked me and wanted to help me out.

It wasn't bad to realize that I had a lot to learn about sex, because if you recognize your development needs, you can fix them. The other positive was that my motive to improve was not totally selfish. I wanted to be able to make it a good experience for the girl and be able to have her happy to see me the next day.

NDJ Life Lesson:

It really doesn't make sense to do things for the sole purpose of being accepted by others. The need to seek approval from your peers as a way to define self-worth is a hard habit to break.

9. Jim's Pizzeria

Before you are accepted into the small-p/small-r thing, you would never, ever consider going to Jim's Pizzeria. Instead, you went to Carl's Pizzeria, which was like a minor league baseball team compared to Jim's, which was the New York

Yankees of pizzerias. The food at Carl's was good, but it was not where the action was. Carl's was a place to get something to eat. Jim's was the official after-school headquarters of the Pack Rats, their affiliates, and female groupies.

There were certain booths that were unofficially reserved for Joe Fazaro and his direct reports. Jim's was a large restaurant that could easily seat one hundred people, maybe more. The food was spectacular, especially the sausage pizzas. The parking lot was filled with great cars, and everyone knew everyone. On a Friday or Saturday night, I could not imagine any outsiders, young or old, walking into Jim's, looking around, and deciding to stay.

Besides serving as a focal point for food and socializing, Jim's was the communication center for the gang. On Friday night, you would first go to Jim's to find out if there were any parties scheduled or if there was going to be a problem with La Raza. As for parties, the Pack Rats would crash parties, which was a way to meet new girls outside of North High or a way to get into fights with people from other schools.

Crashing a party (showing up uninvited) was a scary proposition. Typically, a handful of Pack Rats (three to five) and/or their affiliates would drive to some address outside of North Denver, park their car, and walk into someone's house. Even if two cars loaded with Pack Rats showed up to crash a party, they could always expect to be outnumbered by the kids from the other school. It takes a lot of balls to walk into a house, walk down the stairs to the basement, and act like you are giving them a break for taking time out of your schedule to show up.

There is usually someone that will say, "Who are you guys? Where are you from?" If the party was chaperoned by a strong adult, there was an outside chance that the adult could persuade the Pack Rats to leave. It would depend on how it was handled. If the adult tried to intimidate or bully the intruders, it would be a mistake. If the Pack Rats were outnumbered three or four to one, it still would be a mistake to try to muscle these guys out of the party. If the other kids got physical and started fighting because they outnumbered the Pack Rats, that would be a real big mistake.

It was always possible to win a battle with the Pack Rats but never possible to win the war. I can remember a night at Jim's Pizzeria when five or six Pack Rats walked through the door after getting the shit kicked out of them at a party they crashed. The party was in Wheat Ridge, an upscale suburb west of North Denver. The party was held in this old barn out in the middle of a great big field. These guys walked over to the corner booth, and within minutes, Jim's Pizzeria was empty. There were ten cars driving west to find the field with the barn.

In the movie *West Side Story*, a gang fight is depicted when ten of the Sharks and ten of the Jets face off, with each gang member lined up against his rival. In the movie, the gang members are eye to eye, and the impression you have is that there is going to be ten separate fights, at least at the beginning.

In the real world, gang fights are chaotic and brutal, probably more akin to the time in history when the French conquered the world. The Pack Rats knew how to win a gang fight. It was a matter of strategy and surprise. In the case of the barn out in Wheat Ridge, the strategy was to send a half-dozen Pack Rats into the barn to punch out whomever they encountered. Then they would run out the door into the open field where about thirty or so of their compatriots were waiting. What happened next was very predictable. The Wheat Ridge guys, bolstered by the earlier victory, chased the guys from North to catch them outside.

Just like Napoleon used the terrain and troop placement to defeat his enemies, the guys from North knew a few tricks of the trade. The guys from Wheat Ridge rushed outside into the pitch black from a brightly lit barn. This was suicide for the unsuspecting "good guys" because they could not see anything when they first hit the darkness. They were also exiting a narrow door that limited the number of people that could get outside. The guys from North did not square off with each person that came out to fight; instead, they ganged up on each guy that ran outside. There were two or three guys attacking each of the opposition. That is one of the reasons they call these kinds of events gang fights.

The guys from Wheat Ridge were getting the crap kicked out of them when they could hear the sound of sirens and see the flash of police lights in the distance. As a part of the fight strategy, an exit plan had been discussed. There were three ways into the field. If the police sent cars from all three directions, the guys from North would have been screwed. Again, and somewhat predictably, the police did not think to block all exit roads.

The outcome was never in doubt. North High sent a reminder message to all of the other schools that they would not allow their students to be ganged up on, even if they deserved it. Of course, West, East, and Manual would not be impressed with this message. They knew how gang fights worked, and they knew defeating a bunch of jocks from Wheat Ridge was no big deal.

After any major event, everyone headed back to Jim's Pizzeria to evaluate injuries and compare war stories. All of the girlfriends and groupies were there to welcome the troops back and listen to another tale of conquest. After all, it was important to know that all was right in the world.

The guys from North Denver were inconsiderate bullies and deserved to get the shit kicked out of them when they crashed the party. However, since justice is always in such short supply, ultimately the injustice of their behavior won out and the "good guys" got the shit beat out of them. It was important for the girlfriends and groupies to know that the formula was still working.

NDJ Life Lesson:

There is a lot of injustice in the world, but it should not make us cynical. There will always be bullies and sometimes the "bad guys" triumph over the "good guys."

However, the vast majority of people are the "good guys," and ultimately justice will prevail. Sometimes it just takes a long time for it all to happen.

8. Scotchman Drive-In

The Scotchman Drive-In was a key landmark along the long, time-traveled route followed by all North Denver guys and chicks when driving around, or "cruising." There were two official routes that were used for cruising. One route traveled south down Federal Boulevard to Speer Boulevard heading east into downtown Denver. As you approached the Speer Viaduct, you could turn left on Zuni Street and shorten the trip by fifty percent. Both routes ended at Jim's Pizzeria.

I never ate anything at the Scotchman Drive-In. For one thing, I wouldn't allow food in my car. Another less obsessive reason was that the food at Jim's was too good. The Scotchman was just a place for malts and shakes and cherry or vanilla Cokes.

Unlike Jim's Pizzeria, the Scotchman Drive-In was not off-limits to other schools. There were probably three main reasons that the North Denver guys let outsiders drive through or park at the drive-in:

1. The Pack Rats wanted to show off their cars.
2. The Pack Rats wanted to meet girls from other schools.
3. The Pack Rats needed a neutral site where information could be exchanged between schools/gangs.

There was always an understanding that visitors could not get out of line when they came to the Scotchman. They could not "burn rubber" or race their engines as they drove through. And it goes without saying that they could not hit on our girls or be loud or disrespectful. It was always a big deal when some guys from West High School paid a visit to the Scotchman.

You could spot a car from West High from the moon. Every car from the west side had dice hanging from the rear-window mirror. Most of them had fender skirts covering half of the rear tires. All four wheels had Moon disc hubcaps, and the cars were lowered, allowing a minimum clearance between the undercarriage and the road. Their favorite colors were red, black, or red and black. You would never see a guy from North High School drive a red car.

What I loved about the Scotchman was the cars. My three favorites were: Jerry Gennadus' '63 midnight-blue split-window coupe fuel-injected Corvette; Rich Ido's '62 426 gold Ford with a black landau top and chrome reverse rims; and Richie Falconi's '62 409 Chevy, white with red interior. The 409 Chevy was my most favorite car of all.

In 1963, 45-rpm records were in style. When I played my favorite pop music records, I would daydream about the 409 Chevy. I could visualize how it might feel to be behind the wheel, and I imagined the sounds of the engine, transmission, and radio. If someone asked me, "When do you think you would own a 409 Chevy," I would have probably said, "Never." As it turns out, I bought a '64 409 Chevy with eight thousand miles on it in 1966.

NDJ Life Lesson:

When I have tried to predict the future, I have been wrong the majority of the time. When I have tried to project for

something to happen in the future, I have achieved it the majority of the time. You have to project in order to predict.

7. Steady Girlfriend

Driving by Skinner Junior High was a good idea. It is not necessary to reinvent the wheel each time you want to achieve something. It is better to pay attention to what the winners are doing and do the same thing. I have always been creative, but I learned that the best way to achieve a goal is to do *all* you can to succeed. That may mean following a proven path, exploring new methods, and most of all, never giving up.

I would drive my '50 Mercury west from the parking lot at North to Lowell Boulevard and then turn north toward Skinner. If I spotted some girls that looked interesting, I would pull over and see if they wanted a ride. I would scout down Lowell until I reached 41st Street and then head east. It was on this route that I met Becky Wright.

Becky was a good student and came from a great family. She had a perky look to her and always seemed to be smiling or just ready to smile. She had perfect teeth, short brown hair, and she was slender and athletic. She never wore sexy clothes, and it wouldn't have mattered if she did; you couldn't stop looking at her pretty face and that great smile.

After meeting her every day after school for a couple of weeks and meeting her parents, she was finally willing to let me pick her up in my car. Most of the girls at Skinner would have wanted to be seen by the other girls in a cool car, but Becky was not interested in impressing anyone.

At some point, I asked Becky to go out on a date and she accepted. We drove to Jim's Pizzeria for dinner and then went to the Scotchman to hang out. The main thing was to be seen by others and to find out what was going on. The other main thing was to impress Becky Wright. Going to Jim's was big, the Scotchman was big, and being acknowledged by the Pack Rats was big to everybody but Becky. To her, none of that meant anything. She had decided to go out with me because she liked me. Nothing had prepared me for something like this, and it would be too late by the time I figured out that Becky was a "what you see is what you get" kind of person.

At the end of our first date, I parked my car on the street in front of her house. I looked at her but was too afraid to try to kiss her good night. I walked her to the door and chickened out again. I got back in my car, drove to the end of the block, and said to myself, "I am really stupid if I don't go back to Becky's house, ring the doorbell, and kiss her good night." So I did.

At some point we parked at Inspiration Point, a big make-out place that was high on a hill with a view of…well I don't know what the hell the view was. The view I remember involved steamy windows. But you probably have guessed that Becky was a "good" girl and that was that. My theory that all girls in ninth grade were meant to give guys hand jobs was quickly disproved. Somehow, I got the idea that she would say yes if we were going steady. So, I offered Becky my class ring and asked her to be my steady girlfriend. She said yes, took the ring, and attached it to a chain around her neck. As soon as she had my ring around her neck, she made sure that I knew her answer to my advances was still no.

Going steady with Becky was the right thing to do but for the wrong reason thing again. But this time I didn't recognize that I made the right move for the wrong reason. I eventually concluded that I made the wrong move for the right reason. I was about to learn a tough lesson. I asked Becky to go steady in order to get in her pants instead of asking her because she was a great girl, really better than I deserved. I decided I really didn't want to be tied up with a good girl that didn't put out. I eventually asked for my ring back. Becky cried. Remember my life lesson about injustice? I eventually got my "just desserts" during my senior year at North.

Between the summer and the fall when school started again at North, Becky had had a transformation similar to mine but much, much better. She had gone from this great-looking ninth grader to one of the top ten most attractive girls at North High School. It was an amazing day, a day when all of the guys were talking about this great-looking chick from Skinner. At some point during the day I ran into Becky. Guess what? I got exactly what I deserved. She totally ignored me.

NDJ Life Lesson:

You will find that most of the time you get what you deserve. There are no shortcuts in life and few second chances. If you have the wrong intentions, you may achieve short-term success, but ultimately people will find you out and you will lose.

6. Joe Fazaro Fight

Four months into my junior year, we got word that a there was going to be a new leader joining the La Raza gang. His name was Jesse Montoya, and he was transferring from a school in Grand Junction, Colorado. Grand Junction had a large Hispanic population and a lot of migrant workers. We heard a couple of rumors about Jesse: 1) He was big and strong, and 2) He beat the shit out of the former La Raza leader the first time he met him.

The Mexicans had a new leader, and they were getting braver by the minute. I remember the first time I saw Jesse Montoya. He was huge—over six feet tall and probably 220 pounds. He was confident, and he looked just plain mean. He had three Mexican girls walking with him. The girls wanted to be noticed when they were with Jesse. Most of the time, the Mexican girls were almost invisible unless they were fighting with each other.

The Mexican girls had their own gangs. There were four or five separate girl gangs affiliated with La Raza. The Pack Rats' girlfriends and female groupies did not have gangs; they relied on the guys to protect them from the Mexicans, both male and female. In the '60s, a lot of the girls had beehive hairdos, and it was rumored that the Mexican girls had razors hidden in theirs. Most of the time, the female Mexican gangs left the Pack Rat chicks alone. However, with Jesse on the scene, the Mexican girls became much more threatening.

Eventually, word got back to Joe Fazaro that the girl gangs were getting more aggressive. If that weren't enough, they told everyone that Jesse was looking for Joe Fazaro. Jesse was going to kick his ass.

I could not believe what was going on. It was impossible to imagine how things might change if Joe wasn't the number-one guy. It would definitely create a new balance of power and probably lead to an all-out war with La Raza. The Pack Rats wouldn't stand idle and let Jesse pick them off one at a time. If Joe lost, who would be next in line to take his place? If there weren't anyone to take over the leadership role of the Pack Rats, the only other option would be to have several Pack Rats jump Jesse, kick his ass, and then proceed to have an all-out gang war with the remaining members of the Mexican gang. Choosing this option would undoubtedly piss off every single guy at West High School whether they were Mexican or not. It could also piss off some people at East High School and Manual High School. Just by sheer numbers alone, the Pack Rats and their affiliates—the small-p/small-r guys—would get wiped out if West, East, and Manual decided to join forces with La Raza.

It was about twenty minutes before first bell one morning in December when I saw Jesse Montoya walking with a girl in a counterclockwise direction around the hall on my left. I was standing at the corner and then noticed Joe Fazaro walking in a clockwise direction to my right. I knew that they would see each other within a minute or two.

Joe wore horn-rimmed glasses and was carrying a notepad and a book. When he turned the corner, Jesse was about twenty feet away. There was no doubt in my mind what was going to happen next. Joe immediately dropped his pad and book, reached for his glasses, flung them off to the side of the hall, and without saying a word, put his fists up to begin the most memorable fight I have ever seen.

Jesse pushed his girlfriend aside and continued to walk toward Joe. There was no banter, no words, and no hesitation. Neither person had the advantage, although Jesse was much bigger and physically looked to have the best of it.

I realized at that moment that I had never seen Joe Fazaro fight anyone. I had just heard a few stories and reasoned that if Joe was the head guy of the Pack Rats, the stories must be true. What I was about to see would without question become "The Story," forever replacing all of the old stories about Joe. And for those of us in the Class of 1963 or 1964, Joe Fazaro would be the guy that kept La Raza from taking over and changing everything for everyone.

When you see someone that is truly exceptional as an athlete, dancer, singer, or whatever, it is hard not to notice. Joe Fazaro was an exceptional fighter. He was so tough and strong it seemed unreal, he was so mean it was scary, and one of his most amazing attributes was that he was absolutely fearless.

Joe Fazaro dismantled Jesse Montoya in about two or three minutes. At the end, Jesse—seeing that Joe would not let up—ran down the hall into Mr. Evans' office. Joe straightened himself up, picked up his glasses, pad, and book, and started walking toward Mr. Evans' office. He walked at his normal pace and arrived a few minutes after Jesse. Naturally, everyone followed Joe to see what would happen next. We could see Jesse talking to Mr. Evans. Next thing, Joe walked calmly into the office, and when he got close enough to Jesse, he dropped his books again and punched Jesse right in front of Mr. Evans.

Even Mr. Evans had to be surprised because nobody ever challenged the Dean of Boys or his authority. Mr. Evans pulled Joe off of Jesse and it was over. Joe Fazaro was suspended from school for three days and the rest of us breathed a lot easier knowing that things weren't going to change anytime soon.

NDJ Life Lesson:

When you are in a leadership position, people rely on you to be a winner. In challenging times, they expect you will know what to do and how to do it. Never think that you can bluff your way through things and expect a happy ending.

5. - 2. Became a small-p/small-r guy; Learned Italian; Cool car; Played Pool

It's a funny thing, but all of these experiences played a significant role in shaping my life as an adult. The small-p/small-r guy thing helped me become street smart. Learning Italian helped me develop greater self-esteem and confidence. The car thing was a passion I would never grow tired of, and the pool player thing helped me understand how to win and how to lose.

NDJ Life Lesson:

We all have experiences to share and stories to tell. Most people don't realize it when they do have a story to tell and those that do often miss the lessons that could have been learned. Pay attention.

1. Made Some Friends & Set New Goals

By the end of my junior year, I had made a few friends and knew quite a few people at school and the pool hall. I had made remarkable progress from my days in parochial school, and overall I was much happier.

I realized that I had set some goals, worked to improve myself, and had my share of winners and losers. The key thing was that I was in action, I was experiencing life, I was surviving in a dangerous place, and I was positioned to improve.

I needed to set new goals for my senior year, and I had to at least think about what I was going to do after I graduated from North.

An obvious goal for me was to change pool halls. Fischer's was a good pool hall, but all of the action (gambling) was happening at the Family Fun Center. The Fun Center had its grand opening in 1962 and quickly became the best place with the best players. The pool hall had previously been a vegetable market that was owned and operated by Johnnie and Tony Archer. The two brothers decided to get out of the produce business when they saw a new Safeway supermarket under construction across the street.

I also set a goal to find another Becky Wright. Boy, was I going uphill on this one. The toughest thing to decide on was what to do after graduation.

NDJ Life Lesson:

A lot of people think you have to work hard to get ahead. I think you have to work hard to stay where you are. If you find that you are not working toward some objective, ask yourself this question: How did homeless people become homeless?

Chapter 10

High School Memories: Senior Year
*What Happens When You Become Obsolete?
& Why Won't Things Stop Changing?*

It's funny, but most of my buddies could not wait to graduate from North High School. I didn't feel the same way. For one thing, I had no plans for the future. I also concluded that there would never again be a place or time when I could get in my car and drive a little more than a mile to locate over a thousand girls. I was correctly sensing the fact that what I knew and could do at North to be somewhat successful would not apply to any other place on the planet. I was acutely aware that my place in the social hierarchy of North High School was coming to an end. In less than nine months, all of the things that meant so much to me, like knowing which public park to use for fighting, understanding where to hang out at in the smoking area, and countless other pieces of gang-related knowledge that made up the Pack Rat survival guide were going to be absolutely worthless pieces of information. My fellow comrades and I would be as obsolete as bobby socks, Howdy Doody, hula hoops, Jerry Lee Lewis, and pink cars to name a few. God, it had taken two full years for me to get this cool, and I only got to be cool for a little while longer. Where was the justice?

If that weren't bad enough, there were more changes to deal with. Most noteworthy was the fact that the Mexicans were apparently breeding like rabbits, and the balance of power in North Denver had shifted yet again. Now it was about sixty percent Mexican, twenty-five percent Italian, and the rest was…well, what difference did it make what it was? What did this mean? It meant more policy changes for the Pack Rats. It was numbers that forced the Pack Rats to create a small-p/small-r rung on the gangland ladder. Now, believe it or not, the powers that be had decided that there were some Mexicans that somehow could fit into our little gang world. In the Class of 1964 there would be Mexican Pack Rats.

Most notable of the new Latino Pack Rats was Robert Vigil. He was five feet four inches tall and about 185 pounds of total muscle. His skin looked like leather, impervious to pain. It looked thicker than a normal person's skin as though it was three or four-ply thick. When Robert joined the Pack Rats, he immediately became the number-two guy, second only to Joe. I doubt that Mexicans would have been eligible to become Pack Rats had it not been for the extraordinary pugilistic abilities of Robert Vigil. Oh, yeah, I almost forgot: Robert's nickname was Doberman.

I think drafting key people to join the Pack Rats was another example of Joe Fazaro's leadership and pragmatism. I am not sure that there was a single Pack Rat other than Joe that would have made the decision to embrace certain Mexicans. But true to form, Joe did the right thing for the overall good of the gang and to maintain a foothold in the old neighborhood that was rapidly disappearing.

NDJ Life Lesson:

In your life, you will have dozens of chances to become obsolete. Your work-related skills, spouse-related skills, friendship skills, and father/mother skills can all go out of fashion or into disrepair. Embrace change as the catalyst to keep enhancing and expanding your skills.

Chapter 11

High School Memories: Senior Year
Meet Doberman

It was a Saturday when the doorbell rang. I went to the front door to see who was there and nearly fell over when I saw Robert Vigil on our front porch. I tried to think of what I had done to piss Doberman off. He had never spoken to me before, so I knew he wasn't ringing my doorbell to chew the fat. I thought about just hiding behind the door and pretending that no one was home, but I was sure that he had a purpose for being there and that he would probably come back later.

I was trapped, so I opened the front door. At that point, I still had an aluminum storm door separating me from Doberman. Unfortunately, it was winter so the screen door was covered by a glass partition that slid up and down, forcing me to step out toward the porch to open the aluminum door. Once I did that, I was totally unprotected. I knew if I showed any fear at the arrival of one of my "gang mates" my small-p/small-r status would be history. I opened the door and stepped out onto the porch.

Doberman reached out his hand, and introduced himself. "I'm Robert Vigil. My friends call me Doberman." He went on to say that he noticed my '50 Mercury at school and wanted to know who had done the work on the interior—the white and blue Naugahyde seats and door liners. Amazingly, he had just purchased a '50 Mercury with the exact color gray as mine and wanted to duplicate my interior. His Mercury was a four-door, which usually meant that the car was not cool, but the '50 Mercury was an exception to the rule. The rear doors were hinged on the back of the car, enabling the front door to swing open to the left and the rear door to swing open to the right. This was quite unique, and the styling of the doors and shape of the roof made the four-door '50 Merc really cool.

Within a few weeks, Doberman's Mercury was the mirror image of mine, including the painted undercarriage, engine bolts, and Scavenger pipes. It was amazing to see both of these cars parked next to each other in the parking lot. They were beautiful, and the fact that they were almost identical made people want to look at them all the more.

My '50 Mercury caused me to meet and become "friends" with the number-two guy in the Pack Rats. This relationship had both pluses and minuses. I had access to parties and people that I never had before Doberman. The relationship also exposed me to more danger, more fights, and more Mexicans.

The best example of more danger, fights, and Mexicans came on a Thursday night at the Baja Club in downtown Denver. The Baja Club was a 3.2 beer joint five nights a week, but on Thursday it was a dance club that served soft drinks only. They used to call it "Coke Night," as in "Coca-Cola Night." They had a live band and charged a fortune for admission and another fortune for a soft drink.

Each week, the Baja Club was packed with high school kids from all over Denver. The surfer phenomenon was just emerging on the music scene, and the Baja Club featured one of the most popular Beach Boy-type bands, a local group called the Astronauts. Along with the change in music, there was a change in style and appearance. Blonde, shaggy hair was in, leather jackets and the *Grease* look was out.

It seemed that literally overnight the Pack Rat look looked terribly outdated. In fact, people at the Baja Club would look at the north side guys and chicks and make fun of them behind their backs. The girls from North still wore their beehive hairdos, and there were not a lot of Italians or Mexicans with blonde hair. A lot of the north side guys still wore their hair in a pompadour style and used a tube of Brylcreem every week to keep their hair from ever moving.

It was on a Thursday night, when the club was featuring surfer music, that the new surfer-style students from JFK High School decided to bully and make fun of the people there from North High.

It began when the girlfriend of a football player from JFK bumped into Freddie Villanueva's date on the dance floor. The girls had words and surprisingly, the football player's girlfriend wanted to get into a fight. She was a big girl, much bigger than Freddie's girlfriend, and looked to be very athletic. Freddie was trying to keep the girls apart when the football player boyfriend moved in to confront Freddie.

The boyfriend was about six foot two, two hundred plus pounds, and was wearing a high school letter jacket with a football insignia. In a matter of seconds, all of the kids from both schools were facing each other on the dance floor. Everyone knew that they would be 86'd if a fight broke out inside the Baja Club, so both sides agreed to go outside. We knew we were outnumbered—about thirty to twenty—and that we didn't have all of the toughest guys from North. We did have the second toughest Pack Rat, Doberman, but after that there were sort of ordinary guys like Freddie and me. Oh, and by the way, Freddie was a midget too at five foot six.

When we got outside, we walked about a quarter of a block down the street to get away from the entrance of the Baja Club. At that point, Freddie faced the football player and they had words. Doberman was on Freddie's left, and I was on Freddie's right, just a few feet from this guy with the big mouth. Doberman told Freddie to go after this guy, but instead Freddie continued to exchange words. He was definitely reluctant to get into a fight. The football player's girlfriend told Doberman to shut up and said that if Freddie knew what was good for him, he should just back off. Doberman looked at me and mouthed the word "three." He then mouthed "one, two, three." When he reached three, we both hit the football player in the face. I hit him in the mouth with my left hand and Doberman hit him in the head with his right hand.

I remember reaching as high as I could to hit this guy in the mouth. I cut my middle finger on his tooth. Doberman really smacked this guy at the same time and, yes, the bigger they are, the harder they fall. This guy hit the pavement. The very next instant, Doberman smacked this guy's girlfriend. Then all hell broke loose, and everyone in the street was fighting everyone else, guys and girls included. Someone hit me in the back of my head, knocking my glasses off. It was dark, and I remember being on the pavement searching for my glasses. Somehow I found them, put them in my jacket pocket, and got back into the brawl. It was impossible to tell if we were winning or losing. The key thing was to see people from North that I knew continuing to fight. As long as I could see that happening, I knew I still had a chance to win.

Within a few minutes after the fight broke out, we heard sirens, and shortly after that we saw the flashing lights from police cruisers converging on the scene. At that point, everyone started running. I ran across a parking lot and down an alley. I had to try to get back to my car that I parked a couple of blocks south of the Baja Club. I had to keep from getting caught by the police and keep from accidentally running into some of the kids from the other school. With my heart pounding and adrenaline pumping, I needed to keep my composure and get home safely. I decided to take as direct a route to my car as possible. Initially, I thought of taking a long route that would get me as far away from the fight scene as possible. I could go six blocks north, ten blocks east, and then nine blocks south until I circled around to my car. But I scrubbed that plan because I concluded that the longer I was on the street, the chance that I would be spotted by the police or students from JFK would increase.

When I got to my car, I couldn't wait until I got the door unlocked and was inside behind the wheel. I turned the key, hit the starter button, heard the engine turnover and start, and eased out from my parking place. A couple of blocks went by when I reached the major intersection that would take me back to North Denver and my ultimate destination, which of course was Jim's Pizzeria.

As I drove alone in my car to the pizzeria, I knew that I no longer wanted to be a small-p/small-r guy. I had just been involved in a senseless gang fight, and the guys that I thought were cool were nothing more than moronic bullies. I decided to immediately begin distancing myself from Doberman.

NDJ Life Lesson:

There is a price to pay when you decide to hang out with the wrong people. You may find yourself in a situation that is way beyond anything you yourself would create.

Ultimately, there is no benefit to being a part of any group for the sole purpose of avoiding loneliness. At some point in your life, you must find a way to be happy with yourself, by yourself.

Chapter 12

High School Memories: Senior Year
Izadore

I had become very comfortable being a regular at Fischer's Pool Hall. I knew all of the people that played there, had a good relationship with the owners, and knew how the tables played like the back of my hand. At the same time, I knew at some point I would have to go to the Family Fun Center pool hall. It was getting harder to win money at Fischer's. I had established myself as one of the better nine-ball players, and as a result, I was running out of people that would play me without a spot for money. Another problem was that there were very few new players showing up at Fischer's. The new players and potential marks were going to the Fun Center.

It was a Saturday morning at Fischer's when a guy by the name of Izadore and his mini-entourage strolled into the pool hall. Accompanying Izzie were three girls that were not particularly good looking, but at the same time they all were sexy in an unusual way. The first thing I noticed about these four was that they didn't dress or look like anybody you would expect to see in North Denver. Izzie's hair was unusually long for that era. The colors of his clothes were loud and brought him instant attention. The girls wore a lot of makeup and made it clear that they wanted to be noticed. But the most important thing about this foursome was that Izzie was carrying a pool cue case.

It was shaping up to be a pretty interesting Saturday morning. Before long, Izzie walked up to me, introduced himself, said that he normally played at the Fun Center, and asked if I wanted to play some five-dollar nine-ball. I asked him if he would play for two dollars on the nine and one dollar on the five-ball. He said no. In doing so, he established himself as the more confident and aggressive player and probably the player willing to gamble the most money. I had twenty-seven dollars in my jeans pocket and was worried about not having enough money to play at the five-dollar level. I always felt that I needed at least ten times the price being played. Nine-ball is a fast game, and it is not unusual to be four or five games down in a match before settling in and getting your bearings. Another problem was that it was always harder for me to play aggressively on short money. When I played on short money, instead of focusing on winning I focused on trying to avoid losing.

I looked around the pool hall, and there was no one that I could borrow twenty dollars from. I also realized that if I didn't play Izzie, there wasn't anyone else for me to play. I was anxious to play someone and win some cash. So, I pulled out a coin to flip and said, "Call it for break."

It had been a long time since I played someone that I didn't know, and I was nervous. Izzie seemed calm, cool, and looked as though the five-dollar speed limit was no problem at all. It turned out that Izzie's father was a dentist and his family had a lot of money. Izzie drove a new '64 Chevy Impala 327. It had a four-speed transmission, and chrome rims with narrow whitewall tires. It was turquoise blue on the bottom with a white top. It was a pretty car, not bad-looking. It was different, like Izzie.

I started very fast. I rarely missed a shot and was playing as good as I was able. In a flash, I was forty to fifty dollars ahead, thinking that Izzie would raise the white flag of surrender any minute. But guess what? Izzie was different, and he seemed unfazed about being down. When he paid me for winning, he had a thick roll of twenty-dollar bills. When he was sixty dollars down, he asked if I would raise the stakes and play for ten dollars per game.

I believed that if I said, "No, let's stay at five dollars," I most likely would be closing the door on future matches with Izzie. It was obvious that he liked the action, he liked to gamble, and he liked being on display to his girlfriends. I also believed that if I decided to quit while I was ahead, that would definitely have ended my chances of winning more money from Izzie forever. So I said, "Rack 'em up."

I had never played ten-dollar nine-ball. I would soon find out that ten dollars was over my speed limit. Izzie proceeded to win eight straight games. I was forced to unscrew my stick and admit defeat. It was a sickening feeling to have been up sixty dollars thirty minutes prior and end up losing twenty dollars. That was an eighty-dollar turnaround, which was a very large amount of money to me at that time. The expressions of Izzie's ever-adoring girlfriends added to my feeling of nausea.

I was a better player than Izzie, but it didn't matter because he got the cash. What I didn't realize was that Izzie was a better gambler than I was. Because I was convinced that I could beat Izzie and win a lot of money if I played him again, I decided it was time to go to the Family Fun Center.

NDJ Life Lesson:

In order to win, you must quit playing while you are ahead.

Never believe that making a bad decision today will lead to more opportunities to win tomorrow.

Chapter 13

High School Memories: Senior Year
Introduction to the Family Fun Center

My pool game continued to improve to the point where I felt I was ready for the big leagues—the Family Fun Center pool hall. On the front door of the Fun Center was a sign that read, "No Gambling and No Guns." Ten minutes after walking through that door, you knew that no one was paying any attention to the gambling provision on the sign, and you had to wonder if the rest of the sign's message was being ignored as well.

Johnnie Archer, who co-owned the pool hall, was flamboyant and a flashy dresser with a big diamond pinky ring. His brother, Tony, was very quiet and the total opposite of Johnnie. Johnnie played pool occasionally and gambled while Tony cooked in the kitchen.

The Fun Center had seventeen tables: 1 three-cushion billiard table, 3 five-foot by ten-foot snooker tables with pockets as tight as a mouse's ear, and 13 four-and-a-half by nine-foot Brunswick pool tables. Every table had green felt. There was a long snack bar with about a dozen stools and six tables for food service. There were two areas near the snack bar that had pinball machines and other arcade games.

The Fun Center had a much different look and feel compared to Fischer's. One major difference was that there were very few young people at the Fun Center. There were a lot of businessmen wearing coats and ties. Because the crowd was more mature, there was the feeling that there was a lot of money in the establishment. I also felt that it was going to be a hell of a lot harder to get in.

There was a snooker table close to the cash register that was designated the "A-table." The other snooker tables were designated as the "B" and "C" tables, and the rest of the pool tables had no special designation.

The A-table was reserved for golf games, and it was the best, most highly maintained table of its kind in the pool hall. Only the best players could use the table. This was the arena of the players, the big-money games, and the sweaters. The A-table accommodated sweaters by providing ample seating and good viewing. The B and C snooker tables were reserved for golf games during the day and were used by the B and C players.

Golf is a game played on a snooker table. There can be a maximum of seven players per game. Each player has one ball. Balls are assigned to players before the start of every game. Each table has a pill box that looks like a red rubber jar. Inside the jar are little, round, black and white pills that are flat on one side and numbered from one to seven. At the beginning of each game, one of the players shakes the pill box and randomly gives a pill to each one of the players. The person that gets the one-pill is assigned the yellow two-ball; the two-pill is assigned the green three-ball; the three-pill gets the brown four-ball; the four-pill gets the blue five-ball; the five-pill gets the pink six-ball; the six-pill gets the black seven-ball; and the final pill gets the red snooker ball with no number.

The game begins by placing the yellow two-ball on the spot that is used to rack the red balls when playing snooker, and the cue ball can be positioned anywhere within the "D" located at the head of the table. The D is a semicircle located on every snooker table. On the flat portion of the D there are three spots. One spot is located on each end of the straight line, and a third spot is located in the middle of the straight line. When conventional snooker is played using the numbered balls and fifteen red balls, the D is used to spot the two, three, and four-balls.

Snooker Table

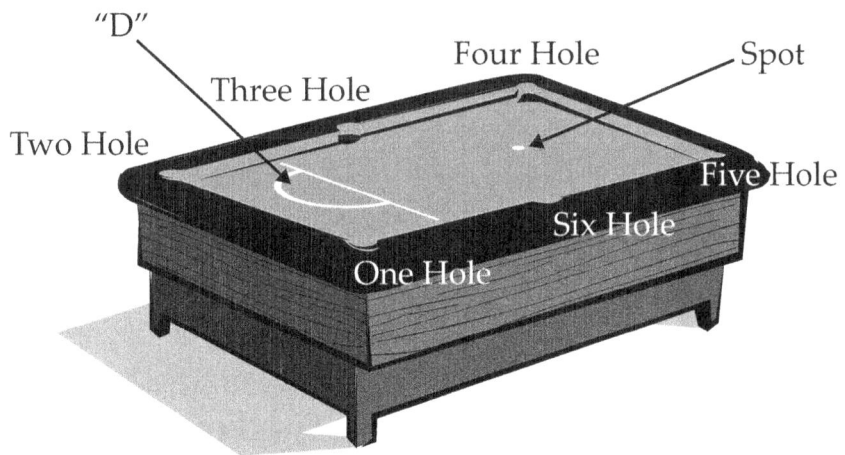

The corner pocket on the right side near the D is called the one-hole. The corner pocket on the left side near the D is the two-hole. Then comes the next sequence of pockets: the side pocket on the left (the three-hole), the remaining corner pocket on the left (the four-hole), the adjacent corner pocket (the five-hole), and the side pocket on the right side (the six-hole). In field golf there are eighteen holes; in snooker golf there are six holes. The winner is the first person to complete the course, holes one through six. The six-hole is referred to as the out-hole.

The game is played on a large five-foot by ten-foot table with small snooker balls and narrow, tight pockets. When there are seven players all trying to pocket their ball in the one-hole at the beginning of the game, the path to the pocket is often blocked by the balls of other players. Conversely, after the initial break, other players' balls can block your ability to even hit your ball, let alone advance it closer to the one-hole. Golf on a snooker table is a game of strategy, patience, bank shots, and safeties. When you have an open shot to make a pocket and advance to the next hole, you had better not miss.

The game is usually played for a fixed amount of money for the game and a smaller amount for each time you scratch. In 1964, a typical "ring game" in which there are three or more players would be played for five dollars per game and fifty cents per scratch. A scratch is taken each time you shoot the cue ball into any hole, when you hit another ball before striking your own ball, and when you are unable to hit your ball when it is your turn to shoot. If you hit another player's ball before hitting your own ball, which is referred to as a "bad hit," there is an additional one-dollar fee that goes to the player assigned to the ball you hit. Also, your ball is removed from the table and the remaining balls that were moved because of your scratch are relocated to their original position. Prior to shooting a shot that has the possibility of resulting in a bad hit, the balls that may be moved are "marked" with spit. The shooter lets the others know that a bad hit may occur, and it is their responsibility to wet the end of their finger and touch a spot close to the ball or balls that may need to be relocated back if a bad hit takes place.

A good ring game with seven top players can take an hour or more to play. Players can accumulate ten to fifteen scratches, and the loser of the game has to pay double. In fact, there are six losers and one winner, but the big loser is the person that "sold out." Since each person's shot is determined by the departure of the preceding player, the person that shoots before the eventual winner is the official loser. If the player assigned the four-ball wins, the owner of the three-ball is the loser and pays double. If the three-ball had ten scratches, the player would pay the owner of the four-ball five dollars for the game, five dollars for scratches, and double for selling out for a total of twenty dollars. The other five losers would pay five dollars for the game plus scratches. A winner could collect between fifty to sixty dollars for winning a game. In 1964, that was a lot of money for a kid that was seventeen with a '50 Mercury.

There was only one problem: I had only played nine-ball at Fischer's Pool Hall and had never played a game of golf on a snooker table in my life. I watched the A players and thought to myself, "This game is unbelievable." I knew I wanted to play on the A-table someday.

I also remember looking around at the pool hall and the people, hoping I would never forget the impressions and sights that the Family Fun Center had provided me on my first visit. I had no way of knowing that I would frequent the Fun Center two to three times a week for the next twenty-seven years or that the sights I was so focused on would not change more than one percent over the next quarter century.

My first visit to the Family Fun Center turned out to be another one of those defining moments. Ahead of me lay experiences, lessons, victories, failures, friends, and enemies that helped shape me as a person. The competition that I found at the Fun Center provided the backdrop to obtaining a wealth of knowledge that I would use to effectively compete in the world of business.

NDJ Life Lesson:

There are always new experiences that await you if you are willing to seek them out.

You must get up, get out, and move. Pick up the phone, read the paper, say hello, stir the pot. Do not wait for things to come to you.

Chapter 14

High School Doesn't Last Forever
Introduction to the Real World

During most of my senior year at North High, I worried about the future. In particular, I worried about what was going to happen to me after I graduated. My parents seemed to be waiting for me to figure out what I should do. I'm certain that their parents didn't provide them with any direction, so they were simply following the example they experienced as young adults. In my mind, I only had two options: I could try to get some kind of job or I could join the Armed Forces.

The Vietnam War was always in the back of my mind. If I didn't go to college, I believed I would be drafted, so it didn't make much sense to try to get a job. If I enlisted, I could at least pick the branch of the Armed Services that would give me the best shot at surviving the war. Using that logic, I joined the Navy Reserves in the middle of my senior year. I picked the Navy because I was pretty sure North Vietnam did not have a big-time Navy. This decision didn't stop me from worrying, but it narrowed the focus of my concerns.

At least I had a plan, and I would be taking the initiative instead of waiting to get drafted and ending up in the Army.

Joining the Navy Reserves meant that once a month I was required to attend meetings at the Federal Reserve Center. I think it was during my second month when I was issued my uniforms, peacoat, sailor hat, and duffel bag. Included in my duffel bag was a single v-stripe insignia that I was supposed to sew on the sleeve of my shirt. The single stripe designated me as a seaman recruit. To earn a second stripe, I would have to successfully complete boot camp training. My reserve unit was scheduled to attend boot camp in August or September, just a few months after I graduated from North High School.

I can't remember my parents' reaction to my plan to enlist. I knew that I needed to get their permission to join the Navy because I was still only seventeen. I think they agreed with the logic I used to make my decision.

It was at this point when I realized that everything had changed. One day I woke up as a high school student, drove my hot rod car to school, and worried about finding Izzie to play some more nine-ball at the Fun Center. Then, in the blink of an eye, I woke up and found that I would be looked at and treated as an adult. I could join the Navy, leave North Denver, and if I got lucky, shoot some guy from North Vietnam. I was genuinely worried now because I realized that I didn't feel at all ready to be an adult. I had absolutely no skills, unless you considered playing pool a skill.

The hardest part of my dilemma was that I had absolutely no one to talk to about my concerns and worries. I felt alone. To the outside world, I had to pretend to be in control, confident, and move forward with my life as if I knew what I was doing. It is times like that when you just have to have faith that everything is going to work out. Somehow, everything will be fine.

After joining the Navy, I could get back to the things that were really important, things like girls, cars, and playing pool. After all, I was a big-deal senior that knew his way around the block, having survived the day-to-day violence that made North High such a special place. And best of all, there was a brand-new crop of sophomore girls that would be looking for a cool guy with a cool car. Armed with a good attitude and an unmistakable air of confidence, I was able to date quite a few cute girls. There was one girl that was quite memorable; her name was Cheryl Weston.

I remember thinking to myself when I asked Cheryl if she wanted to go to the Scotchman Drive-In to get a Coke, "Cheryl is pretty nice-looking, wears a little too much makeup, and seems very different from the rest of the girls." Boy, did I get that last one right. The amazing thing about Cheryl was that she was the one calling the shots, not me, and it was that way with everyone she was with. She clearly stood apart from the rest of the girls in the way that she dressed, acted, and talked. I would describe her as a Katharine Hepburn type in that she possessed a level of confidence, maturity, and sophistication that I had never seen before.

Cheryl accepted my invitation, gave me her address, phone number, and directions to her house, and told me when I should pick her up. Nothing about her style made me feel uncomfortable or like I was being bossed around. She got her way by saying things in a certain manner and with a smile or gesture that just made you want to do what she wanted you to do.

I picked up Cheryl right on time, and I remember how different she looked from the other girls I had dated. She was wearing pants, which was very unusual for girls or women to wear during the '60s, and a really cool tweed jacket and matching beret. I am a sucker for women that like to wear hats. After we made our appearance at the Scotchman, I asked her if she wanted to go for a drive. She said sure and told me that she knew a place where we could go park and make out. It actually never dawned on me that girls got horny. I thought I was dreaming. Did I hear her correctly?

As she was giving me directions to this destination, she said in a very calm manner, "Do you have a rubber?" All of the cool guys at North kept at least one rubber in their wallet. You could tell because when they took their wallet out to get something, you could see a round circle embossed in the leather. My wallet had a round circle, but it had been placed there a long time ago, and I wasn't sure if it was still good. I wondered if there was an expiration date or something that would tell you if it was still usable. I pulled over, took out my wallet, and looked at my one and only rubber. I saw something that you would expect to find if you were excavating for old artifacts in Egypt. My rubber had become a brittle piece of parchment. We both knew that this rubber was not going to see any action that night or ever.

"No problem," Cheryl said. "There is a drug store near here, and you can go in and get some new ones." The ancient rubber had been given to me by one of my friends. I had never purchased one on my own before. The tone in her voice made it clear that she thought buying a rubber was no big deal. Now I was going to really be tested. I knew there was no way that I was going to let this opportunity not happen just because I was afraid to go into a drug store and buy a rubber.

Cheryl directed me to the store, and I parked and got out. As I walked toward the entrance, I kept trying to think to myself, "What do they call rubbers?" I knew there was a word for it, and my nervous mind was going through my limited vocabulary data bank searching for that word. I walked in, and in the next instant my brain came up with the word I needed in the nick of time. "Condom! Yes, that's it. I need a condom."

There were only two people in the drug store when I arrived. There was a gentleman that I imagined was the owner and a much younger woman that could have been his daughter. I walked toward the man but was cut off by the young woman.

"Hello, can I help you?"

"Not really. Can I talk to the pharmacist?"

"I am the pharmacist," she said.

"Well, then can I talk to him?" I asked and pointed at the only other person that was in the store.

"Father, this young man wants to talk to you."

I walked up to him and said in a very soft voice, "I want to buy a condom."

He didn't say anything for a few seconds, and then spoke in a very loud voice. "Julie, this young man wants to buy a condom, and I don't remember where we keep them. Do you know?"

Yikes! What on earth is this guy doing? Doesn't he know that this kind of thing should be dealt with discreetly?

Julie replied, "I believe we keep them in the cabinet near the register."

By then I was totally embarrassed, but I stood my ground and managed to buy three condoms. I thought I'd better get more than one so I could avoid being in this same situation for a while.

When I got back in the car, Cheryl gave me directions to the make-out spot. In a short while, we arrived at our destination. I suggested we get in the back seat. Once we got in the back seat, I began to unbutton my jeans. Cheryl said that we didn't have to rush, and then she grabbed me and started making out. From that point on, she orchestrated everything that would happen and when it would happen. This experience was a lot different from the wham-bam approach that I used during my first encounter. Thankfully, Cheryl knew how things should go and had no problem giving me direction. About an hour after we got in the back, we were getting out of the car again to get in the front seat. I realized that I was very lucky to have had this experience with Cheryl, and I wondered how long it would have taken me on my own to learn what she taught me that night. Fortunately for me, I wouldn't have to find out about foreplay (and much more) the hard way, so to speak.

Cheryl was ahead of her time. She was a prototype for today's modern woman. She was independent, self-assured, classy, sexy, and smart. I knew that I was way over my head being with her and that even though she seemed to enjoy our experience together, I was pretty sure that it was going to be a one-time thing. The nice thing for me was that Cheryl never did anything or said anything to me that made me feel unworthy. Quite the opposite. She acted as though she was happy to be with me. What a classy gal she was. I think every young man would feel extremely fortunate, as I did, to spend some time with a gal like Cheryl.

NDJ Life Lesson:

Be honest with yourself because you don't know what you don't know.

When you are honest with people, you create the possibility that they will teach you.

The exception to this NDJ Life Lesson: Know when you don't know what you should know or have pretended to know.

When you are honest with people in this circumstance, you create the possibility that they will betray you or become unhappy with this revelation. Why? Probably because you have been pretending to be something you are not. People never like to be lied to.

It is essential that you find a way to learn what you should know on your own.

After I joined the Navy, I thought that the next four years of my future was more or less up to Uncle Sam to worry about. I believed that being a seaman was a lot like being a sophomore at North High: I would show up and try to figure out how to survive. I needed to determine who the Joe Fazaro's of the Navy were and come up with a plan to fit in.

The thing about North High School that you must not forget is that you can never let your guard down. No matter what signals you are getting from the Pack Rats that ran the place, like Joe Fazaro nodding at you or Doberman acting like you were his best friend, you could wake up tomorrow and get door popped by any one of them on any given day. As long as you went to North High, the number-one priority was survival.

At North, there was an imaginary organization chart that existed in the minds of the students. Just as in business, the people at the top of the org chart seemed to have more power and more perks. Since this hierarchy existed in the minds of people, you could never be sure of where you stood in the overall scheme of things. The top guys like Joe, Doberman, and about six to ten of their close associates were universally thought of as the people running the show. The top guys determined who the small-p/small-r guys were and provided the leadership necessary to remain in control and prevent La Raza from taking over.

How you were viewed in this hierarchy determined by a great many things. The imaginary level you were ranked at helped determine the approximate location you could park in the parking lot, the parties you would be invited to, the fights you would be allowed to watch, and the girls that would be willing to give you the time of day, to name a few. No matter where you ranked, there was always the possibility of moving up or down in the food chain. You always had to worry about some guy wanting to move up, or maybe he just didn't like the way you looked and wanted you to move down. In either case, the quickest way for that guy to get your position on the imaginary org chart was to kick your ass. It seemed impossible to me that anyone could envy me or want to depose me from a make-believe position to enhance his stature and somehow improve the quality of his life, but before the year was over, I would become the target of one of the many nutcases running around North High.

I managed to become a target when I inadvertently pissed off one of my classmates during one of our physical education classes (although classmates may not be the best way to describe the whack jobs that made up a large part of the graduating class of 1964). The Phys Ed instructor was also the wrestling coach. The wrestling team was the only team that North High School ever produced that could compete with any of the other schools. Our football, basketball, and baseball teams were consistently awful. We ended up at the bottom or next to the bottom in the rankings every year. Our biggest hope was that we would pull off a big upset every now and then. And to everyone's surprise, the football team and basketball team gave us some great performances and a few unexpected victories.

The wrestling team, on the other hand, was a perennial winner. Somehow, we managed to put together a strong team every year and had a few of our strongest performers compete at the state championships. One of my cousin's best friends was on the wrestling team and lettered all three years as a varsity member in the 160-pound weight class. His name was Bob Casagrande. As chance would have it, I met Bob at Tommy's house when I was on one of my weekend visits. He was a great guy, and I got to ask him about what it was like to be on the team. I remember asking what his best wrestling move was. He showed a move he used to outmaneuver one of his opponents, and the tricky move allowed him to pin his man in a matter of seconds.

Okay. Let's get back to that fateful day when I was in Phys Ed and Mr. Moles, our teacher and the varsity wrestling coach, decided to pair us up for a wrestling exercise. Naturally, he selected the pairings based on weight. In class that day was a new guy, a sophomore named Dean Naismith. Dean had tried out to be a member of the varsity team but was beaten out by Tommy Lopez, who was a two-year letterman and one of the stronger members of the team. But because Dean showed promise, he was put on the junior varsity team and was a lock to succeed Lopez the following year.

Dean and I were about the same height and weight, so when it was time for the smaller guys to wrestle each other,

I was matched up with him. Our teacher played the role of referee and awarded points for takedowns and escapes during the match. We all kept score in our heads as we watched the usually futile efforts of our fellow gym mates. To reduce the chance of injury, Mr. Moles started each match from the down position where one wrestler is down on his hands and knees and the other is alongside him with his right arm around his opponent's waist with his left hand gripped around his left arm. Once in this position, Mr. Moles yelled "wrestle" and the match began.

When it was my turn to wrestle, Mr. Moles told me to take the top position, and Dean took the bottom position. I thought about Bob Casagrande's favorite move, the one that he showed me when I was over at my cousin Tommy's house. I thought to myself, "Why not try it?" A split second before Mr. Moles yelled wrestle, I jumped the gun and made the move. Probably because Dean did not expect me to know anything and because I started a millisecond before he was ready, the move worked like magic. The next thing I knew, I had both of Dean's shoulders touching the mat, and Mr. Moles wasn't sure if I jumped the gun or not. It happened so fast, the only thing left for Mr. Moles to do was count to two—with a pause in between—and it was over. Dean was furious and wanted a restart. He told Moles that I started early, which I did, but it was so close, and since the match didn't really count for anything, Dean was denied his second chance. Dean wanted me to wrestle him again after PE class was over. I declined and told him to forget about it, that I just got lucky. My little prank caused Dean to make me his number-one enemy.

I had no way of knowing how pissed off Dean was, and because he was a sophomore, I really didn't know anything about him. It was a few weeks later on a Friday night that I had a chance to find out a lot more about Dean, his temper, and the fact that he had decided to take my place on the imaginary org chart. Somehow, Dean found out that I was going to be at Fischer's Pool Hall. Apparently, he decided that the time was right to even the score, so he and his good buddy, Mike Miller, were waiting for me in the parking lot. Mike and Dean were always together, and they were hard not to notice. Dean was short like me, and Mike was at least six foot one. Waiting in the parking lot at Fischer's was a pretty good move on their part. I was by myself.

When I walked out of the pool hall I noticed two guys get out of a car and walk toward me. I couldn't make out who they were, so I kept walking toward my car, which was close to the car they had just exited. As I got closer, the parking lot lights made it possible for me to recognize both Dean and Mike. I didn't get any sense of impending danger, and with both of them about twenty feet from me, my first thought was that they showed up to play pool. Without a word spoken, when Dean was about six feet from me, he ran right at me and punched me in the nose. Immediately, blood gushed out of my nose. It was kind of amazing and scary at the same time. The amazing part was how much blood came out, and the scary part was how much blood came out.

Dean had decided to punch me out and then choose me out. Sort of an odd approach, but I guess he wanted to say what he wanted to say almost as badly as he wanted to punch me in the nose. As I was bent over trying to keep the blood from my clothes, I pulled out my handkerchief and attempted to slow down the red river. All the while, Dean ranted and raved about our wrestling match. He said something about getting his rematch tonight, now, in this parking lot. At that very moment, things did not look good, but I have always believed that I must have an angel watching out for me. This most certainly stems from my Catholic upbringing. However, unlike most of the things I learned in catechism class at St. Catherine's, my belief in angels was reinforced as improbable things happened in ways that kept me safe when all seemed lost.

Do you remember me mentioning Harry Marks? He was the ex-marine that worked part-time at Fischer's. Harry had just driven up to go to work and got out of his car just about the time Dean smacked me in the nose. Then when Dean started yelling at me, Harry headed toward us and managed to get Dean to calm down and stop screaming. Meanwhile, I was concerned that my nose was broken. I decided that if I was able to stop my nosebleed, my nose was probably not broken. I told Dean that if my nose wasn't broken, I would come back out and give him his rematch. If I couldn't stop the bleeding, I would meet him at a later date to settle things.

In the head, I was able to get the bleeding to stop. I waited a couple of minutes to make sure the bleeding was in check and then I headed back to the parking lot where I knew Dean was waiting. My mind was racing, and I'm sure my adrenaline level was close to maxing out. My first concern wasn't Dean—it was Mike. With him there I had no chance of coming out on top. I was certain that Mike would jump in to help Dean if I was winning the fight. With that concern, I headed toward the cash register where Harry was standing. I asked him if he would act as a referee and make sure Mike didn't make it two against one. He didn't want to leave the pool hall unsupervised, so I couldn't count on him to watch out for me. With that in mind, I knew I had to try to get Dean to meet me after school on Monday. I was pretty sure that wasn't going to fly, but I couldn't think of any other way to postpone the fight. As I walked outside, the air was cold. I decided to walk slowly until I was about ten feet from Dean, then rush toward him and just smack him in the nose to even things up.

There were still quite a few people in the parking lot waiting to see what was going to happen. They wanted to see more fighting, even though they didn't know Dean, Mike, or me. There is an age-old belief that "curiosity killed the cat." That belief was just about to validate itself. As I walked toward Dean, two carloads of guys pulled into the parking lot. They almost seemed to have been beamed down from the Starship Enterprise. There was a screech of rubber as one of the drivers slammed down the brake pedal. Then four doors opened and five or six guys exited the car. The noise, the chaos, and the frantic behavior of the newly arrived invaders caused everyone to shift their attention from Dean and me to the crazy people that had just shown up.

The two carloads of guys were looking to get revenge for something that happened earlier that evening. It seemed that one of the cars in the pool hall parking lot matched the description of the car they were looking for. The car had been seen driving away from a popular Westminster High

School hangout that had always been considered off-limits for anyone from North.

Without so much as a "fuck you," the new arrivals started to fight with anyone and everyone in the parking lot. All of a sudden, Dean, Mike, and I were on the same side, and we found ourselves in the middle of a huge fight without having the slightest idea why. I got hit and tried to return the favor as often as I could. When you are in a gang fight, there are no rules. Hitting from behind, kicking, low blows, and even biting are things that you have to protect yourself from. During the fight, I managed to maneuver to one of the highest points of the parking lot. I threw a punch and hit someone in the shoulder. This guy decided that matching up with someone that could see him did not give him the advantage he was seeking, so he moved away from me and got closer to a couple of other guys that were going at it. At that moment, I was not fighting anyone, but my little voice told me that I had better turn around. When I did, I found some guy coming up on me fast, getting ready to clobber me in the back of my head. This guy decided that he could sneak around and hit or kick people that weren't aware of his presence. He was so confident in his strategy that he didn't bother to take off his eyeglasses. Because I was at a higher elevation than the guy running up on me from behind, it was like punching downhill for me. That, plus the energy he was using to run up on me, caused this weasel to receive the most powerful punch that I ever delivered. It was a punch that nailed him right between the eyes. I remember seeing his eyeglasses break in two and watching him get knocked down and probably knocked out. What a sweet punch.

After a few hectic minutes, Harry came running out to the parking lot, yelling that he had called the Westminster Police and that they would be showing up at any minute. Harry's announcement caused everyone to stop and head for their cars. That's how it ended. Harry saved me twice that night.

Because I was careless and decided to embarrass Dean in gym class, I found myself in a situation that put me in physical danger. The only time I let my guard down—forgetting that survival was my number-one priority at North High—I literally got a bloody nose, and it could have been much worse.

Finally, graduation night came. I remember standing in line waiting to be seated for the ceremony. I looked at the faces of my classmates and realized that I may never see most of them again. I wondered if anyone else was thinking about it.

NDJ Life Lesson:

When you embarrass someone or act like a smart-ass, you never really know how hurtful your actions are. It is totally up to the person you mistreated to decide and then further decide if they want to even the score. Never, ever imagine that you really know what the victim of your abuse is capable of doing.

Chapter 15

Navy Career Sinks

Two or three weeks after graduating from North, a friend of mine told me about a new pool hall that opened up in Grande Lake. Grande Lake was a popular vacation destination for people that wanted to experience the Rocky Mountains and all of the outdoor activities that go with them. According to my friend's friend, this new pool hall was filled with easy marks where there was strong action just about every day (and always on the weekends). A couple of buddies and I decided to give Grande Lake a try. We had to wait until Sunday to go because my friend had to work at his dad's Italian market every Saturday.

When Sunday came around, we decided to get up early that morning and head up to Grande Lake. Danny Polidori came by to pick me up in his dad's pickup truck, the one he used to deliver groceries. Next, we headed to get John Marseco, who lived across the street from Mr. Polidori's market. It was about a two-hour drive, so we left around eight a.m. The drive up to the lake was uneventful, and we arrived a little after ten a.m. As soon as we got to Grande Lake, we located the pool hall and found out that they didn't open for business on Sundays until noon. We had a couple of hours to kill, so we decided to see if we could get lucky and meet some girls.

Before you knew it, I saw this girl riding a horse. She was heading in my direction. I looked up at her and asked if she wanted to give me a ride, and before you could say "Gene Autry," I was sitting on this huge horse behind this cute gal with my arms wrapped around her. To make sure my buddies saw us, I yelled over to them and said something like, "Yippee-yi-o-ki-yay!"

After that brief moment in the limelight, my horse-riding experience went downhill fast. I didn't know anything about the girl, and I had no idea how much danger I put myself in when I climbed up on this horse. As soon as I was situated with my arms around the girl, she let the horse know she wanted to get going with a little kick from the heel of her shoe. Apparently, this horse didn't like hauling two people around at the same time and wasn't too happy about being kicked on top of it all. To express his displeasure, our mighty steed actually reared up on its back legs, but not like Silver did with the Lone Ranger. Both front feet were definitely off the ground! I began to slide off of the back of the horse, so instinctively I did all I could to stay on and hold tight. After that brief moment of protest, our horse seemed to accept having both of us and proceeded to trot down this dirt road we managed to find.

At that point of our journey, I was able to talk to this gal, and I sized up my situation. I found out that her name was Jenny and that she was visiting her grandparents. She said they owned a cabin just outside of town and that she went horseback riding nearly every day. By this time, we were at least a quarter of a mile outside town. The thrill of meeting Jenny, waving *adios* to my two *amigos*, and being the first one to be in position to score with a girl was losing its appeal. In reality, I was on the back of this horse being bounced along a dusty, dirty road. All the while, I was reminded of how bad horses smell. Once I got Jenny to start talking, she wouldn't stop. She held her equestrian skills in very high regard. She was also an endless source of information about animals in general but horses in particular.

I was ready for my great outdoors experience to end. I asked Jenny to turn the horse around and head back to town. I had become annoyed with her and was developing a genuine dislike for the way she talked nonstop about herself and how talented she was. I managed to find the biggest, snobbiest, pain-in-the-ass chick in Grande Lake. She turned the horse around, and we began our return trip to town. Once again, I bounced along. Then I made a huge mistake. I asked her if she could get things to smooth out a little bit and get the horse to stop bouncing me around. As soon as the words left my mouth, I regretted them. Jenny told me that our ride would be much smoother if she could get the horse to canter. Once again, to get the horse's attention, she gave it a little kick in an effort to shift gears from trotting to cantering.

She hadn't learned that this horse didn't like to be kicked. Period. Instead of rearing up on its back legs like before, the horse took us back to town in a full gallop. You cannot really appreciate how fast a horse can go until you are riding double on its back. We flew down the dirt road out of control, both of us hanging on for dear life. The next thing that happened was bad. The dirt road ended and merged into a paved road that ran perpendicular to it. When the horseshoes made contact with the asphalt at full speed, it caused the horse's legs to slide out from under him. Essentially, our horse went skidding onto the street just like a baseball player would slide into second base. Somehow, Jenny managed to remain on top of the horse as it slid. All I can remember was the thought that I should try to hold my head up away from the asphalt. My right leg was under the horse as we skidded to a stop. I was unconscious for a brief period, and at some point, I tried to lift my head to see what happened. I remember seeing what appeared to be a church with people coming out of it in the distance. After a while, someone knelt over me. He said, "I'm a doctor." Is that unbelievable or what? I go skidding into this street with part of me under this huge horse right when church is being let out, and one of the first parishioners to see this horrific accident was a doctor.

Somehow, I found myself in this clinic; Grande Lake didn't have a hospital. I think I was going into shock. I remember how the sound of the glass shelves in the medicine cabinets lining the room vibrated against the weight of metal implements used to operate on people. That small sound caused by the vibration, which was caused by nurses and doctors walking near me, was unbearable. I was writhing in pain. Because I wasn't eighteen yet, the doctors had to contact my parents before they could operate on my leg and before they could give me anything for the pain. Finally, someone came over to me with a syringe. The second the needle penetrated my skin, the morphine took effect, and my pain was gone. I will never forget what it felt like to get such an immediate reaction from this drug. Morphine was something that I never imagined I would use or need.

My friends waited for five hours before I was patched up enough to be driven home. I was so doped up that I slept the entire trip back to Denver. When I got home, my mother and father were able to see for themselves the various injuries that the doctors in Grande Lake described to them. My right leg was broken, and the top of my right foot had been split open and stitched back together. I had lacerations covering the right side of my body as if I had been used as some kind of Brillo pad to clean up the street. I had managed to keep my head up away from the pavement, which kept me from sustaining any head injuries.

I found out that Jenny was virtually unscathed. Somehow, she had managed to keep the horse between her and the asphalt. The horse was lucky too, managing to avoid breaking any bones. For the most part, it sustained cuts and bruises while sliding to a stop on the street.

I was told that it would take eight to twelve weeks for me to get back on my feet. Then I would need some physical therapy to regain the strength and range of motion in my right foot and leg. I would not be able to attend my Navy Reserve meeting. Not showing up at a reserve meeting was a huge deal. It was rumored that the Navy would send the Military Police to investigate anyone that was absent. To avoid seeing the Military Police come to my door, I was required to get a note from my doctor to validate my explanation for not attending the meeting. The Navy had zero tolerance for anyone that did not want to keep the commitment they made when they decided to join the Reserves and swore an oath to serve their country. Because of the Vietnam War, there were a lot of draft dodgers and a lot of people that enlisted got cold feet and wanted out.

I managed to recuperate, get rid of the cast on my leg, and eventually get rid of the crutch I was using to help me walk. My lacerations were just about all healed, all but the big one I had where my right foot split open. Physically I was okay, but I couldn't run or bend my right foot like I used to before the accident. In August, about ten weeks into my recovery, I attended my first Navy Reserve meeting since May. At the meeting, we received orders to attend boot camp at Treasure Island, California just outside of San Francisco.

I knew that I couldn't run and that it would be impossible for me to complete my boot camp training until I was fully healed. Even then, my right foot wouldn't bend properly, and I wasn't certain if it would ever fully mend. At the end of the meeting, I went to see the corpsman who was the top medical guy in our reserve unit. I told him about my accident and that I didn't think I could complete the boot camp training. Because there were so many guys trying to get out of the Reserves, the corpsman was very skeptical about the extent of my injuries. He asked me to take my shoe off and show him my injured foot. What he saw was a black scab that covered almost the entire top of my foot. When the doctors closed the wound, they used stitches that don't get removed but rather dissolve over time. As that process takes place, an ugly black scab forms. Our genius corpsman examined my foot and said that he thought it would be okay by the time I got to boot camp. So that was that. The amazing thing was that our "medical expert" corpsman worked selling stereo equipment in the real world. It was only in the pretend world of the Navy Reserves that he was able to play the role of doctor.

I told my parents I would have to go to boot camp in about a month. I also told my girlfriend, the one that I took to the senior prom. So, she decided to have a going-away party for me at her dad's pizzeria, which of course was Jim's Pizzeria.

Finally, the time had come. The party happened on Saturday night, and I went to the airport Sunday afternoon to catch a plane to San Francisco. My girlfriend even went to the airport to say goodbye. I was about to take my very first airplane ride, and I imagined that there were going to be many other firsts coming my way now that my Navy adventure was underway.

All of the other seaman recruits from our reserve center were on that plane. When we landed, there were Navy personnel waiting for us. After we claimed our duffel bags, we were escorted to a large school bus type vehicle. It took about an hour for the bus to get to the base. We filed out of the bus and were told—I mean, ordered—to form a line, and we waited for the platoon leader to tell us what to do next.

It turns out that Treasure Island was a training base for the Marines as well as the Navy. What this meant for us was that there were more people to salute. That sounds fairly innocent at first blush, but when you are not accustomed to saluting anyone in the first place and the standards for a proper salute for a Marine were quite a bit more intense than saluting people at the reserve center, the idea of saluting a lot proved to be a problem for the slow learners.

We were marched to our barracks and assigned a footlocker and a bed. Just as I started to unpack my duffel bag, I heard my name. "Santone. Seaman Recruit Santone." I raised my hand and this guy with a lot of stripes on his sleeve came over to me. He had my personnel folder and said, "It looks like you expressed some concerns about your ability to perform the training tasks and that you thought we should postpone boot camp training. Is that correct?" He continued to look at my folder and said, "There is a notation that you have a problem with your right foot." I was totally surprised that our stereo-salesman corpsman documented the discussion I had with him four weeks earlier.

This guy asked me to show him my foot. He looked at it, tested it for flexibility, and asked me to get up and walk away from him and then toward him. Then, out of the blue, he said, "You don't belong in boot camp, and I'm not sure you belong in the Navy." He told me to put my stuff back in my duffel bag and follow him to the infirmary.

At the infirmary I was assigned another bed, and I was introduced to another defective SR. His name was Russell. It wasn't very difficult to spot Russell's defect; he weighed over three hundred pounds and was about five feet eight inches tall. This guy was fat. I had never seen anyone close to Russell's weight and condition. It looked like everything he did required a maximum effort on his part—walking to the drinking fountain, bending over to pick something up. Whatever he did was a chore. Accompanying most of Russell's movements were a wide variety of noises, a majority of them breathing related, but there were also some gurgles that you really couldn't tell where they came from. On top of all of this, it didn't take much to get him sweating. He was a mess.

Russell and I were told that reservations were going to be made so we could return home the next day. After that, the commanders at the reserve centers would determine our next steps. We were given permission to have dinner at the mess hall, which was located about three blocks from the infirmary. As we walked there, we could see that we were going to encounter a couple of Marines. When we got close enough, I stopped and saluted. Russell decided to skip all of the formalities because he viewed himself as a short-timer, and on top of that, his total focus was on the food he was in route to. The Marines stopped us and asked Russell why he didn't salute. Before Russell could say anything, the Marine told him to get down and do push-ups. I thought he was going to die after the first one. It was painful to watch, but Russell really could have avoided all of this if he had not tried being a smart-ass. When it was over, we got to the mess hall, got our food, and found a place to sit. I tried to eat whatever it was I had on my plate, and it was awful. Russell seemed to have no problem eating his dinner and mine.

The next day, I flew back to Denver. Tuesday night I went to Jim's Pizzeria to get some good food. I ran into my girlfriend, and she couldn't believe what had happened. For whatever reason, she just didn't buy my story, and I was pretty sure that would be the last time I would ever talk to her. In one day, my world went completely upside-down. I had a game plan for my future, and then I had none. I had a girlfriend (sort of) and a day later she wouldn't talk to me. I left Jim's, got in my dad's car, and as I drove away, I was once again worried about the future, just like I had been before I graduated North High School.

NDJ Life Lesson:

It is absolutely impossible to predict the future. At the same time, it is important to have a plan for the future.

When you plan for the future, it means that you have established a goal and have defined the things you believe you need to do to attain your goal.

As life unfolds, things may happen that affect or invalidate your plan.

The important things you must understand are:

Never fall in love with your plan. If you do, you will be reluctant to change it or abandon it altogether.

In life, you will be amazed at how many people have clung to a useless plan that would have worked if it were not for a bad break or some other event that could not be anticipated.

When change happens that causes your plan to not work, you must determine whether the goal that the plan was intended to accomplish is attainable.

When you need to change your goal is when you need to be at your best.

Establishing goals, planning, experiencing change, needing to let go of your plan, establishing new goals, and starting over again are really what the "ball game" is all about. Get used to it!

Chapter 16

Remember Faye?

A few weeks after my Navy career was derailed, I had an unexpected visitor drop by to see me. It was Faye, my ex-girlfriend. I hadn't seen Faye since her parents put the kibosh on our relationship. They forbade her from dating anyone that wasn't Jewish. It was a bad break as far as I was concerned because I really liked her and we enjoyed being with each other.

I was in my backyard sitting on the grass in the shade of our maple tree enjoying a beautiful late-summer day. Faye was driving her mother's car, a car that I had never seen before. When I saw the car slow down and move closer to the curb, I immediately recognized the driver. She pulled up to where I was sitting. Then she asked me to go for a ride; there was something she needed to talk to me about.

Faye looked great. I was more than happy to see her and find out what was going on. I got in the car, and as soon as she pulled away from the curb, Faye told me about her problem. As we drove, it seemed as though she was going to a predetermined destination. When I asked her where we were going, she said it was a place where we could be alone.

By the time we got there, Faye had told me the whole story about her parents and their desire to control her life. They had made arrangements for her to marry a man from a very successful family, a family that attended their synagogue. The wedding had already been planned and scheduled. It was going to happen the third weekend in October—in just six weeks.

Faye told me that she hardly knew her husband-to-be. The way she talked about him it was clear that she wasn't even remotely attracted to him, that he was a lot older than she, and she implied that he wasn't very good-looking, at least not to her. Some of Faye's girlfriends knew the future groom, and the picture they painted was one of a controlling, chauvinistic know-it-all.

I couldn't really understand why she was telling me all of this. Yes, we both liked each other for a brief time, but why would she make a beeline to my house? Then, the method to her madness showed itself, and when it did, I would be tested in a way that would really define the kind of person I was, a test that would either build my character or create the need to rationalize my behavior so I could continue to stand myself.

In the blink of an eye, Faye slid from behind the steering wheel to a point where we were virtually nose-to-nose. We started making out, and as we did, she was doing things that could be described as giving me the green light, which then escalated to an on-ramp that led exactly where I wanted to go. Somehow, I forced myself to stop kissing her and got back to the key issue at hand: What did she want from me?

In route to our make-out destination, I told her that my plans to be in the Navy went south after my horseback riding accident, and I told her that I was trying to see if I could get accepted to Colorado State College in Greely, Colorado. If I couldn't find a way to go to school, then I would look for a job. Faye used this information to answer my question, and her answer explained her supercharged passion.

Faye was very direct. She didn't want to marry this guy, she liked me from before, and she hoped that we could somehow come together so she could bail out of her wedding. She knew her parents would throw her out in the street if she refused to get married, and she knew that we hadn't really gotten to know each other intimately when we were together before. Maybe it was the pragmatist in her that caused her to play the sex card with me. She knew there wasn't enough time for us to romance each other and fall in love, so she must have believed that she would need to let me drive the car before I would buy it, so to speak.

Now, this is where a person gets to reveal their true character. It would have been totally—I don't know if it's because Faye is Jewish—kosher for me to "drive the car" and then say "this car is not for me." Think about it. I'm eighteen years old, perpetually horny, Faye is really, really cute, and I really, really would like to drive. But what else do I know? I know that there was no way I could lead Faye along to believe that there was some possible future with me. I essentially got out of the car, or off of the car, and told her that I wouldn't be able to help her. I pointed out that while I would love to be with her, she would probably regret having sex with me because it could only make a difficult situation more difficult. She knew I was right. She moved over to get behind the steering wheel, started the car, and drove me home.

Like clockwork, I received an invitation to Faye's wedding. I attended. She looked beautiful, and the ceremony was powerful, especially when they broke the wine glasses. I'm glad I got to see her again. I'm really glad that I made the decision I did and never for a minute thought about doing something else. I never saw Faye after that. She was a really neat gal.

NDJ Life Lesson:

There are people that will tell you that there is virtually no such thing as simply black or white or right or wrong.

Often, those same people will try to discredit the right-or-wrong thinkers and describe them as simplistic or unsophisticated.

They believe that there is a multitude of actions that are acceptable, which can be found in the endless shades of gray that separate a person's choices.

There are times, especially when it comes to issues involving character and integrity, that there is only one choice.
End of discussion.

Deep down inside, most people know the right thing to do and the wrong thing to do. The shades of gray that they describe are a by-product of the rationalization they use to explain or justify why they did the wrong thing.

Chapter 17

My Career Begins

Following my discharge from the United States Navy and the brief notion that I might be able to go to college at Colorado State College in Greeley, the time had come to get a job. I can honestly say that up until that point in my life, I never had the slightest idea of what I would do to earn a living. My parents didn't have the slightest idea about the things they might have been able to do to help prepare me for when I would have to face the world as an adult. In defense of my parents, neither one of them knew just how much they did not know about being parents. They were certain, however, that they were giving my sister and I much more support than their parents had given to them.

Nonetheless, I had to figure out what I could do. At age eighteen, I'm sure that I had never heard the word "nepotism" before. But I would benefit from this age-old practice of helping members of your family to gain employment at a company who has an employee related to a prospective new hire. I was given a huge advantage in terms of landing my first job when my uncle pulled some strings and found an entry-level position for me at Samsonite Luggage.

What had happened without my knowledge was that my mother put a hammerlock on my Uncle Tommy, one of her younger brothers. Even though my mother and her sisters and brothers did not get along very well, my mother must have played some kind of trump card that rendered my Uncle Tommy powerless to dismiss her request. She asked him to help me get a job at Samsonite and use his vast influence to make it happen. Uncle Tommy was the closest thing to a white-collar worker in the family. Having spent over thirty years at Samsonite, he had worked his way up to supervisor of quality control. What this meant was that he could wear clean clothes to work and return home with relatively clean clothes at the end of the day. In addition, he was issued a professional-grade micrometer that he toted in a high-quality leather holster attached to his belt. He was instantly recognized as part of management because of the holster and his tidy appearance.

Well, pull strings he did; good old Uncle Tommy came through. I was expected to go the Personnel Department, which was located adjacent to Samsonite's main plant and production facility. There I filled out an employment application and received some employee orientation material. I was told to report to the Samsonite Luggage Foundry—which was located about six blocks from the main plant—on Monday morning, only four days hence. My job was described to me as a hand fork operator. I would be provided with all of the details about my duties on Monday.

Once I got out of the personnel department and into my car, I decided to drive by the foundry to see what I could see. I had the address, and I thought it would be a good idea to locate the building before I had to report for work. That way there would be one less thing to worry about. Within a few minutes I reached the foundry building. It was a gray, concrete, nondescript structure with windows that were painted gray so that you couldn't see in and people couldn't see out.

Finally, Monday morning arrived, and I reported for work twenty minutes before the seven-a.m. start time. Before reporting to work, I spent about thirty-five minutes in Winchell's Donuts, which was located about two blocks from the foundry. There was no way that I was going to be late. After all, this was the first day of my adult work life. I was eighteen years old and a mere forty-seven years away from retirement. Think about that for a minute. Elementary school lasted seven years and junior high and high school took five years to complete, but my career was something that would take more than four decades to wrap up. During the upcoming year, I would have a great deal of time to think about what it would be like if, like my Uncle Tommy, I spent forty years or more working for Samsonite.

There was a small waiting area just inside the front door of the foundry. The manager of the foundry and some administrative people occupied the offices adjacent to the waiting area. Shortly after my arrival, a person that identified himself as the shop foreman took me down a short hallway that led to the front entrance of the stamping plant. I was told that the building was divided into three sections: the management and administrative offices, the stamping plant, and the foundry. The stamping plant contained huge machines that made the metal parts used in the luggage products. The foundry was located in the rear of the building and was separated from the stamping plant by a huge concrete wall that extended well beyond the roof in order to create a firebreak. The foundry housed two large furnaces used to heat magnesium, which was used to make the frames and latches for the suitcases, briefcases, and other types of luggage. The advantage in making the frames out of magnesium was that it helped to make Samsonite luggage lighter and stronger. A disadvantage in working with magnesium was that it was a highly volatile material that created an ever-present risk of fire.

After entering the stamping plant area, all communication between the foreman and me required us to yell at each other. The noise made by over twenty-five giant steel-biting, steel-chewing, and steel-spitting machines was astonishing. The door that separated the office area from the stamping plant area could better be described as an exit and entry point separating two planets. My first impression of this new planet—formulated during a two-minute walk with the foreman on my way to meet the person that would train me to perform my job—was that it appeared to be extraordinarily hostile, hot, dirty, loud, unfriendly, foreign, scary, unforgiving, and unbelievable.

We walked past the stamping machines to another door on the left. The foreman walked to the door, opened it for me to see in, and described the area as the cafeteria and break room. Across the walkway that we used to go past the stamping machines was another entrance without a door. This entrance led to a wall that caused you to stop and then choose right or left. Both choices led to a large locker room that housed lockers assigned to the workers where they kept a clean change of clothes. The locker room also contained a lavatory and about six or seven shower stalls. On one of the walls there was a large community sink with a shelf just overhead. The sink was about twenty feet long with a long silver water pipe containing small holes. Stepping on one of several footrests beneath the sink could turn on the water. On the shelf there was borax soap and some kind of jelly substance that resembled dirty Vaseline. These were industrial-strength grease and dirt removers. I was assigned a locker and told that most of the guys used padlocks to keep their lockers secure. What that meant was that if I wanted my locker to be secure, I would need to buy my own padlock. The foreman, who was a loyal company man, did point out to me that the soap and grease remover were provided by the company.

After the locker room visit, we reached an area that had a machine that looked like a cement mixer, and there was a huge pile of sawdust, at least four feet high, on the floor. This was where I met the guy who was going to train me, a guy named Jesse Mason. Jesse was also a hand fork operator. I know it's not a good thing to judge a book by its cover, but Jesse could have been a poster boy for the Greaser guys I had my fill of at North High. He had the pompadour haircut with a ton of hair oil, and he had a white T-shirt with a pack of cigarettes bulging out of one of his rolled-up sleeves. He had the look, the posture, and the attitude of the guys that wanted you to think they were tough, someone you would not want to mess with.

The foreman had talked to Jesse about training me before we met, so after a brief introduction, I was instructed to listen and learn from Jesse since he had been working there for nearly a year. The foreman left, and it was time for me to begin my training program. It might not be right for me to describe my training as a program. Something that took less than forty-five minutes to complete probably doesn't deserve to be called a "program." Reality was beginning to set in. I was going to learn what I was going to be doing every day for as long as I worked there as a hand fork operator. Did I really need to spend three years in high school preparing for this? Perhaps this was what they meant when they said, "I feel like I'm being underutilized." My God, what the hell was I doing there?

Jesse's training began immediately. He pointed over at the machine that looked like a cement mixer. He walked over to it, and I followed. When we got close, I could see that there was no cement in the large steel bowl that was slowly rotating as if it were mixing cement. Instead, there were metal parts that had come from one of the huge machines located in the stamping plant. There was also a brown, dirt-like substance included the mixing bowl. Jesse showed me how it got in. He took a large square-faced shovel and used it to scoop up some of the sawdust adjacent to the machine and emptied it into the bowl, which was seventy-five percent full of the metal parts. Jesse explained that the metal parts were coated with oil that the stamping machine operators applied to the rolls of steel as they were fed into the grip of the giant machine. The oil kept the feeding mechanisms and stamping dies lubricated and less likely to jam up, lock up, or stop. It was the machine operator's highest priority to have his machine never stop producing parts, never get jammed, and to never have the die—which determined the shape of the metal part being stamped out—become damaged.

The incentive given to the machine operators to be diligent in their duties and to maximize each machine's productivity was money. The number of parts an operator's machine produced determined their paycheck. Usually, one operator could manage three or four machines. It would not be practical to have the machine operators count the number of parts they produced and just as impractical to have Samsonite managers validate the operator's count numbers. Instead, the parts that were stamped out were put into wooden boxes two feet high and two feet wide. When a box was full, the stamping machine operator placed it on the outside of the yellow line that delineated the stamping machine area from the walkways used by non-operator personnel to navigate their way around the plant. It was Jesse's job to use his hand forklift to transport the boxes to the oil removal machine and then to a large walk-on scale to be weighed. Each part had a specific weight that did not vary. It became a simple matter of taking the total weight of the wooden box and its contents, subtracting the weight of the wooden box, and then dividing that number by the individual part weight to determine the number of parts in the wooden box. That number determined the dollar value used to pay the stamping machine operators. Paying people an amount of money based solely on the number of pieces they produced was referred to as piecework.

Most of the people working in the stamping plant were pieceworkers. They worked extremely hard in order to make as much money as possible. The unrelenting, brutal nature of their job and the harshness of the workplace created a perfect environment for people to produce at the highest levels possible. It sounds like a contradiction, doesn't it? But what happens is that the people working in this difficult environment realize that the only way to cope, the only way to survive the monotony and the mind-numbing boredom is to make as much money possible. Because a union maintained the company prices for each individual part, operators could produce parts at a level where a person with no real skills could earn a pretty decent living. By a decent living, I mean that the people could afford to live in small houses, drive older used cars, and retain a standard of living that they had when they were growing up. It meant that their lives could be a lot like their parents' lives—not better but not worse either. So, believe it or not, the pieceworkers jobs were highly prized. All non-management personnel were members of the union, and the pieceworkers were the top earners within the ranks of the union membership at Samsonite.

In addition to learning how the cement mixer and oil removal machine worked, I was shown how to use my hand forklift and how to maximize the number of boxes I collected. Doesn't that sound pretty good? I previously described this area as a place with sawdust all over with a cement mixer type of machine spinning dirty metal parts. Now, since it was part of my ball game, I described it as the Oil Removal Facility. See how people can make themselves sound a lot more important than they really are? Jesse explained that the key to my job would be to keep the boxes from stacking up in the walkways just next to the stamping machines, and it was important to get as much oil off the parts as possible so that weight of each box was not padded by oily parts, which of course weigh more than clean parts.

The more oil left on the parts the better it was for the stamping operator. The weight got inflated, and so did his paycheck. Conversely, it was not considered good form to overdo the oil removal process. A machine operator can look at a box and calculate how much money he should get paid. If his boxes appear to get lighter and lighter, it means the hand fork operator may be a little overzealous in the application of sawdust, and from the operator's point of view, he is getting screwed by the fork operator. As you can see, the stamping plant had its own set of unwritten rules that affected how people fit in, how they interacted, and where they were on the food chain. Just like at North High, there was an imaginary org chart, and you were going to be placed somewhere on that imaginary hierarchy whether you liked it or not. However, unlike North High, there was also a real organization chart defined by senior management. The real org chart represented a hierarchy of functions performed by people. The hand fork operator function I had been assigned to was located at or near the very bottom of the chart. The location of your level, or function, had a direct bearing on the amount of money you were able to earn when performing the functions assigned to each job description.

Once Jesse described the hand fork operator job to me, he had me follow him around the plant as he performed his duties. We began at the Oil Removal Facility where earlier he had emptied the contents of four wooden boxes into the mixer, added sawdust, and hit the start button. The mixer had taken about three minutes to complete its cycle. Jesse showed me how to lower the mixing bowl and remove the parts by reaching in and pulling the dried parts toward the lip of the mixer and into the wooden box. Then the boxes would be set on top of each other, and the hand forklift was positioned near the bottom box. The box below the top box could be grabbed and rocked slightly forward, which allowed the metal tongue of the hand forklift to slide under the bottom box. Once that balancing act was over, the boxes could be pulled back against the body of the forklift with your left hand, and then you could use your right hand to pull the forklift back in order to support the weight of all of the boxes as they were pulled toward the operator and kept from falling out of control.

Every day, Jesse collected hundreds of boxes, picking each one up to empty its contents into the mixer, unload the mixer, pick up three of the four boxes so they could be stacked on top of each other, and then push them to the scale to be weighed. Each box and its contents weighed about thirty to thirty-five pounds.

It was finally my turn to demonstrate to Jesse that I was paying attention and able to do the work. In a very short amount of time, I realized that my job was physically demanding. I struggled with the awkward boxes and tried to figure out how Jesse made it look so easy to use the hand forklift. Another factor was endurance. The boxes weren't really that heavy at first, but as time went on, the boxes took on the feeling of a relentless force exerting itself in an endless parade of wood and steel.

Part of what I was going to have to do to perform my job at a satisfactory level involved increasing my strength and stamina, and another part involved improving my balance and technique. That first day on the job was unbelievably hard, and things remained that way for about three or four weeks. As time went on, I did get stronger, and I was able to figure out some better ways to do things, allowing me to exert much less effort to accomplish each task. After the first month, I was able to collect all of the boxes produced during the day shift, clean most of the oil off of the pieces, take the boxes to the scale to be weighed, return the total weight slip to the press operator, and most importantly, meet my boss's expectations. I had never thought about quitting or complaining to my uncle about the awful job he managed to get for me. This was the beginning of my career, and it was my first glimpse at what it was like to be an adult. I couldn't believe, nor could I have ever imagined, that I would find myself in this situation. But there I was, and there I would stay until I figured out what I could do to make things better.

I developed a simple philosophy as far as work was concerned. I decided that no matter what my job duties were, I would do the best job possible, and I would find a way to exceed my boss's expectations. It didn't matter if I liked the job or not; I wanted my boss to want to keep me over all of my peers. I hope you noticed that I didn't say that I would *try* to exceed expectations; I said that I *would* exceed expectations. And I didn't say that I would use my personal assessment of my performance; I would use my boss's assessment of my performance no matter how unfair or incompetent. And, to make sure that I was accomplishing my goals, I asked my boss for suggestions and what he believed a great hand forklift operator would be like.

I'm sure there are people that would describe me as a suck-up or worse. I know what a suck-up is: someone who wants to earn the boss's favor by pretending that they would like to be a great hand forklift operator and by saying things that appeal to the vanity of their supervisor. I, on the other hand, wanted to know whom my boss thought was a great performer and then attempt to perform at that level or better. I figured out that even if I thought I was doing a terrific job, it wouldn't matter unless my boss agreed.

No matter where you go, as long as there are other people there, you will be judged, categorized, evaluated, tested, reviewed, categorized again, generalized, critiqued, liked by some, disliked by others, and all of this takes place in the first minutes and hours after you arrive. I cannot emphasize enough how important it is to make a good first impression, even in a loud, dirty, dingy factory. The good news is that it is possible to be prepared and not leave it to chance when these important first impressions are formed.

I learned the value of being prepared when I was going to school at St. Catherine's. It was the preparation that I put into every test and every homework assignment that allowed me to achieve high grades and position me as a front-runner to get a scholarship to Regis High School. I would be able to use my understanding of the importance of preparation and my strong work ethic to my advantage throughout my career.

But for now, suffice it to say I had been dealt a tough hand of cards, and it was up to me to decide how to play my hand. There are a lot of different ways to go, some a lot easier than others. There are ways that lead to losing and ways that lead to much different results. Am I being vague here? Yes, only to point out that I could lose, have a different result, or kid myself that I found a way to win with this crummy hand. The different result involves not losing, not winning, but rather breaking even in a manner of speaking. I had a job, income, a car, good health, and by not screwing myself with self-pity or some other bad move, I remained intact and ready to seek out a better opportunity.

After a couple of months of working at Samsonite, I managed to keep the stamping machine operators and my boss, the shop foreman, relatively happy. As for me, I was much stronger, I learned how to deal with the noise (earplugs), and felt as though I was accepted as a good worker by the guys in the plant. At the same time, I knew I had to find a way to get out of there and that I had better start coming up with some kind of plan.

It was on a Monday, a day very close to my six-month anniversary as a Samsonite employee, when a couple of things happened that I could not have anticipated. First, the shop foreman asked me to go with him to the lunchroom.

I followed him and then waited as he opened the door, allowing me to enter the combination lunch and break room first. It was just a few minutes after starting time so there weren't any people on break. The shop foreman—his name was Manuel Rodriguez—asked me to take a seat and then proceeded to sit across from me. He began by saying that I had done a good job and that he was happy with my work. Next, he informed me that they were going to add a fourth punch press operator to the production line and wanted to know if I was interested in the position. Essentially, I was offered a promotion, a position performed by the highly compensated pieceworkers. I was totally surprised by Manuel's offer. To be honest, for a brief moment I was very happy to move up and away from my hand forklift duties and in a direction that paid a lot more money. Or at least I thought it did. I asked Manuel how the punch press operators were paid and what he thought I could make doing that job.

Before Manuel talked about money, he wanted to describe what the job entailed. Manuel explained that the punch presses are used to assemble steel rods approximately an eighth of an inch in diameter. The rods were bent on a special hand-operated machine that took straight rods and bent them so that there were four rounded corners. Once the rods were bent, they were taken to the punch presses for assembly. The operator took a single bent rod out of a large wooden box and held the open ends of the rod so that they touched each other. Next, both ends of the rod were joined together permanently by using a T-shaped connector. The top of the T was held together by the hands of the operator and positioned so they were lying in the channel provided by the connector. A straight rod was placed in the connector channel that ran north and south to form a T. When all three rods were in place, the operator stepped on a foot pedal that causes the press to come down onto the open connector with great force. In one down-and-up motion, the punch press completed its task, which was to close the channel of the T-connector and bind the three ends of the rods together. Next, the other end of the middle rod was placed in the north and south channels of a second T-connector, and the original rod was guided into the remaining open channel that forms the top part of the T. Again, the operator stepped on the pedal, and the center rod was connected to the original rod. The original rod with four bent corners was joined together by a center rod and two T-shaped connectors. The final product looked like the letter D on the right side of the rod, and the left side looked like the reflection of a D in the mirror. Once assembled, the rods were sent to the main factory building for more assembly.

    Ultimately the rods were used as the frame for the separators of a suitcase that separated clothes. The frame was covered with a material stitched together by people using industrial sewing machines and heavy-duty polyester-like fabric. The seamstresses created an outer casing that resembled a very thin pillowcase, and the frame that was assembled using the rods was used to slip inside the open end of the pillowcase. Once inside the casing, the open end of the pillowcase was sewn shut. Lastly, the separators were integrated into the suitcase, which was lined with a material similar to the one used to make the pillowcase. The lining of the suitcase matched the colors of the pillowcase material covering the frame, and the final step of assembly involved sewing the separator onto a strip of material that extended from the lining near the center of the suitcase.

After I got the more-than-you-would-ever-want-to-know-about-suitcase-separators speech, Manuel wanted to stress one important point: About fifteen percent of the people that operated a punch press were missing at least one finger. He said the monotony of the job caused people to daydream, lose their concentration, and in an instant, they lost part of their hand forever. As for the pay, the top press operator made a little over four dollars per hour. In 1966, four dollars an hour was huge money for a guy just out of high school. And it was enough money for most people to live in a small house and raise a family. He said the top operator, John LaMotte, was very fast and that it was incredible that he could produce at that level. Manuel believed that a good press operator could make about three dollars to three fifty per hour. Both of those numbers were a lot more than what a hand forklift operator made, and it was a lot of money at that time. I told Manuel that I definitely wanted the job and thanked him for giving me the opportunity. When we left the break room, we headed straight for the punch presses. I was introduced to John, and Manuel asked him to show me how to perform my new job.

Now there I was, a punch press operator. The promotion didn't really change anything from the standpoint of wanting to get out of the suitcase biz. But now I was making good money. It took four or five weeks for me to get up to speed and start producing big-deal paychecks. On my best days, I produced at a rate equal to three thirty-five an hour. On my worst days, I made about two seventy-five an hour. Again, this was big money at the time, especially if you were nineteen years old.

"What to do with all of this cash?" I wondered to myself. It took me about a millisecond to come up with an answer. Get a cool car. I had sold my 1950 Mercury just before I went off to see the world as a seaman recruit. When my military career came to an abrupt end, I purchased a 1959 Opel. Nobody had ever heard of an Opel at that time, and neither had I, but my dad knew a guy who had one and wanted to sell. The Opel was a German car built to compete with the Volkswagen Beetle. It had a very small four-cylinder engine, pee-wee tires, and it had the unique feature of being a stick shift four-speed transmission with a shifter mounted on the column of the steering wheel, just like an American-made three-speed. When I bought it, the exterior was really weathered and in need of a paint job. My dad, the house painter, decided he could become a car painter. So, he painted my little Opel metallic green. The new paint job served to highlight all of the bodywork that had been previously done, which in some ways made the exterior problems stand out even more. Go figure.

I asked my dad if he would cosign a loan so I could get a nice car. He agreed to do it and asked me what kind of car would I be looking to buy. I told him I hoped I could find a 1962 Chevrolet Impala Super Sport that had four-speed transmission. So the search was on. I kept looking in the newspaper and looking for cars with "For Sale" signs in their rear window. After a few weeks went by, my dad came home from work and told me about a car that one of the painters wanted to sell. He said he thought it was a '63 or '64 Chevy, and he knew it had a four-speed transmission. My dad said that the guy was getting married and wanted a more economical car, a car that would get good gas mileage and low insurance premiums. The only other information my dad had was that the car was green and that Wolfgang, the Polish painter, had taken good care of it. Dad asked me if I wanted to go see it, and of course I said yes. All the while I thought to myself, "What are the chances that I would want to buy Wolfgang's Chevy?" And I believed the chances to be about zero. Nonetheless, I didn't want to upset my dad by not going, so the next day we made plans to meet Wolfgang and see his green machine.

It took about thirty minutes to get to Wolfgang's place. Dad parked about half a block away and on the opposite side of the street from where Wolfgang's house was. I got out of Dad's Chevy Nova and walked on the sidewalk toward the address that we were looking for. As I got closer, I saw an unbelievably beautiful, dark metallic green 1964 Chevrolet Impala Super Sport with chrome reverse rims, oversized blackwall Goodyear tires, and a special insignia on the front fender just behind the front tire. The insignia read "409." I could have fainted! I couldn't believe it, but I was looking at one of the neatest looking cars I had ever seen. And, as if it were one of the final scenes in a movie with a very happy ending, this car was a 409. For an instant, I was transported back to the day at North High School when my cousin took me to see Rich Ido's 426 Ford. The moment Rich started the engine, I heard a sound that most people would never hear or at least would only hear as a spectator like me. Being the guy behind the steering wheel, turning the key on, and hearing the 426's engine come to life, creating a loping, rumbling sound was an experience reserved for people whose parents were both doctors, like Rich Ido's parents. Surely a guy like me would never have that kind of experience, right? How about dead wrong, or better yet, how about double dead wrong?

I don't know if I had ever consciously dreamed of having a 409, my favorite muscle car, but on a subconscious level, I must have obsessed with this dream of dreams. There was nothing in life that would have made me happier than that beautiful Super Sport Chevy 409. Honestly nothing. Just saying "409" gives me a sense of joy and gratefulness to this very day and will for my entire life. Thank you, God.

Yes, I bought Wolfgang's car, and I can still remember driving it home. It was summertime, and I had all of the windows rolled down. My journey took me west on Speer Boulevard. There was a stoplight on Speer located just before you got on the elevated portion of roadway. It was at that stoplight that my memory of my 409 is etched permanently in my mind, for it was there that the sound of my car reverberated back toward me as it was deflected by the large buildings on both sides of the roadway. When the light turned green, I accelerated slowly, and when it sounded right, I shifted into second gear and continued to accelerate. The sound of my car was unbelievable. It was a deep rumble, a sound that projected power, a sound that could not be mistaken for anything other than a 409. Yes, Rich Ido's 426 Ford had a special muscle car sound, but the 409 produced an unmistakable, rich, and finely tuned sound that made it stand out in my mind above all of the others.

I kept my '59 Opel and drove it to work and also when the weather was bad and the roads were too icy. The 409 had a special parking place off of the street and close to the house. Another reason I kept the Opel was because the big Chevy only got about nine miles per gallon of gas. The two four-barrel carburetors sucked up a lot of petrol, but on the plus side the price for a gallon of gas was about thirty-five cents.

One of the unforeseen benefits of getting a really cool car was realized when I went on my grand tour to show off my new ride. I went back to the Scotchman Drive-In to let all of the north side guys and gals check out my new ride. I also went down to Jim's Pizzeria to see if anyone I knew was hanging out so I could show them my gorgeous car. During one of my visits to Jim's, I ran into a friend of a friend of mine. Her name was Barbara Busch, and for some crazy reason we seemed to really get along well whenever we were together. Barbara was very sweet and innocent. She graduated from Holy Family, a parochial high school in a fairly nice section of North Denver. She was having pizza with a couple of her girlfriends, so we didn't have much time to talk. Our chance meeting led to me inviting her to go out so we could get caught up on what was going on in our lives. She gave me her address, and we were set to get together Friday night, just a few days away.

By the time Friday rolled around, I had come up with a game plan for my Friday night date. The first and maybe most important piece of the plan was to make sure my car looked perfect, which meant I had to decide when I would wash it, polish the chrome rims, vacuum the interior, and make sure the windows were spotless inside and out. The next piece of the plan was deciding what I was going to wear and making sure that whatever it was was clean and pressed. Of course, what that really meant was making sure my mom knew what I needed to have pressed. Then I had to decide where we would go, and lastly I had to make sure I could find Barbara's house. The address she gave me was in Wheat Ridge, a pretty upscale neighborhood located west of North Denver just before the foothills that were next to the good old Rocky Mountains. I hadn't been to her house before, and Wheat Ridge might as well have been located on the moon from my standpoint. I couldn't imagine what people that lived there did for a living.

As I drove my new car toward Wheat Ridge, I couldn't help but think to myself how lucky I was and how grateful I was to be me. I think that is something I have always done. I have always tried to notice what was going on in the present and to appreciate the times when I felt truly blessed, or better yet, truly lucky.

When I got to the street name Barbara gave me, I made a right turn and proceeded into a subdivision that was just amazing. All of the houses on both sides of the street were huge. They were brick, and the neighborhood looked brand-new—nothing out of place, nothing in disrepair. The subdivision was immaculate. And then I saw the numbers I had been looking for—Barbara's address. I didn't know if I should pull into the driveway or park on the street. A small detail, but I didn't want to make a bad impression. I didn't want to look or act like I was as out of place as I was, like I didn't belong in a neighborhood like this one. I decided to play it safe and park on the street.

When I walked up to the door, Barbara answered. She had been waiting for me. Inviting me in, I was introduced to Barbara's parents. Both of them looked like they were going out on the town themselves. They were both dressed up, or at least it looked that way to me. After the introductions, they told Barbara to make sure she was home by midnight and that they were going to stay home to watch a little TV. I thought to myself, "I wonder what they wear when they *do* go out." It was a little bit like *Make Room for Daddy*, a sitcom on television about a family and the things that they had going on in their lives. On that show, the parents seemed to always be dressed up and ready to go out, just like Barbara's parents. Maybe that was the way people looked when they lived in great big houses. I figured I'd get a chance to find out if Barbara and I wanted to see more of each other.

After I went through the pre-rehearsed description of my car, its horsepower, gear ratios, and about fifty more very noteworthy features of my 409 Chevy, I began to talk about the other things going on in my life. The most dominant aspect of my situation was my job at Samsonite. I guess that was one of the reasons I liked being with Barbara; I didn't feel like I had to put on an act with her. I could talk to her about almost anything. I had forgotten how much I enjoyed being with her and thought to myself that I should have tried to contact her a long time ago.

When I described the stamping plant, the foundry, and my duties as a punch press operator, I couldn't help but mention how worried I was about being like John LaMotte, the guy running the punch press on my left. When I described my situation to Barbara, I did it in a way that allowed me to talk about things that I didn't even realize were bothering me, like the fact that our machines faced the exterior wall and how all of the windows along the wall were painted a gray color. I told her I wouldn't doubt that there was probably a name for that color—probably "real gray," which superseded "factory gray," the longtime champion of factory interior décor choices. We both laughed, and I guess that was another thing I liked about Barbara; she laughed when she thought I was trying to be funny.

Our date went well, and we started seeing each other on a regular basis. Having Barbara to talk to helped me figure out some of the possible options that I had available to me. Before Barbara came into the picture, I had a desire to improve myself but lacked the confidence and maturity to figure it all out by myself. Her willingness to listen and offer suggestions had such an enormous impact on my attitude and myself in general. With her, I seemed to be able to overcome the inertia that kept me where I was, which was the beginning of the path that John LaMotte had traveled when he was a much younger man.

As time went on, I took steps to improve my life. The first thing I did was get myself scheduled to take the civil service test. If I passed this test, I would be eligible to work at the post office. Next, I asked my dad if he knew anyone in the electricians' union. I wanted to find out what I needed to do to become an apprentice electrician. I found out, and guess what? I needed to take another test. My dad pulled some strings and got me scheduled to take the electricians' test. Thankfully for me, those union guys stuck together, and my dad was the kind of guy that everyone liked. He was a real man's man and a stand-up guy. The third piece of my work enhancement program fell into place when Barbara talked to her father about my situation. Her father was a big-deal director-level manager at the Public Service Company of Colorado (PSCCO).

Overall, I was doing things to try to help myself. I took the civil service test and felt that I did okay. I took the test to become an apprentice electrician. I felt that I did okay on the written part of the test but wasn't sure about how I did on the physical part, which would determine if I had the manual dexterity required to perform the everyday tasks of an electrician in the field. Essentially, the test was made up of a wooden board with about seventy-five small holes drilled into it. There were metal pins stuck into all of the holes, which were at varied distances from each other. Some of the pins were only one-fourth of an inch apart while others were a half-inch apart. There were small washers in a tray located at the top of the board. The test involved taking a pin out of a hole, putting a washer on it, and placing the pin with the washer back into the hole it came out of.

Another test consisted of turning the pins over and putting them back into the hole. Each end of the pins was colored red or blue. The board was set up with all the red ends up while the blue ends were hidden in the holes. Both dexterity tests were timed. I was always lousy at doing things with my hands. I was clumsy, and my fingers were stiff and didn't seem to work very well together. The person administering the test knew my dad, so after my first attempt at the washer test, he told me that what I had just done was a warm-up. Then I did it again, and I found out that I was still warming up. I did it a third time, and finally I must have gotten warm enough to go on to the next test. Again I needed two warm-up tests in order to complete the turn-the-pins-over test. I was told that I had passed all of my tests and that I would receive something in the mail when there was an opening for an apprentice.

Then, I went to the Public Service Company's headquarters building in downtown Denver. I went to the Personnel Department and completed a job application. I was told that I would be contacted if there were any open positions that I might be qualified to fill. About a week later, the person in the personnel office called my home, and my mother took a message. The message said that I was invited to attend an in-person interview for a job as a clerk in the engineering department located at the Holly Street Service Center.

I interviewed with a man named Willis Bashore. Mr. Bashore was one of the nicest men that I had ever met in my entire life. He could see that I was a little nervous and told me not to worry. He said we were going to have a nice chat.

He described the duties of the clerk position and asked me how I felt about doing that kind of work.

After my meeting with Mr. Bashore, I was introduced to Merlin Olsen, the manager of all administrative and building maintenance personnel. Mr. Olsen asked me what I thought of the clerical position that Mr. Bashore talked to me about and what I thought were the most important aspects of the job. It was at this point that I realized what was happening. Mr. Bashore explained to me what the clerk was expected to do, and Mr. Olsen asked me what I thought the clerk was expected to do and what I thought were the most important parts of the job. I realized then that Mr. Bashore's friendly, low-key conversation style of interviewing was not as spontaneous as it seemed. Instead it was the old tag-team maneuver that you saw in all of the fake wrestling matches. It was "Tiger Man" Bashore softening me up, and then with the touch of a hand, turning me over to Merlin "The Terminator" Olsen to polish me off. Fortunately for me, I was so impressed with everything during my interview—the office facilities and the appearance of the employees, especially the guys with the window offices dressed in suits with white shirts and ties—that I soaked up everything I saw and heard like a sponge. I had never been in a professional office environment that was so big, and to me, so very impressive. It made me feel like some of the smartest people that I could ever imagine meeting were in this building working on engineering projects that I could not begin to fathom. I was confident that I could do a good job describing the responsibilities of the position to Mr. Olsen.

However, the second part of the question was something different. Mr. Bashore didn't tell me what the most important part of being a clerk was. In a flash, I realized that they wanted to see how I thought and how well I could do under pressure. I thought for a minute about what I had been told: a clerk files all of the correspondence and engineering drawings, trims blueprints, creates mailing labels, runs errands for engineers, updates engineering manuals, unpacks inbound mail, and keeps the administrative supply room stocked. I thought about those tasks and realized that Mr. Bashore did not emphasize any one task over another. So, my answer had to involve something else, not the tasks. And then, voilà! It came to me. A clerk had to be thorough and accurate in carrying out his duties. A clerk should be good at following directions and making sure that he understands what the engineer wants him to do. That was my answer, and that concluded my job interview at Public Service Company of Colorado.

Two weeks went by, and unbelievably, I received three letters in the mail—one from the post office, one from the electricians' union, and one from PSCCO. All three employers had accepted me. I was given start dates and hourly rates of pay. I was expected to call and confirm my acceptance. Can you imagine how great it felt to be escaping from Samsonite Luggage? Don't get me wrong; I was glad I had been given a chance to make some money, and I got to see what it was like to be a factory worker. The latter made me realize how difficult it was to work in a factory, and for the first time ever, I made the connection between education and working, between education and income, and between education and lifestyle. Before Samsonite, I really didn't get it. It's embarrassing for me to admit, but I guess I needed to have a building fall on me before I understood what became so painfully obvious.

Now, I needed to make a decision about which job to take. It really wasn't that difficult for me to do. When I thought back to my experience with the electricians' union, I realized I had been given an enormous edge when I was taking the manual dexterity test. I doubt that I would have been able to hide my clumsiness when they were training me, and sooner or later I would be let go. Even if I could have somehow gotten my hands to work right, there was another reason for me to factor out the electrician's job: most of the lighting was located in the ceiling or above whatever was to be illuminated. I know, sometimes I wonder about me too. This revelation led me to remember that I had a strong fear of heights and hated to be on ladders or scaffolding. So that was the end of that job offer.

Next, I thought about the job at the post office. To make this decision, I decided to get in my car and drive downtown to the main post office just to look around. There appeared to be three things going on at the same time. First, I saw the letter carriers with their bags heading out to deliver mail. There was another epiphany coming my way again. What I realized was that all of these guys worked *for* the post office, not *in* the post office. What that meant to me was that about six months a year I would be working outside in the cold, and for about three months I would be working outside when it was too hot to be outside.

There were also post office personnel inside the post office; however, the ones that were manning the counters and taking in mail seemed to be much older than me. I concluded that it would take a lot of seniority to get one of the inside clerk jobs.

Then there was the third kind of post office worker who could not be seen. They were the ones located in the bowels of the building, the post office people that nobody ever saw. They did sorting, and probably some more sorting, and then after they got some seniority, they got to sort some more. I imagined that the post office career path might not be the best move for me.

So, I took the job of clerk at the Holly Service Center working for Public Service Company of Colorado. I had always been impressed with the PSCCO headquarters in downtown. It just seemed like the people you saw enjoyed their work and their environment. I couldn't be sure, but that was my impression. Then, my memories of the engineers, the draftsmen, and the sense of being around a lot of smart people made me excited and glad to accept the job offer.

I imagined that I would be jumping for joy when I turned in my two weeks' notice at the stamping plant, but that was not the way it happened. Inside I was jumping for joy, but when I went to work and handed in my resignation, I did not do in a somber way, but for sure I kept my emotions down. I wanted to appear low key about the whole thing. I chose to be this way out of respect for all of the workers that I was leaving behind. I knew that many of them would remain at Samsonite as long as Samsonite would let them be there. I knew how hard these people worked, how harsh the environment was, and how difficult it would be for most of them to ever leave the factory. I was so grateful for my situation and filled with a sense of curiosity about what the future held for a guy that was just about to become North Denver Johnnie.

NDJ Life Lesson:

I got a tremendous break when I reconnected with an old friend who was willing to ask her father if there was any way he could help me get a job at the Public Service Company of Colorado. In my career, there were people that helped me get ahead. Some of them recommended me for promotions, helped me get challenging assignments that advanced my standing within the department, or acted as a mentor by providing me with the benefit of their knowledge and experience.

Unless your father owns the company, every person that has achieved any level of success has received a break from someone at some time. Always remember the people that helped you, and always look for people that you can help.

Chapter 18

Colorado Sid and North Denver Johnnie

At this point, my life was just about as good as it could be. I had a good job with a great company, and there were opportunities for advancement. I was driving a Chevy Super Sport 409 that, in my mind, was perfect in every way. My pool game was continuing to improve, and I was thinking about playing in the Denver Open Nine-Ball Tournament. The only thing that would make things better was to find another girlfriend like Becky Wright.

What a difference a year makes. It hadn't been long since I was working in a dark, too cold or too hot, dirty, dangerous, and incredibly noisy factory with very little opportunity for advancement. I was driving a metallic green 1959 Opel with dents, noticeable body putty attempting to cover up additional dents, and a paint job that highlighted all of the problems and attracted attention because it was a fluorescent, metallic, lime-green color never before seen on the open roads in Denver.

I owed so much of my good fortune to Barbara Busch. Had she not come along and given me a sounding board to describe my troubles, offer suggestions, and ask her father to help me get a job interview at Public Service Company, I have no idea where I would have been at that point. Just about the time that I was starting my new job, Barbara started college at Northwestern University just outside of Chicago. It was a prestigious school, and it was the school her father graduated from. As a prominent alum, Mr. Busch used his contacts to get Barbara accepted, but that may not have been necessary because she had a 4.0 GPA and was interested in pursuing a degree that would qualify her for law school down the road. Barbara was a real star on the rise, and she was someone that helped me beyond anything she could imagine. We remained friends, and I will always be grateful to her and Mr. Busch for their help.

At this point, my life was focused on work, my car, the pool hall, and trying to find a new girlfriend. I continued to improve my pool game, and because I was making pretty good money, I started playing for higher stakes. It didn't take long for me to realize that it took a lot of different skills to become a top-level pool player and make money doing so. For the most part, I tried to improve my abilities by practicing, practicing, and then practicing some more. I wanted to be able to look at a shot and feel secure about my ability to pocket the ball and get the cue ball in the right place for my next shot. Naturally, it was important to be confident as a pool player, be able to execute the shot, and get shape for the next one. What I discovered, however, was that shot-making was something all of the good players could do, especially when they were practicing by themselves. The good-money players had a lot more going for them than just being able to pocket balls; they could do it under pressure, and they could do it over and over again.

I found out in a hurry when I started playing for higher stakes with good players that there was an element of pressure far in excess of anything I had experienced before. I found myself looking at a shot, a shot that wasn't really that hard to make, and thinking to myself, "What if I miss?" All of a sudden, the confidence I had when I was practicing was nowhere to be found. It was replaced with doubt and worry. Instead of focusing on making the shot and getting the shape I wanted, I was focused on how much money I was playing for, and I was trying not to lose instead of trying to win. It was easy to see—after I managed to consistently lose to players that I felt I could beat if I played well—that I needed to learn some new skills or forget trying to be a big-money player.

I had been fairly successful playing in the golf game on the A snooker table. I won my share of games, maybe a few more than most, but that was when I was playing in a ring game with several other guys and risking relatively small amounts of money. When I stepped up to playing one-on-one for a lot more money, I wasn't even close to the same player I usually was. I knew it, and to make matters worse, my opponents knew it. They seemed to know that sooner or later I would "dog it," or choke, when the game was on the line.

The guys that I played with in the golf game saw me as a pretty good player, someone that didn't choke when I needed to make a shot. One of those guys was Sid Barcelon.

Sid was a big-money player and probably the most respected and well-liked guy in the pool hall. For some reason, Sid and I hit it off really well, and he seemed to like me. As I said before, everyone liked him, and I wasn't any different. I really enjoyed being around this guy. For one thing, he always seemed happy and had a new joke to tell. Most of the time, he had a new story to talk about. Most of Sid's stories were about gambling. He played pool for money—a lot of money when he could find someone to play him—and he gambled on just about anything. One story had him pitching quarters next to a brick wall behind the Fun Center for one hundred dollars a shot. Sid was the Bruce Jenner of the pool hall; he could do everything well. He could play pinball machines like a wizard, he could play a strong game of golf on the golf course, and he bet on every NFL football game all season long, namely because one of his money-making enterprises was taking bets on football games. Over time, Sid managed to develop a loyal following of bettors and eventually became a legitimate, big-time bookie, taking in between thirty and forty thousand dollars in action every week.

It was rare for me to bet on football, but once in a while I would get a hunch about a game. When that happened, I called Sid. The smallest bet he would take was one hundred dollars, and the vig—which was how Sid made a profit—was the standard ten percent. As long as Sid had someone betting on one team and somebody else betting the same amount on the other team, he couldn't lose. Sid would get to keep the ten percent that the loser gave him when he placed the bet, and he would pay the winner off with the loser's money. The trick to being a good bookie was to have a high volume of bets wherein the total amounts bet for each team were the same. When that happened, which it did most of the time, Sid would essentially pocket five percent of the total handle.

When he couldn't balance the money bet in a given game, Sid called up another big-time bookie, probably Jimmy Piccoli—better known as Pic—and make a bet that would protect him from being a big loser when a lot of money was bet on one team and not much on the other. When Sid laid off a portion of his bettors' action with another bookie, he was essentially creating a break-even scenario, which was much better than taking on the total risk himself. Most bookies deep down inside are gamblers and will occasionally take on the risk themselves by not laying off the action. Sid was very familiar with this kind of scenario. He had firsthand knowledge about the consequences of being too greedy and not laying off bets when the action was too one-sided.

Not too many people knew that this was Sid's second attempt at booking football bets. Several years earlier, he failed to lay off some bets and lost just about everything he had. That mistake put him out of business as a bookie. I found this out when Sid and I were having one of our two a.m. breakfasts at the Village Inn Pancake House. Most gamblers will tell you that there is nothing better than a steak and eggs breakfast in the wee hours of the morning after you had a big win and got the other guy's cash. Sid told me that it had taken him over three years to get a big enough bankroll so he could take another shot at being a bookie. With that terrible experience permanently etched in his mind, there was no way in the world that he would ever put himself at risk like that again.

When Sid told me this story, I realized that even he could screw up, and another thing that I learned was that he screwed up, but he never gave up. In order to pay everyone off when this happened, he was forced to go to Pic for an emergency loan, a loan that cost him about fifty percent more than his original loss. Sid's bettors were loyal because they believed he would pay them when they won a bet and would do so immediately. Sid knew he could never be a bookie again if he didn't pay everyone off.

Sid's second attempt at booking bets was a very lucrative proposition; his weekly volume was about forty thousand dollars, allowing him to pocket two thousand, sometimes more. He made more money when there was a shot at winning both bets because the point spread created the possibility that neither player would win. The way that could happen was if one of the bettors got three and a half points by choosing the underdog and the other bettor had to give up four and a half points for choosing the favorite. In this circumstance, the underdog would lose if his team lost by four points, and the other player would also lose because his team needed to win by five points to collect. This was the sweetest kind of bet from Sid's standpoint because he not only collected the vig, but he also got one hundred percent of both bettors' bets. It wasn't uncommon for Sid to have a three to six-thousand-dollar-bet bet on a single game. And when the bettors both lost, Sid's take could increase from two thousand a week to a whopping eight thousand. As time went on, Sid's personality and likability turned his nice chunk-of-change bookie business into a big-deal bookie business where the weekly profit reached twenty thousand or more. Can you imagine having that kind of weekly income? And it was all in cash.

Sid was always at the Fun Center, usually playing in the golf game each afternoon. It was in this circumstance that Sid and I became friends. I remember Sid asking me where I lived and where I went to high school. I told him I lived in North Denver, I went to North High School, all of my family lived in North Denver, and my parents grew up in North Denver. At the end of my story, Sid decided that just about everything about me had a link to North Denver and out of the blue decided to call me "North Denver Johnnie." He kiddingly told the other players in the golf game that we should all think of me as North Denver Johnnie. As the golf game continued, Sid said things like, "North Denver, that was a nice shot." After that, every time he talked to me he called me North Denver.

As fate would have it, I ended up having a shot to win the game. I had a three-rail bank, which sounds a lot harder than it was because my ball was in a perfect spot for me to try the shot and I didn't have to do anything with the cue ball to play safe. I hit the shot, and when my ball came off the third rail, it looked like it just might go in. When the ball was about six inches from the out pocket, it was easy to see that it was going to go in and that I was going to win the game. When the ball fell in the hole, I yelled, "North Denver!" Everyone in the pool hall could hear me. From that time on, I always said, "North Denver!" after every big win. Sometimes I would shout, "North Denver Johnnie!" when I made a great shot to win the game or when I won a hotly contested game and the competition was very strong. My nickname became a permanent part of my pool-hall image, and Sid and most of the other players at the Fun Center knew me as North Denver Johnnie.

Sometime later, I told Sid that if I was North Denver Johnnie then he should be Colorado Sid. I chose this name out of respect and wanted him to know that he was someone I admired and called friend. Over time, people close to Sid referred to him as Colorado Sid. I always greeted him as "Colorado" and he always greeted me as "North Denver."

As our friendship strengthened, I asked Sid for advice on just about anything. He was the type of guy that saw almost everything as either black or white, and whichever color he chose to paint his answer or viewpoint, he did it with absolute certainty, clarity, and confidence. When Sid gave advice, for the most part people paid attention. The fact that he had become a highly successful bookie and was making really big money added to his credibility amongst his peers. At some point, I asked him what he thought I should do to stop choking when I played pool one-on-one for a lot of money. I really wasn't sure if he was going to give me any help, because it was a little bit like asking Coca-Cola if they wouldn't mind telling me the formula they used to make Coke. After all, Sid was a big-time gambler. Why would he want to help someone else learn how to become a big-time gambler?

Sid didn't hesitate in answering my questions about choking, betting, losing, winning, and anything else I talked to him about. And as with everything else, Sid's remarks were straight to the point, no punches pulled. He started by telling me that one of my big problems is that I played every game the same, and I played every person the same as everyone else. I didn't understand anything he was saying. Of course I played every person the same as everyone else. I tried to play my best, and I tried to be consistent in my approach. Sid said that I didn't understand and went on to explain how he approached each opponent and developed a strategy to help him beat the person he was going to play.

First of all, he compared my approach to his. In my approach, I didn't do anything differently, no matter whom I played, and for me to win I would have to play at my best and hope it ended up being better than the guy I was playing. All of the pressure to perform was on me all of the time. Sid, on the other hand, sized up his opponent as the game went on. If he was playing someone for the first time, he would try to determine their strengths and weaknesses and get a sense of the their temperament and speed limit. Sid watched everything his opponent did, how he approached each shot, the person's shot selection (e.g., Was he choosing the best shot to shoot?), and how good his ability was to play shape, draw the cue ball, shoot bank shots versus long shots, spot shots, and so on. Sid developed a player profile for each person he competed against, and he would observe players that were playing other people to gain insight about their game before he ever played them. In Sid's mind, his player profile gave him an edge. He told me that every player had strengths and weaknesses. If you could identify some of the weaknesses, then you could try to exploit them.

To play pool at a high level, you needed a strong offense and defense. You play defense when you cannot make a shot; you need to play a safety and leave the cue ball in a position that will make if difficult or impossible for your opponent to make his next shot. In nine-ball, the balls are pocketed sequentially—first the one-ball, then the two-ball, and so on. When you can't make the two-ball, you try to move the two-ball and the cue ball to a spot where your opponent either cannot hit the two-ball on his next shot, or if he can hit it, you leave him a very difficult shot to make. Sometimes, you must leave him a shot that he can make, but if you have a choice of leaving him a bank shot, a long shot, a shot off the rail, or a shot that will make it difficult for him to get shape for the next shot, you can choose to leave him a shot that is not one of his strengths. Maybe you leave him a bank and he slams the bank shot in. The next time this circumstance presents itself, you will try to leave him a different type of shot. While the game progresses, Sid adds details to his player profile and looks for ways to take advantage of his opponent's weaknesses and tendencies.

Sid's analytical approach to the game gave him an edge that he believed took some of the pressure off of his game and added pressure to his opponent's. He explained how he always looked for things that might get his opponent out of their comfort zone. Sid might try to raise the stakes and play for more money than his opponent is comfortable with, or he might try to disrupt his opponent's rhythm by deliberately slowing down the pace of the game (e.g., taking more time to evaluate his shot selection, pretending to line up a wrong shot but then selecting, lining up, and executing the correct shot after some more deliberation). By looking at the wrong shot, your opponent may get the feeling that you are about to make a big mistake and then get frustrated because you never actually make the mistake. Eventually, they may even realize that you have been screwing with his mind by pretending to be unsure about the proper shot selection.

The part about choking and missing shots when you were playing for a lot of money was an area where Sid believed he had superior abilities, and it was his confidence in himself to handle the pressure and perform better—not worse—when he was playing for big money that was the most important factor in his ability to win and win big. Sid said that he had watched a lot of big-money games, and at the end of the day, the person that handled the pressure the best was the person that won. Even if the loser seemed to be a better player from a technical standpoint, it was the person that didn't choke and didn't miss the easy shots that ended up with the cash. He said the bigger the stakes, the easier it was to win against most people. They just couldn't execute when they got over a certain amount of money, and because of that, Sid thought of himself as a virtual lock to get the money every time. Naturally, I asked him how he managed to become so confident and if there was ever a time when he choked.

Sid told me that he always looked at things from the standpoint that he was both physically and mentally stronger than most people. He stood about five feet nine inches tall and weighed about 225 pounds. At first glance, he seemed overweight with a waistline bigger than a person of his stature should have. But the longer you looked at him, the more you realized that his waistline was about the same circumference as his chest. He had a beer-barrel physique with strong-looking arms and huge forearms. Sid's body was as unusual as everything else about him, and as a result, he was a much more formidable physical specimen than he appeared at first glance.

Growing up, Sid had three older brothers that were all pretty tough guys, and they mentored Sid to be the toughest one of the bunch. Like most things, Sid paid a pretty good price for his eventual dominance, learning how to fight by fighting and losing and fighting and losing until one day he stopped losing. He used this same formula to develop his mental toughness playing pool—by playing and losing and playing and losing, and eventually, as he did with fighting, he stopped losing. Sid used his strong will and steadfast belief in his mental and physical abilities to overcome adversity when he played pool, lagged coins, played golf, or did anything that put him in a win-or-lose situation.

Sid told me that when he was learning how to fight and getting his ass kicked, he began to realize that there wasn't that much difference in what he had to do to win instead of lose. He said that he didn't have to become a better boxer or puncher. What he did have to do was not quit and wait for his opponent to give up. Sid said that in most of the fights that he lost, he lost because there was a point where he gave up, gave in, and essentially gave the other person the victory. He realized that for the most part, he quit because he gave into his fear of being beaten up. He quit before he had no choice, and he quit when he really wasn't physically hurt that badly. He began to wonder what would happen if the next time he was ready to quit he forced himself to keep going and only gave up when there was no alternative.

He said that it was one of the most difficult things to do because he was going against a key survival instinct that was built into every person: to flee or fight. Each of us has a kind of autopilot that kicks in when we are afraid or threatened. People have their own threshold for accepting potential risk. Sid told me that he believed we have an ability to change our threshold for fear, and in doing so, we are able to accept more punishment and become more fearless. He said it is not easy to believe that you can control your ability to accept fear. The most difficult thing to do is to mentally force yourself to stay and fight and not surrender. The good news about winning the internal struggle and forcing yourself to not quit is that once you do it, you absolutely know that you have separated yourself from about ninety-nine percent of the people on the planet, which Sid said was the most exhilarating feeling he had ever known.

Sid said that being a part of the one percent of people on the planet was like having the Brazilian nuts in just about everything you do in life. "Having the nuts" is street slang for having a poker hand that can't be beaten or having a guy that you know dogs his brains out want to play nine-ball with you for a ton of money. Then Brazilian nuts is the highest form of having the nuts. Since street slang is, for the most part, an undocumented topic, I can only surmise that since Brazil is known for exporting the best pecans and other high-end nuts, the Brazilian adjunct can only be interpreted as a cinch of biblical proportions. To the best of my knowledge, there are only two types of nuts: the stand-alone type and the Brazilian.

Now, you might be asking yourself, "What does any of this have to do with the question he asked Sid?" (which was, of course, "How did he manage to become so confident, and was there ever a time when he choked?"). Sid said that people choke because they are afraid they are going to miss the shot, sell out to their opponent, and lose the game and their money. They are afraid, they are fearful. But when you join the one-percent club, you can become far less fearful than most, and the strongest of the one-percent club members can actually become absolutely fearless and aren't afraid of anyone or anything. When you get rid of being afraid that you are going to miss a shot, your perspective when you are getting ready to pull the trigger on a shot is much like the perspective you have when you are practicing, and you know you can make the shot. Most of the time you do make it.

I believed Sid's advice was absolutely correct, and I knew that it wouldn't be easy to follow his formula for winning and become a member of the one-percent club, but at least I had a strategy, and all I needed was a plan to make it happen. I had a goal, I knew what I wanted, and just like when I was in high school looking to find a girlfriend, I would put together a plan to get me closer to the one-percent members. I also thought that there might be a two-percent club with a slightly lower standard that would accept members that might slip and occasionally become afraid but later recover. Worst case, I knew I could be a two-percent member and maybe fall a little short of where Sid was. I saw him as a guy that was probably in the top one percent of the one-percent club members overall, which would make him absolutely fearless. You probably can tell that for me, Sid was the kind of guy I wished I could be. I guess this was progress of sorts, because for the longest time my cousin Tommy was the kind of guy I wished I could be. Sid had a ton of friends and a ton of money. Tommy had a ton of friends.

I could never know how important my nickname would become as my life progressed. I'm sure that everyone I've become friends with throughout my entire adult life knows that in my younger days I was North Denver Johnnie, and my closest friends know that I still am North Denver Johnnie. The very best part is that my journey takes me to a place where I would never want to be anyone else and where I would be totally grateful to become the person I am. Keep turning the pages, and you will see how it all happened.

NDJ Life Lesson:

Every single person's life is totally unique and totally important to others in some way. Virtually every funeral gathering has family and friends remembering the very best aspects of the dearly departed loved one.

We all know this is true, yet even with the inevitability of death and the knowledge of family members and friends gained in moments of reflection, most people are unable to publicly acknowledge how much our loved ones mean to us and how very important they have been in our lives.

Now, this has to be the craziest yet most common way people live their lives. Only after the losses of one of the most important people in our lives are we able to stand in front of our departed loved one's friends and family and tell everyone what we have most likely never told the person that died.

It is clear by now that the success I have enjoyed thus far in my career came about because someone helped me or shared their knowledge with me. As these events happened in my journey I always tried to acknowledge how much I appreciated the people that gave me a helping hand and how truly grateful I was.

You will never really understand how good it makes the person that helped you feel.

Try to make it a point in your life to say thanks to the people that have made a difference in your life, especially the ones that helped you advance your career. I focus on the career because this aspect of your life has most influence over your quality of life and the contributions you make to people outside of your immediate family.

Chapter 19

Public Service Company of Colorado
Clerk

I was hired by Public Service Company of Colorado to perform clerical work at the Holly Service Center, which was located on the east side of town near the Stapleton Airport. The service center housed the engineering staff and four major engineering departments (electrical, structural, mechanical, and transmission, and there was a large warehouse that PSCCO used to store a variety of electrical equipment and supplies. The warehouse stores included high voltage transformers, wires, and insulators. There was a separate office building adjacent to the warehouse that was used by the crews of electrical workers, and the overall Holly Service Center property was large enough to have parking spaces for the employees, and the large trucks, tractors, and cranes used to install and maintain high voltage distribution facilities.

On my first day on the job, I was introduced to Ken Griffey, who was the other clerk assigned to support all four engineering departments. Ken gave me a very good understanding of what my job responsibilities were and showed me how to do all of the various jobs. The clerk's responsibilities included: filing correspondence, taking Mylar drawings to the blueprint department to get copies, running errands that usually involved taking something to the PSCCO downtown headquarters building, or picking something up. For the most part, it was a very fun and interesting position.

As I gained experience and got to know some of the engineers and draftsmen, I began to get a basic understanding of how electricity was produced and how it was distributed to the customer. The Electrical Engineering Department was the largest group, followed by Mechanical, Structural, and Transmission Engineering. The ME Department was my favorite because of the nature of their work, and I liked the people in that group the best.

Mechanical Engineering was responsible for all of the equipment and facilities that were used to produce electricity. PSCCO had four coal-burning power plants, one nuclear power plant, and it was in the process of building a hydroelectric plant. It was amazing to see the enormous amount of equipment, facilities, and people needed to produce and distribute electrical power for all of the PSCCO customers. There were times when I went to the plants on an errand and got to see the huge coal-burning furnaces, generators, cooling towers, what seemed like an endless number of valves, and mountains of coal. The nuclear plant was newly constructed but had not gone online yet. They were working to achieve certification from the state and federal nuclear regulation boards. There was a hydroelectric plant under construction that I thought was the most interesting plant of them all. The hydroelectric plant was called Cabin Creek and was located in the mountains about twenty miles west of Denver. The Cabin Creek plant was designed to use water from a natural lake to spin two giant turbines and deposit the water into a manmade lake. There were two huge pipes running from the natural lake to the turbines and from the turbines to the man-made lake.

The nifty part of Cabin Creek was that the lake where the water came from would get the water returned to it because there were two additional pipes running back up the hill with pumps that sent the water eight hundred feet back up to the lake. It took a tremendous amount of power to run the pumps. The power to run the pumps came from the coal plants, and the pumping would only be done between midnight and four a.m.

It turns out that the coal plants were more efficient when they produced power at a consistently high level. The plant operators would slow down the production of power during the late evening and early morning hours when the demand was significantly lower than during peak usage hours. Reducing the plant's production during low-demand time and then later increasing the generator production to meet peak-demand requirements caused the plant to use more coal than if the generator production were kept at a consistently higher level. The Cabin Creek plant allowed the plant operators to continue running the generators at their peak efficiency when normal customer demand was low, because the peak-efficiency power generated during the off-hours could be directed to the Cabin Creek plant to run the pumps. The pumps would send the water from the artificial lake that was created when the water was sent plummeting downhill through the massive pipes in order to propel the hydroelectric generator. The beauty in this engineering marvel was that PSCCO was able to generate much more power when the water was sent downhill to the hydrogenerator than it took to pump the water uphill to be recycled. The new power generated by the Cabin Creek plant was used to meet the ever-increasing power requirements during peak demand hours.

Fred Easton was the mechanical engineer in charge of the Cabin Creek project. My desk was located just outside of his office, and over time I was able to talk to him and he was willing to share some of his knowledge to help me understand what his project was trying to accomplish. Fred was very generous to take time out to answer my questions, and I was a curious, starstruck kid who thought Mr. Easton was the smartest person I had ever met. As I became more proficient in performing my clerk duties, there was time when I really didn't have anything to do. This didn't happen every day, but I felt I could take on some additional responsibilities if someone gave me a chance. Because I was familiar with the Mylar drawings and the process used to produce blueprints, I could see that the penciled drawings became more and more faded and in some cases almost illegible. The blueprint machines exposed the Mylar to a tremendous amount of heat and pressure, which gradually erased lines and lettering. I saw this as an opening for me to take on extra work and gain some drafting experience that would hopefully help me advance someday.

Before I could ask my boss, Merlin Olsen, if I could take on some extra work tracing the worn-out Mylar drawings, two things would have to happen. First, I would have to demonstrate that I could produce high-quality lettering and numbers. To make this happen, I had to practice my printing ability. In the Mechanical Engineering Department, all of the draftsmen had very good, distinctive drawing and printing abilities. Drawing straight lines and using a protractor and templates to trace the drawing portion of the worn-out Mylar was not very difficult; it was the lettering and numbers that presented the challenge. For some reason—perhaps it was the extraordinarily high demands the nuns at St. Catherine's placed on everyone to have excellent penmanship skills—I was able to catch on to the distinctive lettering style used by the draftsmen.

Looking back, I think I had good instincts about what it would take to advance, and I had a tremendous work ethic, which I developed while watching my father do things around the house and listening to him talk about his job when we were having dinner. My dad was a house painter. He was the crew foreman and was responsible for supervising all of the other painters assigned to work on the job. My dad described all of his projects as "the job" when he talked about his work during dinner. I think he thought about his work as a series of jobs that he was assigned to, and because he only worked on one job at a time from start to finish, the only time he expanded his description was on the first day of a new job when he might say something like, "We started work on Menninger's today," and after that it was "the job."

I remember the Menninger job in particular because my cousin Tommy and I got to work on it during summer break when I was fifteen years old and Tommy was seventeen. My dad was always working. When his Monday through Friday job ended, he worked Saturday and Sunday to make some extra money painting houses. Somehow, he became fairly well known by some wealthy people living in a prestigious, upscale community called Cherry Hills. He was much more than a guy that just slapped paint on a wall; my father was a skilled craftsman with good taste and a masterful ability to use colors, textures, and workmanship to showcase the architecture and design of a client's high-priced home. He got extra work though referrals, and there was always a strong demand for his talents.

I never really got a complete understanding of how much money he made working on the side, but I'm pretty sure he made more on Saturday and Sunday than he did when he worked as a foreman Monday through Friday. This created a huge temptation to quit his union job and become an independent contractor with his own business. I think he was tempted to go it on his own, but at the end of the day, he knew that there were a lot of things he didn't understand when it came to running a business versus running a crew of painters. And he placed a lot of value on the benefits he received from his employer and the painters' union. There are many ways to define success, and I think most of the time my dad felt that he was making pretty good money for a guy without a high school diploma, and I know he really did enjoy his work.

My dad's two brothers didn't seem to find their niche in the workplace. Uncle Nick, the oldest brother, didn't really have a steady job, and he seemed to always be working on some kind of deal that would result in a big payoff. Unfortunately, Uncle Nick's big payoff never materialized. Uncle Tony, my dad's younger brother, was a bartender, and it seemed to me that he was working at some bar one day and working someplace else the next time I saw him. His wife, Aunt Sophie, was a waitress and seemed to have a steady job. Uncle Nick had two kids. Both were adopted. The boy was named Nicky Berry and the girl was called Sylvia. My cousin, Nicky Berry, was just about the strangest kid that I had ever met. I could never figure out why he seemed so peculiar in the way he spoke and the way he behaved. He was nice, but very different from anyone I had ever met. And Sylvia had her own set of traits and behaviors that put her in a league all her own as well. Neither of Uncle Nick's children was Italian, which in and of itself made them seem different from the rest of the clan, but that was not the icing on the cake, so to speak. The thing that made them seem so unusual wasn't going to come into focus until Nicky Berry decided to come out of the closet, and believe it or not, Sylvia had a closet of her own to evacuate. Yes, Uncle Nick's adopted children were gay and lesbian. What are the odds?

Uncle Tony and Aunt Sophie were my favorite relatives on my dad's side of the family. They didn't have any children, and they really enjoyed trying to spoil my sister and me with presents or a little extra spending money that Uncle Tony would magically pluck out of my ear. He would come up to me and tell me not to move a muscle, that something had just flown into my ear. He told me to stay still while he slowly moved his hand closer to my ear, and then wham! He acted as though he caught something mid-air that had just flown out of my ear. With his hand closed, he pretended the flying creature was now in his grip. He made a lot of facial expressions as he described the event, and no matter how many times he did it, my eyes were riveted on his closed fist, waiting for him to show me a little ear monster. He built up the suspense and then slowly opened his hand to reveal another gift for me. He usually gave my sister and me some kind of special money, like a silver dollar or a two-dollar bill. My Uncle Tony was a really neat guy and very generous, just like my dad.

My work ethic was also influenced by my experiences with my mother when she "helped" me with my homework. Her idea of helping with homework consisted of me doing it and then doing it again to make sure I got it right the first time, and then depending on how important the homework assignment was, studying some more and doing it again just to get an advantage over my fellow classmates. She wanted to make sure that I got a scholarship to Regis High School and that she could brag about my academic accomplishments to her brothers and sisters. All of my uncles and aunts lived in nice neighborhoods, owned their houses, and seemed to have a lot more money than us. We lived in a small, rented duplex that in North Denver, east of Federal Boulevard. All of the nicer neighborhoods were located west of Federal Boulevard. I think my mother wanted to be able to have something that was better than her siblings, and sadly, she used my grades and academic accomplishments as a way for her to show everyone what a great mother she was.

There is no doubt in my mind that I had a very strong work ethic that was based on the example my father set and on a fear of failure instilled in me by my mother. If there was one thing I was sure of, it was that I would do whatever it took to make sure I exceeded the expectations of my boss and outperform my peers with whom I competed for advancement. As a clerk working to support an engineering department, I was able to consistently receive above-average performance appraisals from my boss. I made sure I understood what management expected of me, and I tried to exceed their expectations on every assignment—every day and every time. I virtually never missed work, was never late, and always approached my duties with a sense of enthusiasm and positive energy. I wanted to somehow advance my career, get promoted, and make more money, but I wanted to keep my job above all else. My fear of returning to the days when I worked at Samsonite as a hand forklift operator and punch press operator was the strongest motivator of all. Having worked in a brutally harsh, dirty, and dangerous factory with no windows, I vowed to never forget where I came from and to do everything humanly possible not to return.

Then, one day out of the blue, I got a telephone call from Merlin, my boss. He asked me if I had some time and that he would like me to come to his office. I said, "Yes, I have some time, and I will be right over."

Ken Griffey, the other clerk I had been working with, could not help but overhear my conversation since our desks faced each other. When I hung up, he looked at me and said something like, "Don't worry. Merlin just wants to tell you about a job opening."

I didn't have time to ask Ken how he knew that was why Merlin called, so I just said, "Okay, thanks."

When I got to Merlin's office, he asked me to sit down, and he proceeded to tell me about a job opening in Transmission Engineering. He said that Dean Miller, the director of the department, would like to meet me and tell me about the position. He asked if I would be interested in talking to Mr. Miller, and of course I said yes. Merlin picked up the phone, called Dean, and the next thing I knew I was walking down the hallway to meet with the director.

Dean was a high-energy, enthusiastic, well-spoken, and extremely competent manager. He walked fast, talked with a lot of enthusiasm, and always gave me the impression that he really enjoyed being the director of the Transmission Engineering Department. When he shook my hand to thank me for coming to talk to him, his grip that was strong, and he made eye contact as a way of letting you know that he was the boss. He told me I could call him "Dean" and then described the job opening that he had in his department. He said that he had gotten some good feedback about me from some of the people in Mechanical Engineering. He had also reviewed my performance appraisals and was impressed with the job I had been doing as a clerk. He described what my new responsibilities would be and wanted to know if I would be interested in joining his department. He asked me to think it over, but he wanted me to give him an answer by Friday.

My consistent high-quality job performance and positive attitude were being rewarded when I was offered a promotion to work in Transmission Engineering as a rear chainman in a survey crew. I had worked as a clerk for a little over four years, and I was being given an opportunity to work in an area that offered much more of a challenge, more money, and the possibility for further advancement. The Transmission Engineering Department was responsible for performing all of the civil engineering work necessary to construct new transmission high-voltage power lines and reroute existing lines. The high-voltage power lines were the link between the power generating plants and the transformer substations that were located close to the final destinations of the electricity, which are the houses, businesses, and other end-users of power. The high-voltage lines transported electricity at 115KV or 230KV. The transformer substations received the high-voltage power and—using a transformer—reduced the voltage to a level that was usable by their customers, which was usually 120V. The substations transported the stepped-down power to individual customers via overhead low-voltage power lines or underground power lines.

On one hand, it seemed like a no-brainer for me to accept this promotion, but on the other hand, there were many factors that I had to consider. Being a member of a survey crew meant that my days in the nice, warm Holly Service Center were going to be significantly reduced. I would have a drafting table to work on when I was in the office, but I was going to be working outside at the job site approximately seventy-five percent of the time, and the locations of my job would be literally all over the state of Colorado. About one-third of the time I would be working in the mountains or at locations that required staying in hotels or motels for weeks at a time. Usually I would be able to be home for the weekend, but the out-of-town duty was something that I would need to think about.

Another important aspect of the job was that it was very physically demanding. As a member of a survey crew, I would be hiking in the mountains where the air was thin, breathing was difficult, and I would have to carry equipment used to perform my job. All of the other people working in Transmission Engineering were fit, strong, and rugged, including Dean Miller. There were no soft positions and no soft people in this group. If I said, "Yes, I would like to be a member of the department," I would have to get into shape and somehow get mentally and physically tougher than I had ever been. Another reality I had to consider was that if I took the promotion, then someone else would be hired for my old job as a clerk. If I couldn't cut it in the TE Department, then I would most likely be let go, and I would find myself out of a job and out on the street.

During the time, it took me to walk back to my desk, I managed to come up with some compelling reasons to say "no thank you" to Dean Miller's proposal. I never imagined myself turning down a chance for advancement. Now I was beginning to see why those guys in the Transmission

Engineering Department were making so much more money than I was. They were taking on more responsibility, their jobs were more demanding, and they were willing to take on more risk. The guys working on those survey crews were tough, rugged, unafraid, strong, and self-confident. The $64,000 question was: Could I be one of those guys?

I sat down at my desk. Ken Griffey looked at me and said, "Well, are you going to take it?" I didn't say anything, and then Ken let me know that they had talked to him about the position a few days earlier. He told me that they were big on seniority at PSCCO, and that was why he was talked to first. When he turned them down, he was sure that they would want to talk to me next. On one hand, I was relieved that Ken knew what was going on, so I didn't have to be vague or evasive, just in case he didn't know anything about the opening. I was also glad they talked to Ken first. He was a good guy, a good clerk, and he deserved to be given the opportunity before me.

The obvious thing to do was find out why Ken turned down the promotion. He said that he hated working outside when it was cold and didn't like it when it was too hot either. He couldn't see being out of town and away from his wife and child. He was a real homebody and didn't mind admitting it. He said the extra money would be great, but it wasn't worth it to him to make those kinds of sacrifices to get it. He had talked to Bobby Green and Larry Weaver, two members of the TE survey crew, and found out that when they went out of town, they always worked a ton of overtime so they could get done as soon as possible. They loved it, and they were making really good money. For Ken, overtime wasn't something he wanted; it boiled down to the more time away from home, the less attractive it was for him.

I decided that it might be a good idea for me to talk to Bobby Green and Larry Weaver. Luckily for me, I found out that both of these guys were in the office, so I started retracing my tracks back to the Transmission Engineering Department. When I got there, I saw that Bobby and Larry sat right next to each other. I made a beeline in their direction, but before I could introduce myself, Bobby said, "I guess you want to know what it's like working in the Transmission Engineering Department, right?"

"Yes, thank you. It would be a big help to me if I could learn a little more about the job and how things are done." I got one of the chairs that wasn't being used and rolled it over to their area so that I was seated between them. Bobby was much more animated than Larry, and he started telling me what he thought were the important aspects of being a rear chainman. He began by telling me that if I had a problem working in bad weather or had a problem going out of town to work that I should stop thinking about taking this job. I told him that I had never worked outside before and never had to go out of town. I asked him how he dealt with those issues when he was a rookie in the department.

He told me that the most important thing when you're working outside and the weather is either very cold or very hot or raining or whatever, is to have the right gear to help you handle it, and that it was of utmost importance to have a pair of great boots. From there, you needed to get thermal underwear and wear many different layers of clothing, like a thermal undershirt, a wool shirt, and a water-resistant sweater or vest. You needed really good gloves and something for your head. Bobby said that once he got the best gear to wear when the weather was lousy, the weather became much less of a problem. And when you were busy working and moving around doing your job, the weather wasn't that hard to deal with. But if you didn't have the best gear, then all you could think about was how cold it was or how uncomfortable you were. It became the center of the universe for you. Larry Weaver nodded in agreement.

I asked Bobby to tell me about some of the other guys in the department and what it was like working with them. He didn't hesitate for a second. He said that all of the other guys were great to work with as long as you can carried your weight and showed them you could do your job and do it well. The thing they didn't want to see was someone that was lazy or sloppy, and didn't really want to get the job done and done right. Bobby said all of the guys were good at their jobs and were willing to do whatever it took to get the job done correctly and on time. If that meant working overtime, especially when they were out of town, then that was what they would do. They didn't like being around someone that complained about the overtime or the travel. It was what it was, so you had better be the kind of person that could deal with it.

Larry just nodded his approval of everything Bobby was telling me. I thanked both of them and headed back to my desk with my head spinning around like a top. I really never imagined that I would even think about turning down a promotion, especially one that would increase my salary by almost twenty percent. When you added in the overtime that was almost guaranteed, the pay hike was going to be more like twenty-five to thirty percent. Another important aspect of the promotion was that I would be learning skills that could lead to more possibilities down the road, just like for Bobby Green, who started as a rear chainman a little more than five years prior but had moved up to the level of head chainman and junior transit operator. Larry Weaver, an extremely bright and somewhat introverted kind of guy, was a senior transit operator who was being groomed to become team leader of one of the survey crews. The rest of the day flew by, and I would have to give Mr. Miller my answer Friday morning, in two days.

I remember walking to the parking lot and seeing my car, which was parked far away from any other cars in the lot. As I got closer to my Super Sport 409 Chevy Impala, I thought about how much money it would take to be able to go into a Chevrolet showroom and buy a car like mine when it was brand-new. Then, as I was driving home—where I grew up—I asked myself what kind of money I would have to be making to get my own place. Now, for the first time, I was able to make a connection between my job and the quality of my life. I realized that the promotion into the Transmission Engineering Department was my ticket to becoming self-sufficient; I would no longer have to depend on my parents. I always knew that it would have been impossible for me to have my 409 Chevy if I had to pay rent for an apartment, pay for utilities, pay for food, pay to get my clothes cleaned and pressed, and all of the other perks that I had by living with my parents.

My original plan was to join the Navy as a way of growing up and becoming independent. When my horseback riding accident put an end to my Navy career and I got a job at Samsonite, I put growing-up plans on hold. I had wanted to leave home and find my way in the world, but it was much easier to stay put, and when I took out a car loan for my 409 Chevy, my budget took a major hit, especially when you added in the cost of my little Opel commuter-and-bad-weather car, auto insurance, gas, and upkeep for my hot rod.

The next thing I thought about was my dad and the tough job he had been doing for all of the years I had been alive. Then I remembered the guys I worked with at Samsonite. Most of them were married and had children. Their jobs were tremendously hard, but that was what it took for them to support their families. Now I realized that my job as a clerk wasn't the kind of job you could support a family with; it was barely the kind of job that I could use to support myself if I had to be totally self-sufficient. I thought about the crummy little apartment I would have to rent and tried to imagine how I would be able to furnish it. I wondered where it would be located. It probably wouldn't be a place where I could park my 409 and not worry that someone would try to steal it or maybe just key it as a way of expressing dissatisfaction and anger about their own personal circumstances.

Before I was less than halfway home, I knew I had to accept the job offer in the Transmission Engineering Department.

A huge reason that would force me to take the job was the fact that my salary as a clerk had topped out; I was making the maximum for my pay grade, which was seventy-eight hundred dollars. The first year I didn't get an annual raise was 1971, and my salary was frozen if I didn't find a way to move into a higher pay grade. If I didn't take this job, I might not get another chance for advancement.

From that moment on, I decided to think about things I could do to increase my chances for success in my new job. The first thing that came to mind was the advice Bobby Green gave me when I asked how he dealt with the challenges of working in bad weather. He said that you needed great boots, thermal underwear, water-resistant clothing, high-quality gloves, a down-filled jacket, and something to cover my head and ears. I had to figure out where I needed to go to buy my new work clothes and weather-proofing gear. As I got closer to home, I decided to put my thoughts into a written plan that I could use to make sure I didn't forget to do or get something that would help me be successful at work.

Next, I thought about my first day on the job at Samsonite and how I had been able to deal with all of the issues that I faced when I first started working there. I remembered how hard it was for me to lift the heavy wooden boxes all day long, and I thought about the awful working conditions in the factory. I remember thinking to myself that I somehow had to find a way to deal with anything and everything that made me want to quit my job. I knew how devastating and embarrassing it would have been for my mother if the son that she bragged about to her brothers and sisters couldn't handle working at Samsonite. Failure wasn't an option then, and once I accepted my promotion, it still wouldn't be an option.

During my interview with Dean Miller, he told me that if I accepted the rear chainman job I would begin working in his department the week after next. That meant, including both weekends, I had nine days to prepare for my new assignment. I decided to ask my Uncle Joe, the father of my cousin Tommy, where I should go to buy my boots and all of the other clothing that would help me handle the weather. I thought he would be the best one to ask because he was an avid outdoorsman. He loved to go fishing and deer hunting. He even had a Jeep that he used when he went on one of his hunting or fishing trips with his older brother and some of his other buddies.

From my experience at Samsonite, I knew I would get stronger and my stamina would increase just by doing the job. However, in this case, I decided that I should try to be proactive and figure out a way to get stronger and improve my stamina before I started my job, and it was something I could continue to do while I worked in an effort to get stronger faster. I always thought it was kind of amazing when I found an answer to a question because of something I had stumbled upon a few weeks earlier. In this case, I remember seeing an interview on television of a guy named Arnold Schwarzenegger, who had won the Mr. Universe bodybuilding contest. He said that he started lifting weights because he was a scrawny kid when he was growing up and the other kids used to like to bully him. So, he started lifting weights, and in a short amount of time he noticed how much stronger he was getting and how his body responded to the weightlifting program. He said that he kept setting new goals for himself by adding more weight or increasing repetitions to his lifting exercises.

I decided to follow Arnold's example. I went to a sporting goods store and purchased a weightlifting set and a bench for bench-press exercises.

On Thursday morning, I was at work a little earlier than usual. I went down to the Transmission Engineering Department, hoping to get a chance to talk to Dean Miller. He was always at work earlier than most, and he parked his company car in an area reserved for department heads. Knowing this, I waited for his arrival just inside the entrance door closest to the parking space he always used. Like clockwork, Dean opened the door, and with his normal high-energy style, briskly entered the office building. As soon as I saw him, I got up, and in my most brisk walking style, approached him with my right hand outstretched to shake his hand. I said, "Good morning, Dean. I wanted you to know that I am very happy to accept the rear chainman job, and I'm excited to become a member of your department. I haven't told Merlin yet, but I'm going to his office right now to let him know."

By accepting Dean's job offer the way I did, I created positive momentum for myself in the eyes of Dean Miller. Knowing how important first impressions can be, I wanted Dean to see someone with positive energy who was anxious to become a part of his department. I believe that Bobby Green gave me the keys to being successful in my job. I made a promise to myself to never ever complain about the weather, and I mean never ever. I had always been a hard worker, but I knew that I wasn't really sure about how difficult it would be to keep up with the other guys on the survey crew. All I could do was work hard with my weightlifting program and improve my stamina by jogging or riding a bicycle.

When my first day on the job in the Transmission Engineering Department arrived, I rolled into work with a plan and a philosophy that I hoped would give me my best shot at keeping my job. I worried about what it took to advance only when I knew beyond a shadow of a doubt that I had earned the respect of my crew members and believed that Dean Miller was happy with my performance. Having a plan to become a competent, respected, and valued member of the Transmission Engineering Department was a step in the right direction. However, it would all become meaningless if I was unable to execute the plan or if it turned out that the plan was incomplete.

I believe that some of the lessons I learned in the pool hall helped me think about aspects of my job and what I wanted to accomplish in terms of winning or losing. In this case, I thought about playing nine-ball and making a ball on the break. I could see myself laying out a plan in my mind so I could make the one-ball and get shape on the two-ball and then the three and so on. I knew from experience that if I executed my plan perfectly, I could pocket all of the balls and get myself in position to make the key shot, the shot to sink the nine-ball and get the cash from my opponent. What I learned at the pool hall was that after I came up with a plan to win the game, I needed to put a tremendous amount of effort into maintaining my focus on each and every shot. I learned that I could follow my plan perfectly for seven shots and still lose the game and my money if I didn't properly execute the eighth shot to pocket the nine.

Knowing that concentrating on each shot was a must in order to successfully execute the plan and win in pool made me approach my plan to secure my new job one day at a time. At the beginning of every day, I reminded myself to never complain, hustle and keep up, pay close attention to the details of the job, and watch and learn as much as I could about what the other crew members were doing. At the end of every day, I evaluated my performance. I knew if I didn't make this a daily, never-fail part of my day, then little by little I would develop a false sense of security. I might imagine I was doing my job well because I wasn't being yelled at or criticized. Days might go by, then weeks, maybe months, and then one day I would find out that my performance had been subpar. I would look at my supervisor with a puzzled expression and probably ask him why I hadn't been told about my performance problems before. It would be too late to repair my image or change people's perceptions of my poor performance. I would have missed the eighth shot and lost the game. Guess what? That was not going to happen to me because North Denver Johnnie knew how to plan, how to execute, and how to win.

NDJ Editorial Comment:

I have noticed that when people find themselves in a challenging situation, they will try to give themselves a get-out-of-jail-free card.

What I mean by this is that they will look to find another person to tell their story to. They might do something like describe their promotion opportunity as difficult and maybe even a little risky.

The punch line comes when they conclude their story by saying, "All I can do is try my best." They will be granted the get-out-of-jail-free card when the friend replies, "I know you will. After all, that's all that you can do."

People go through this exercise so that someone will know that accepting the promotion means taking on some risk and significant challenge. This someone will also be able to validate that you have vowed to "do your best."

This ritual serves no tangible purpose, however. People who say, "All I can do is do my best," are hedging their bets so that if in fact they do fail, everyone will surely conclude that anyone taking the job is virtually in a no-win situation. They figure that if good old what's-his-name failed when he was doing his best, the deck must have been stacked against him.

Think about it for a minute. When someone says they will take on a new challenge that is fraught with risk by trying their best, what on earth does that mean? Does it mean that up until now they were cruising but now faced with a risky situation they will kick it up a notch and do their best?

Probably not, because before the promotion offer was made, I'm pretty sure they would tell you that they did their best every day.

So this is where the rubber meets the road. What someone really means when they say they will do their best is that they are not going to do anything out of the ordinary. They will show up to the job without a plan and hope that they can somehow handle the challenges as they present themselves and hope like hell that it all works out. But if it doesn't, they can tell their story about how they did the best they could.

I hope you know now that you need to do your best every day to stay where you are. You need to recognize new challenges, assess risk, and plan a way to be successful, not on your terms, but on the terms of your peers and superiors.

If you fail, you have to ask yourself, "Was what I was asked to do impossible?" Probably not. It is more likely that you didn't step up to the level needed. If you know this to be true, then you failed because you didn't do everything possible to succeed. Somewhere along the line you got lazy, succumbed to the weather, or physical effort was required.

I can tell you for sure that someone who is being counted on to be the breadwinner and has a family counting on him/her should never let these people down. I know it happens, but if you read this book, you must find the will to never give up, never let your family and children down, and please...never do anything less than all that is the essence of who you are.

Chapter 20

Public Service Company of Colorado
Transmission Engineering Department

Working in the Transmission Engineering department (TED) turned out to be a tremendous physical and mental challenge. I didn't realize what a big wimp I had turned into after spending four years as a clerk where the heaviest thing I lifted was a three-hole-punch, and the farthest I had to walk in a day was probably equaled by walking around a city block two or three times.

My plan to start lifting weights seven or eight days before I started my new job was a step in the right direction but woefully inadequate. I could not imagine how hard it was going to be for me to just keep pace with my crewmates and carry the 500-foot metal chain and radio while wearing all sorts of layers of clothing and walking around in heavy work boots. Bending, pulling, breathing, lifting, somehow paying attention to what I was being asked to do, doing it, keeping it up for four hours straight, taking thirty minutes for lunch, and hitting it for another four hours. Each day was unbelievably difficult and way beyond anything I had ever attempted to do. And with all of that, I had to follow my plan: never complain and never question the directives I was given. However, there was no way I could hide my exhaustion or pretend that it wasn't extremely hard for me to keep up. Without a doubt, I could see why the lowest position in TED paid fifteen percent more than the top range for a clerk. On day one as a rear chainman, I was making nine thousand dollars per year versus seventy-eight hundred, and the difference in effort and risk between the two jobs was astronomical.

The guys I worked with were used to the pace, and each and every one of them was fit, strong, and each had managed overcome the difficulties I was experiencing. While they were willing to be somewhat patient with a rookie, they had to see progress because patience really was not their strong suit. Since Dean Miller had interviewed me and decided to hire me without conferring with any of his subordinates, I had to believe he was monitoring my progress closely. I'm sure he was hoping that I would be able to hang on and gain the strength I needed to succeed, but at the same time, there was no room for people who couldn't their weight and perform their job. In general, I was learning what it meant to be a member of a survey crew in the Transmission Engineering Department of a major public utility company, and in particular, I was being trained to perform the duties of the rear chainman, the lowest rung on the crew's job responsibility ladder. The one thing I was sure of was that I would have to meet one hundred percent of the crew leader's expectations and at the same time earn the respect and confidence of the other members of the survey crew.

For the most part, a survey crew consisted of a crew leader, transit operator, pole-man/rod-man, front chainman, and rear chainman. TED was responsible for performing the civil engineering work necessary to locate and build new electric transmission lines (115KV/230KV) or relocate existing transmission towers. Like most people, I didn't really understand how PSCCO produced electricity or what was involved in making this indispensable resource available to every house and business in Denver, which at the time was the center of my universe. The short story on how this works is that there are several electric generation plants located in and near Denver, and each plant produces power that is transmitted to electric substations using high-voltage power lines carried by huge transmission towers. Each substation contains many transformers to reduce the high voltage to the level needed to power our lights, appliances, and all of the other gadgets we use every day.

I could never imagine how much my life was going to change when I decided to accept the opportunity Dean Miller gave me. During the next four to five years, I advanced from rear chainman to front chainman to rod-man and then a transit operator working to locate a power line from a substation in Georgetown, Colorado to a huge copper mine that was being established approximately twenty miles away, the route to which would be created via centerline through a virgin forest over a rugged mountain terrain, with an elevation change of more than seven hundred feet from start to finish. Establishing the route used to locate each transmission tower through a virgin forest meant the land was under the protection of the Federal Parks & Wildlife Agency. This in turn meant that every tree cut down to build the transmission line must be within the boundaries of the approved right-of-way proposed by PSCCO and approved of by the agency.

Dean Miller personally drove to Georgetown to become familiar with the area. He told us that the Parks & Wildlife rangers would closely monitor our work and that PSCCO could be fined up to five thousand dollars for every tree cut down outside of the approved right-of-way. To give you some idea of how difficult that assignment was, imagine that you are standing at the beginning of a dense forest looking down at the Georgetown substation. Then pretend there are two orange markers that you can easily see from your vantage point. Next, position yourself so that both markers line up so that an imaginary line appears showing you the starting point and direction for the proposed route. You get lined up, flip you transit scope over so that it is 180 degrees from where the two orange markers are in alignment and the direction that the scope is pointed is the place where the centerline should begin and the precise direction it should take. Now look through the scope. Any tree blocking your view should be cut down. You tell the rod-man which tree needs to go. One of the other crew members uses a fifteen to twenty-pound chainsaw with a three-and-a-half to four-foot blade to cut it down.

Eventually, the elevation change or the distance requires you to relocate the transit up ahead to the point where you have the rod-man pound a wooden 12-inch stake into the ground and then place the tip of the rod on top of the stake so that you can put the crosshairs on the tip of the rod and signal the person to push the tip of the rod down, which creates a small depression on the wood so that a small nail can be pounded into the stake. You double check to make sure the crosshairs are exactly on the nail then move up to where the wooden stake is, set up the transit directly over the nail, then backsight to the wooden stake that you were previously set over. Each time the transit is moved, it is moved because the next point on the centerline cannot be viewed by the transit operator due to the elevation change that lies ahead, which is usually lower than the current elevation of the transit, or because the distance in this particular stretch of right-of-way has become too great to see the next nail head location due to the optics in the transit.

Imagine that the first setup of the transit—which backsights the transformer station and then flips 180 degrees to point into the virgin forest—is repeated over and over until you reach a predetermined location where the direction of the future transmission line changes and angles off in a new direction. The transmission lines are a series of towers that support huge wires, providing a thirty-five to forty-foot clearance between the wire and the ground. The towers are usually six hundred to a maximum of eight hundred feet apart when the ground is flat, and the spacing is significantly reduced when the ground elevation increases or decreases to the point that the distance between the towers must be reduced to maintain the minimum safe clearance between the wires and the ground.

Another factor that comes into play when locating the exact position of every transmission tower is ice. When ice forms on the transmission lines, the weight of the wires significantly increases, causing the wires to sag. This in turn causes the wires to be closer to the ground. Each tower will be located somewhere on the centerline being surveyed so that both the maximum distance between towers and the minimum clearance between the wires and the ground is achieved.

The twenty-mile path that the transmission line will follow has been established by creating aerial photos of the area between the Georgetown substation and the copper mine. Using the photos, the path of the transmission line is drawn, and each location that causes the direction of the line to change is located. Exact coordinates of every angle point are developed, the exact point on the ground is located, and a stake is put into the ground, signifying another angle point where the direction transmission line will change left or right. Every single angle point is physically located on the ground using survey data and geographical locations, such as section corners and the like, to pinpoint the location of every angle tower that will be constructed on this line.

So, when I flipped my transit scope when I was backsighting to the Georgetown substation starting point, my scope pointed to the centerline where the first straight-line span of towers would be located. Trees are cut to allow for the centerline, and relevant elevation data to the right and left of the centerline are used so that towers that will carry the wires can be located. The elevation is determined by the transit operator and the survey crew member, who uses a surveying rod with markings to determine the elevation differences between the transit and the rod cited by the transit operator. Every three feet of elevation change, the survey crew member stops and positions the survey rod on the imaginary centerline. The transit operator takes a reading and announces it to the survey crew chief so he can record it in his notebook. The readings are collected along the centerline every time the elevation changes by three feet or more. In a typical straight-line span in the mountains, hundreds of readings are taken and recorded as the crew heads for a predetermined angle point up ahead. The survey crew will eventually spot the angle point location that has been carved out on the straight-line path.

This is where the rubber meets the road. As unbelievable as it seems, a good transit operator will hit the angle point previously established by hitting exactly on the stake that was pounded into the ground by the advance team and sometimes right on the nail that was pounded into the stake when the location was established. Going through miles of trees and then arriving upon the exact location where the direction of the transmission line will change is an extremely satisfying accomplishment. It validates the importance of making every set-up and subsequent move of the transit perfect every single time, regardless of how difficult it is to deal with the weather or the myriad challenges presented when working in the mountains.

I realized how special it was for me to be a surveyor on a crew for the Transmission Engineering department of the Public Service Company of CO. This was the big leagues, and I was a player in this very tough ball game. It made me realize just how far I had come from the punch press at Samsonite, and it made me have a greater appreciation for what it meant to the quality of my life and future to have proved to my peers and superiors that I was good at my job and understood that I would always be expected to rise to the occasion no matter how difficult the challenge.

At this point in time, I was making the most money I had ever made, and for the first time ever, I was making more money than my dad. I knew how hard he worked and that I inherited his work ethic. I could also see that working hard could only get you so far; you needed to have a special skill set, knowledge base, and experience to earn a salary in excess of fifty thousand dollars, which was an income level I could only dream about. I think I was making around thirty-five thousand including overtime. The main thing for me was that I realized how much I had learned during the past eight years or so at PSCCO. I knew I would continue to look for opportunities to learn more, and it wasn't too long after the Georgetown project was completed that I stumbled into a new area of learning thanks to Larry Weaver, one of the smartest guys in the department.

I used to always get to work twenty to thirty minutes before the eight a.m. start time, but there was one early arrival that would change my life. When I walked in, I noticed Larry Weaver reading a book, so I went over to him and asked what he was reading. He told me he had signed up for a class at the University of Denver Extension Center in order to learn Fortran, a computer programming language. He went on to explain that Fortran was a programming language used by engineers to solve various problems usually performed manually with slide rules and a variety of mathematical formulas. I did not understand anything he told me, so I asked him to give me an example. He knew I understood the process we used in the department to establish a centerline in order to plot the topography of the land and then use predefined templates that represented the wire that would be strung between each transmission tower so that we could achieve a minimum clearance between the wires and the ground.

Larry explained how a computer program written in Fortran could take the input from the field book we created as we took readings along the centerline every time the elevation changed three feet (plus or minus) and automatically plot the topography using a huge flatbed plotter. He went on to say that the way we do this is very time consuming, and the accuracy we achieve is limited to the 0.10. When we calculate our numbers, we limit our accuracy to two digits to the right of the decimal point whereas a computer will easily calculate all numbers to eight to ten digits to the right of the decimal point. We need only feed in the data contained in our field book, and the computer would calculate all points where readings are taken in a matter of minutes and then plot the topography on a plotter in thirty seconds.

Knowing how exceptionally smart Larry Weaver was and that he had gone to college for a couple of years majoring in civil engineering, I imagined that something like Fortran was way over my speed limit. So, I told him that I doubted that I would be able to grasp something like computer programming. In a New York second, Larry said that he didn't think it would be a problem for me. I don't know why he said that, but the next thing I did was ask him where I could go to sign up for the next class. And then, the next thing after that, I went downtown to the DU Extension Center to enroll in the next Fortran class. I paid eighty-five dollars and was scheduled to attend a two-hour class on Tuesdays and Thursdays for eight weeks. Classes started at seven p.m. at the extension center, which was located in downtown Denver.

I went to the same bookstore my mother took me to every year before the start of school at St. Catherine's to purchase my Fortran programming guide. Actually, this was the one and only bookstore that I had ever been to in my life. Over the next year, this particular bookstore would see me one more time when I found myself in desperate need for information that would literally change my life forever. But that story is down the road a little later in my journey.

I can tell you that I attended every class. I had a terrible feeling after the first class I attended and maintained that sense of dread throughout the subsequent weeks until the end. It was the kind of class that you wouldn't get a grade or even any college credit. You would simply be given a pass/fail rating at the end of class. Somehow, I got a pass rating but did not understand a single thing our instructor said. Our professor was one of those guys that was so in love with himself and hearing himself talk that I cannot ever remember seeing him make eye contact with anyone. He actually was not even the least bit interested in knowing if everyone in the class was able to understand his lectures or anything else. He was simply going through the motions, providing information about programming in general and Fortran as a specific set of instructions that most computers could recognize and execute.

After receiving a pass rating, I decided to talk to Larry Weaver about my experience since he had the same professor. I told Larry I really didn't understand what the hell the professor was talking about and asked him if he had any problems understanding the instructor. Larry told me he understood where I was coming from and that it wasn't that uncommon to come out of a class like that with a lot of questions. He told me that the advantage he had was having a computer at home. He was able to use the Fortran programming language to develop simple programs that utilized the Fortran functions and produce easy-to-understand formulas that took keyed-in input and processed it using the formulas for output on a hard-copy report. He told me that once he could see the cause and effect when he used the Fortran functions, it was easy to understand what the professor was trying to say. He told me not to give up, and he told me that Ron Hall, who was data Datapoint (DP) computer hardware and software rep to PSCCO, was going to be teaching a Fortran class at our facility. Before you could say Jiminy Cricket, I was on the phone talking to Ron and asking if I could attend his class.

Ron Hall's class was like a breath of fresh air for me. Every single thing he said I was able to absorb like a sponge. Terms that my old professor talked about became something that I was able to remember, and now I was able to assimilate the terms in the context of a programming language. It was as though the professor described a term, but the language he used to explain the function was like introducing Spanish words into an English-based language. Ron, on the other hand, used the Spanish word but provided the English equivalent so that I was able to make a connection to the previously unknown term in a way that allowed me to easily understand its use and purpose.

I had invested sixteen weeks of my time to learn a computer programming language that had absolutely nothing to do with my job, and I could not explain exactly why I did it. This was one of those times when you had to listen to the little voice in the back of your head. There have been many times in my career at PSCCO when I saw some manual and maybe page through it until I saw something that seemed interesting. Then I stopped and read that section of the manual. Believe it or not, whatever I read seemed to become relevant to me at some point in the near future. This seems almost spooky when you think about it, and I certainly cannot explain it. But what this type of phenomenon tells me is that once again my little voice directs my behavior, and if I pay attention and I'm willing to listen, then somehow I am able to be just the tiniest bit ahead of the pack.

Larry Weaver's prediction of using computers to plot our centerline topography and be able to locate towers, have the computer run through formulas that determine the wire sag between the towers maintaining a minimum of a thirty-five-feet clearance from the ground when fully loaded with ice became reality. Dean Miller immediately saw the value in the new technology and ordered a couple of the Datapoint mini-computers and a new high-tech flatbed plotter located in the downtown office's computer room that was attached to the IBM 360 mainframe computer.

Next, Dean Miller wanted to select one of his people to be in charge of the department's new technology and coordinate with the technical people downtown in order to provide them with the required topographical data needed by the mainframe software in order to produce 24-inch by 36-inch plats that depicted a side view of the centerline, the location of towers, and the sag of the wire between each tower. In my mind, there were three people that Dean could select: Neil Terry, Larry Weaver, or me. All of a sudden, knowledge of Fortran became a prerequisite to performing the job, and the two Fortran classes that I took but could not explain why became a key differentiator in deciding who would be promoted to head the Transmission Engineering Technology department. At the beginning, it would be a one-person department, but it was easy to see that the Structural, Mechanical, and Electrical Engineering Departments would also want to take advantage of computer software that facilitated the automation of various functions within their own areas of responsibility.

At the end of the day, Dean Miller chose the best person for the job: Neil Terry. It was almost unbelievable when I think back about the people in the department. There were four extraordinarily smart people and other average players who were outstanding in terms of specific job-related skills and work ethic. I came in third out of the three candidates for the job, but to me the amazing thing was that I was even a candidate under consideration for the position. I congratulated Neil, and he told me that he would keep me in mind if and when his department started to expand. I knew he meant that, but I asked him why he wouldn't want to add Larry Weaver to his team before me. It would have been disingenuous for me to assume Neil thought I was smarter or better suited than Larry Weaver. Neil told me that Larry told Dean he didn't want the job; he enjoyed doing the surveying work in the field and wouldn't want to be stuck in an office all day.

NDJ Life Lesson:

After spending nearly six years in the Transmission Engineering Department, I finally managed to learn a set of marketable skills that I could use to become an independent, adult member of society.

I could afford to get my own apartment, and I could get married if I found the right girl. All of these things became possible because of what I learned as I carried out my duties, because I found a way to exceed my boss's expectations, and because I managed to earn the respect of my peers.

I was able to make this happen because I looked at every day as a day that I had to prove myself. Every day I reset myself to zero and started my workday. It may seem so very hard to do, but when you think about it, there are a lot of occupations that require a high level of performance every day, every hour. Think about firefighters, policemen, and doctors. They all know that we always count on them to do their best work every day and every hour in each day.

When we hold ourselves to this high standard, it actually does become easier over time, and it is the upside potential when you manage yourself to be the best, not just do your best. Look around. Who are the people you know that perform at a higher level than you? Why is that true? What do you think you could do better? How do you think you can up your game?

One secret that I learned was that I could almost count on being able to accomplish more than another person if I was willing to spend more time working on a given task than my competitor. Remember how the tortoise defeated the hare? He just never stopped. There is a term called "casual overtime." I was always willing to work more than eight hours to complete my work as expected or as a way to exceed expectations. And I didn't worry a bit because I didn't get paid overtime wages when I worked past the normal eight-hour workday because I always viewed it as an investment in my future.
And for me it always paid off.

You need to give whatever effort necessary to exceed your boss's expectations, and never let down the family members that are counting on you.

Chapter 21

Public Service Company of Colorado
Information Systems Department

As they say, life goes on. Neil Terry was doing a great job automating the plotting functions within the department and interfacing with the computer programmers that worked downtown on the mainframe computer. Then, out of the blue, everyone received an announcement letter from the vice president of information systems. In the letter, the VP explained how computer technology was literally changing the way companies did business and that there was a tremendous shortfall of qualified computer programmers available in the job market.

These were the very early days of the technology boom when there wasn't even a way for college students to major in computer science. The letter went on to say that PSCCO management had decided to establish an in-house computer training program tailored to produce qualified computer programmers proficient in the technologies and methods used by PSCCO to support all automated functions within the company. People interested in attending the first six-month training sessions needed to complete the form included with the letter and be willing to take an IBM aptitude test administered by IBM. All test results would remain confidential.

Unbelievable. All of a sudden I have a once-in-a-lifetime opportunity to become a computer programmer. I can't tell you how incredible it made me feel when I was completing the application form requesting to be considered for a position. The second I sent my application back to the Information Systems Department (ISD), I immediately became hugely concerned about having to take an aptitude test. This was one of those things that I absolutely had no understanding of; I assumed that you either had the aptitude for something or you didn't, right? Somehow, I learned a long time ago that when you know you don't know something, you have to admit it and then find out what you can do about whatever it is. It was clear in the letter that if you didn't do well on the test, it was over.

Remember when I went to the bookstore to get my Fortran training guide? I said I would make another important trip to that store sometime in my future. Well, this was the time. I decided to go to my only source of knowledge in my entire life and see if anyone could help me figure out what an aptitude test was. I felt really uncomfortable asking one of the clerks at the store if they had anything that would help me if I was going to take an IBM aptitude test, but admitting to myself that I didn't know anything about this subject forced me to try to figure out if there was anything I could use to help me. And guess what I found? I found a treasure map that led me to something much better than a pot of gold. It would lead me directly to a path that I would follow for the next twenty-eight years, a path that would provide me opportunities beyond any I had ever imagined. The store clerk didn't look at me as if I lost my mind; instead she brought me directly to a section of the store that had computer-related information. Then she located a book entitled *IBM Aptitude Test*. I opened the book to the first page and read "This book is not a real IBM aptitude test. However, it contains examples of questions and exercises contained in a real IBM aptitude test." The idea of the book was to provide the student with questions, pictures, multiple-choice questions, and every other type of question that actually did exist on the IBM Aptitude Test.

I purchased the book, which was about one and a half inches thick, and took it home to read. I had about two weeks to get ready to take the test, so I remembered the countless times my mother had me read and reread every chapter for an upcoming test. Once I started getting used to each of the various sections of the test, I realized that I wouldn't have had a prayer to pass this test had I not practiced and practiced, and yes practiced some more. On top of everything else, the test was timed, and if you were not familiar with test at all, it would have taken the average person about twenty to twenty-five percent of the time allotted just to understand how to perform each section since all five sections were completely different from one another. I literally stayed up all night before the test making sure I could fly through the questions and at least be able to complete the test in the allotted time.

The day of the test came. The tests were handed out, and they were the exact format described in my instruction manual. While there were no identical questions in the real test from my instruction manual, I was able to breeze through the test, completing each section before time ran out. I knew I had an excellent chance of having a very high score. No doubt.

A couple of weeks went by, and then something unusual happened. I had been assigned to be the transit operator on a power-line reroute that located near downtown Denver. When our crew leader signaled us to head out, Dean Miller asked me to take a ride with him in his car. He would take me to the jobsite but wanted to talk to me about something first. I got in his car, and he began by saying that he had some bad news and some good news. I couldn't even imagine what on earth he was talking about. Dean said he wanted to start with the bad news first and then said, "I'm afraid you didn't do that well on the aptitude test." He went on to say that they weren't going to release any of the scores but that my score wasn't high enough to qualify me to be accepted into the training program. "But now I want to tell you the good news," he continued. "I am going to offer you a promotion into our own Technology section at the same pay and grade you would have received if you were accepted into the training program. I can understand if you're disappointed because you weren't accepted, but I hope you will accept my offer and continue to be a member of my department."

I was shocked, in total disbelief. I knew I knocked that test out of the park. Somehow something didn't feel right about the conversation. "I know they told us that we wouldn't be given our scores," I said, "but did they say anything at all about me?"

He hesitated for a few seconds and then said, "They did say that you appeared to be indecisive."

"Indecisive?" I asked. "How could I have been indecisive?"

Dean said he didn't know, but that was what they said.

We arrived at the job site, and he told me to think it over and let him know what I wanted to do.

Okay. Now the wheels in my brain were really moving, trying to process everything I had just been told. First of all, how could they conclude I was indecisive on a multiple-choice test? I didn't fill in the dot more than once for each question, and I didn't erase a dot, fill in a different dot then erase that dot and pick a third dot. Just how can you be indecisive on a test like this? You can't, right? Then why would Dean Miller offer me a promotion at the same level when I failed to score high enough to qualify for the other job? Nobody would do that, right? Well, for sure something fishy was going on. That much I was sure of.

At lunch break, I got to a phone and called one of my friends, Fred Sommers, who was already working as a computer programmer downtown, and I told him what my boss told me. He said he saw Dean Miller meet with his boss, Dwayne Gilbert, the day before. Dwayne told Fred that Dean wanted to keep me in his department and would offer me the same level and promotion to stay. I told Fred that Dean told me I didn't pass the aptitude test, which I thought didn't make sense because of the promotion he offered me. Fred told me he thought I got the second-highest score. So now what was I going to do? That was the $64,000 question, and I had to come up with an answer by the following day.

The next day I got to the office early, hoping to catch Dean after he parked his car and was walking into the building. But this time, Dean got to work earlier than usual. He was in his office, the kind of office that had wooden walls that were about four and a half feet tall, with glass-wall extensions reaching up an additional four and a half feet. This meant that any conversation could be heard by anyone in close proximity to Dean's office. He was on the phone talking to someone, so I just had to wait where I could see when he hung up but try to be far enough away to not be conspicuous. Finally, Dean ended his call. I walked up to the entrance of his office where the wood/glass door was open, and I asked him if I could have a few minutes of his time. He said sure and told me to come in and take a seat. I asked him if he would take a walk with me so that we could have some privacy.

He said, "Sure, no problem."

We walked toward the huge warehouse that housed monster-sized reels of transmission-line wire, huge transformers that were kept to provide back-up to the hundreds of substations in the Denver Metro area, and countless types of hardware needed to support the PSCCO infrastructure related to high-voltage power transmission and distribution. I began by telling Dean that I really appreciated his job offer, but I would rather go to the in-house training program that being offered downtown. I told him this as if I didn't hear him tell me that I didn't qualify for the job downtown. I pretended that none of the things he said to me about being indecisive even happened or mattered. It was my thought that I would be much better off just acting as if my ride in the car with Dean never happened.

I ended by saying, "I would really appreciate it if you would tell the people downtown that I would like to go work for them."

He looked at me with strong eye contact and extended his hand out to shake hands. I told him I was very grateful for the opportunity he had given me five years ago and to let me know if there was anything I could do for him. We walked back to Dean's office, and he wished me well in my new job.

"Thanks, Dean. I really appreciate it," I said as I turned and walked back to my desk. I called my friend, Fred Sommers, told him what happened, and he said he would let Dwayne Gilbert know.

NDJ Life Lesson:

I grew up watching the "Wonderful World of Disney," and I can still remember Jiminy Cricket singing, "When you wish upon a star, makes no difference who you are... your dreams will come true."

Those were the days when kids were able to pretend, but when you get older you are supposed to know better.

Well, I just used my powers of pretending on Dean Miller so that I could avoid a terrible confrontation after I found out he lied to me.

I pretended he didn't say any of the things he actually said. And then I pretended that he made me a job offer but that I wanted the other job downtown that he said I didn't qualify for.

If I was playing poker, you could say I was bluffing. I acted as if I had a winning hand after Dean told me I didn't. I continued to play my hand by thanking him for the job offer but deciding to take the other job as if he told me I could choose either one and that he hoped I would stay with his department.

Because I knew Dean Miller was a very savvy guy, he immediately realized that I knew my hand was better than his. He played along and folded his hand.

Pretending is an important skill to have in your toolkit. There are all sorts of reasons to pretend about things in order to advance your cause.

It was at this precise moment in history when the term "Dress for Success" was coined. The slogan simply means that even if you are not successful yet, you need to pretend you are by looking the part.

I will talk about how important pretending can be in all facets of your life in future chapters, but you have to keep reading to find out.

Chapter 22

Public Service Company of Colorado
Information Systems Department:
Junior Programmer Training Class

Two weeks later, I found myself in the first in-house computer programming training program. Before I showed up for class, I spent several hours and about a thousand dollars upgrading my wardrobe. In my new position, all men were required to wear a coat and tie. I think I had two sport coats, four or five pairs of slacks, three or four ties, and one pair of dress shoes. I had a raincoat I could wear over my sport coat, but I didn't have a heavier topcoat. This definitely reminded me of my high school makeover when I decided to develop a new image. I know there are some guys that don't like to shop for clothes, but I am definitely not one of them. I'm certain I got my ideas about appearance and image from my dad. Even though he was a house painter, when he went out to the dog races with my mom, he was a real stud—good looking, and his taste in clothes was top notch. Once I went out and bought four new sport coats, six new dress shirts, eight ties, four pairs of pants, one pair of dress shoes, and a topcoat, my biggest problem was what to wear on day one.

There were twelve students total. Neil Terry and I were the only two from Transmission Engineering. One student came from Grand Junction, Colorado where PSCCO had a small coal-electric generating plant and a substantial gas distribution facility. His name was Fred Medrano. Believe it or not the other nine students were new hires with degrees in engineering, mathematics, or physics. One of the nine also held a master's degree in business administration. All of the new hires had intimidating credentials and I can tell you for sure that Neil Terry and I were the only people without a college degree.

The instructor made some introductory remarks. "Hello. I am Jonas Markham. I would like you to address me as Mr. Markham. Senior Management has asked me to welcome each of our programmer trainees into the Information Systems Department. Brice Marshall, the vice president of ISD, is out of town and unavailable to be here today. He told me that he plans to welcome you in person when he returns. I have been hired by PSCCO to develop an in-house training program. I am on loan from the University of Colorado where I am a member of the science faculty. The course that you have enrolled in is made up of seven separate sections. I myself will be the instructor for three of the seven sections. There will be four sections that contain areas of learning for specialized programming languages used by the Information Systems Department here at PSCCO. The instructors for programming languages and telecommunications interfaces will be senior in-house technical personnel. The seven sections are Decision Logic Tables; Computer Programming Design; Assembler Language Programming; CICS Telecommunications; Job Control Language; Program Testing and Debugging and PL/1 Programming Language.

"Each section will have at least one intermediate test and a final end-of-section test. Each student will be required to achieve a passing score at the end of the section test, or he or she will not be eligible to continue with the course. At the end of the course there will be a final test, and each student must receive a passing score in order to become a junior programmer in the Information Systems Department."

I had never imagined that anyone in the training class would be tested and that the consequences for getting a D or worse would be banishment from the class. You talk about pressure! What if Mr. Markham from CU was as bad as the professor I had in my Fortran class at DU? I had managed to maneuver myself right into a pickle of epic proportions. I just had to pray and hope and pray some more that this class was going to be my springboard into the future where the water was and not a springboard that propelled me into the side of the pool headfirst.

It's funny, because when I was asked about being promoted from a hand fork operator to a punch press operator by Manuel Rodriguez or from a clerk in Engineering to rear chainman by Dean Miller, Manuel made me aware of the risks inherent in the punch press operator job, and my common sense told me about the risks associated with becoming a rear chainman on a survey crew battling the elements and trying to keep from falling off a mountain somewhere. But somehow, I did not even fathom the possibility that there were any risks associated with this training class—nada, zilch, zero. And because of that, I strolled in totally unprepared to deal with a danger that I didn't even know existed. My biggest asset had always been my ability to anticipate problems and come up with a game plan to deal with them. Now I was sitting there, and I was almost numb with fear, so much so that I was having trouble hearing anything the instructor said after "will not be eligible to continue with the course."

I literally sat there staring at the instructor, watching his mouth move, and then noticing everyone stand up when the instructor apparently told us to take a break. I stood up, and tried to look cool and calm as everyone began introducing themselves to each other. What a day so far.

After break time was up, there were some administrative things to take care of. Each person was given a computer identification code to use when we sent things to the key punch operators to produce punched computer cards and for use on our job control language (JCL) header card so that our punched cards and printouts could be returned to the rightful owner. We were assigned individual cubicle work areas that included a CRT (cathode ray tube) and keyboard that we would use to test the programs we wrote. The cubicles had built-in desks with drawers and a flat table space where we could write or place manuals.

Each person was given a greenie, which was the 3-inch by 6-inch "IBM Programmers Assembler Language Instruction Guide." It was one of those cards that folded into itself three times and had information on both sides of the paper. This card was thought to be the most valuable possession that any assembler language (AL) programmer could own. On this card were the abbreviated form of the most-often used computer instructions and the format for the numerical byte, or bit configuration, that each instruction required in order to be read into the assembler, which produced machine readable and executable code. If I would have asked the person who handed out the green card, "What's this green card for?" and received the answer I described above, I probably would have passed out cold. How on earth could anybody be smart enough to understand, need, or use a greenie?

But guess what? Six months later it would make perfect sense. I have always been amazed by the fact that I seem to find out what I need to know just before I need to know it. A case in point here is that had I not asked Larry Weaver what he was up to when he was reading a book at his desk, I would have not had any idea what Fortran was. Had I not enrolled in the DU extension center class, I would never have had any idea of what a computer programming language was. Had I not enrolled in the second Fortran class I would have never realized that I could actually understand how to write a computer program and that I enjoyed working with technology. Had I not gone to my one and only source for formal training material, the bookstore recommended by the nuns at my parochial school, I would have never been able to pass the IBM aptitude test. Somehow, my little voice, the voice everyone has, has always given me a path to follow.

Something made me pay attention to what was happening in my life, and more importantly, to always pay attention to what my little voice was saying.

I have sometimes wondered if my little voice is louder than most, but after thinking about it for a while, I don't think that is the case. I think I am able to hear my little voice more clearly because it is not competing with any other voices from people giving me advice. That is not to say that the nuns were actually and literally yelling in my ear giving me their religious point of view; I can assure you they were. But I didn't view their input as anything relevant. My little voice was my only source of input about my life here and now.

NDJ Life Lesson:

When you boil it down, my life was changed in an unimaginable way because Larry Weaver was reading a book, and my curiosity caused me to ask him what he was reading.

Next, I started reading the same book and eventually found myself applying to become a student in the first PSCCO in-house programmer training class.

Next, I located another book that would help me prepare for the IBM Aptitude Test.

When I thought about it, Larry Weaver always had some kind of book with him. When we were working on a jobsite, Larry would brown-bag it and pull out some book to read during lunch break.

Epiphany moment: "Maybe that's why Larry Weaver is so smart. He's always reading books!"

When you're in school, the teachers tell you which books to read. When you're not in school, it is up to you. What I'm absolutely certain of is that the smartest people are always reading something.

Chapter 23

Public Service Company of Colorado In-House Training Class:
Section 1—Decision Logic Tables
Section 2—Computer Programming Design

When I was working as a clerk, I remembered Danny Martin talking to me about his job as a draftsman in Structural Engineering. He was working on the façade of one of the company's many service centers trying to enhance the building's appearance. He told me that before anything can be built, at a minimum you needed to be able to visually understand the front elevation of the building. I didn't really know what he meant by that, so he went on to explain that you need to understand how the front of the building looks if you are standing on the sidewalk looking at it. Without that visual picture, you cannot build a building. He said that if you know that and only that, it is possible to construct a building that meets the implied requirements associated with the structure.

Now, I still was not totally getting what he was saying, so he gave me an example. Pretend a married couple comes to you with their two children, says that they want you to build a building, and gives you a sketch of the front of the building. With a picture, you can begin deciding the width of the structure based on lot size and zoning restrictions. You can assume the building is a house, you can deduce that there should be four bedrooms, and the size of their budget will dictate maximum square footage and so on. The main thing is the initial picture required to get the ball rolling.

During the decision logic tables and programming design sections of the class, I realized the same thing was true if you were going to construct a computer program. Before you can start building the program, you must first create a picture of how it will work and how it will look. So instead of using a drafting table, straight edge, and pencils, there are tools specifically used to describe the architecture needed to support the functionality of the program.

Using special templates as design aides and 18-inch by 36-inch white paper with light-grey horizontal and vertical lines (grid paper), each program began with the creation of a program design folder that included a functional description narrative that described the files and explained the purpose of the program, and data records and fields used by the program. If the program was going to be an online-type (CICS telecommunications) program, then a screen layout specifying the locations of the fields would be displayed on the screen would be included in the program design folder. If the program was not an online program, then it was described as a batch program, which required no user interaction to execute, and in most cases, were programs routinely scheduled to be submitted for execution by a computer operator tasked with submitting jobs to run each day using a predefined schedule. Most batch programs produced some kind of paper output whose contents and format had been predefined by an analyst, and this information took the place of the screen design for an online program, which was commonly referred to as a report.

Mr. Markham was the instructor for Sections 1 and 2. When he got in front of the class to begin, I remember thinking to myself, "Please don't be like the Professor at DU" Ten to twenty seconds after Mr. Markham began speaking, I knew that my fears would not be realized. Unbelievably, I had never heard anyone easier to understand. He had perfect enunciation and spoke at what seemed like a perfect rate of speed. He had obviously taught this subject many times. He had what I thought were great visual aids to help convey his teachings. After day one with Mr. Markham, I knew I wouldn't have a problem passing his tests. I have always been a visual person versus an auditory person, and Sections 1 and 2 were definitely in my wheelhouse. These sections lasted a total of five weeks, and I had no problem passing the interim and final tests for both.

NDJ Life Lesson:

In order to build a building or design a computer program, you must create a picture of how it will look.

Using the power of your mind, you can create an image of yourself achieving great things and enjoying great moments.

Before you can become the person you want to be, you must be able to create a picture in your mind of how you will look and how you will act when you see yourself accomplish an important goal in your life.

When you replay these images in your mind repeatedly, you are sending signals to your subconscious that says, "Help me figure out how to make this come true".

When you and your subconscious both strive for success over your peers, it's usually two against one in your favor.

Chapter 24

Public Service Company of Colorado In-House Training Class:
Section 3—Assembler Language Programming
Section 4—CICS Telecommunications Peaches

Our instructor for Assembler Language Programming was Jim Peachinelli, a.k.a. Peaches. His opening remarks were, "Nobody calls me Jim. Not even my mother. Please feel free to call me Peaches."

He was without a doubt the main man in a department of over three hundred people. He was the senior system programming engineer. His cohort, Marko Mistoffi, was also a system programmer, minus the engineer qualification. The reason for the difference in titles was due to the fact that Marko was qualified to work on the operating system, telecommunications, and all system-level software, such as ISAM and VSAM, which were components used by the operating system to access special file types. Peaches was the department's sole firmware programmer, which was the lowest level of code that is burned into hardware devices for special purposes. Every man in the department wore a coat and tie except Peaches and Marko. The reason for this was that their offices were located in the computer room, where the temperature was maintained at sixty to sixty-five degrees Fahrenheit. Also, all computer operator personnel were not required to wear a coat and tie, and female operators all wore pants.

Peaches was about five feet ten inches tall, and he usually wore designer jeans, tennis shoes, and a variety of sweatshirts, some of which reflected his alma mater, Notre Dame. He had an outgoing personality and was very comfortable speaking in front of a crowd. He had been the Assembler Language instructor for several one-of events that took qualified in-house PL1 programmers to an entirely new level of programming. PL1 was considered a high-level language, and assembler language was considered a low-level language. An example might be that a PL1 programmer codes a read instruction in a program, and then that program, filled with hundreds of other PL1 instructions, is read by a compiler. The compiler takes the read instruction and generates about thirty assembler language instructions. The AL instructions are read by an assembler, and the output of the assembler is machine readable/executable instructions. You can see that AL programming was very labor intensive, but at that point in time, it was the only language you could use with CICS that supported multiple users with CRTs on their desks performing various functions like payroll and accounting.

When Peachinelli explained how AL programs were constructed and the complexity and power of each individual instruction, I absolutely thought I had died and went to heaven. I just could not explain how exhilarating it was for me to really understand how a computer worked and to learn the almost magical world under the covers of these giant machines with their memory and registers.

By this point, PSCCO had just upgraded its mainframe computer from an IBM 360 to an IBM 370 Model 155, increasing our computer capacity by a factor of eight to ten. I learned over the next several months that the new 370 presented me with a work environment where precision, complexity, and creativity were going challenge me every day I. I just cannot tell you how grateful I was to have an opportunity like this. For the first time in my life, I realized that it was possible to go to work and really love your job.

When I thought about it for a while, I only knew one person that I thought loved his job: Fred Eastom, the mechanical engineer heading up the Cabin Creek hydroelectric project. You could see it in his eyes that he loved being a mechanical engineer and especially loved the Cabin Creek project. Other than Mr. Eastom, I didn't know another person who loved their job. I have met a lot of people who like what they're doing but hate the boss or the working conditions or the commute or their lack of opportunity to advance. Most people are just not happy with their jobs, and I don't ever remember somebody saying that they didn't love what they were doing but it was okay for the time being. Even that type of person was still hoping that their lot in life might improve.

NDJ Life Lesson:

This is too important to wait until the end of the chapter to say: Burt Bacharach got it right when he wrote, "What the world needs now is love sweet love. It's the only thing that there's just too little of."

At this point in my life, I can remember every time I was in love:

- First Bicycle—26-inch Schwinn, black with chrome fenders
- First Car—1950 Mercury, grey with blue and white Naugahyde interior
- First Girlfriend—Becky Wright, 1962
- 1964 Chevrolet SS Impala 409
- Junior Programmer at PSCCO, 1974

For me there is no better feeling in the world than when you love someone or something, and I think most people would agree with my assertion. Yet, when it comes to choosing a job or career, most people never imagine it is possible for them to find a job that they will love.

Why is this true for most people? It's true because most people go to work to earn a living, and the idea that they are going to love any aspect of what initially starts out as trying to survive seems almost like a contradiction in terms.

Would you ever expect someone to say "I love surviving"? (See Appendix 1, "North Denver Johnnie's Job Choices and Motives for Leaving Old Job.")

My motivation for writing this book was based on my belief that the life lessons learned by NDJ while experiencing the real-life stories depicted here will be a source of self-help and/or motivation for the reader.

In most motivational books you find answers to every problem discussed. In this chapter, NDJ discovered a job and a set of skills that he truly loved. Most readers, at this point in the book, are very likely to anticipate NDJ explaining how to find a job that they will love.

I understand the expectation, but I am sorry to tell you that loving your job is something that happens almost by accident and not by design. NDJ stumbled into a set of circumstances that gave him more than he knew was possible.

The reality of working often produces one of the following opinions people have about their jobs:

1. I like what I'm doing, but I don't like my boss and/or management.
2. I like what I'm doing, but I don't feel I'm getting paid enough.

3. I like what I'm doing; however, it is impossible to get ahead and there really aren't any ways for me to advance.
4. I like what I'm doing; however our work environment and the tools we have to get our job done are subpar, which makes it hard to get up and go to work.
5. I don't like what I'm doing, but it's too late for me to do anything about it.

There are too many variables required before someone is in the situation NDI discovered in 1974. But before you decide that there is no good reason to keep reading this book, please consider the following:

Most people have to work, and they spend about thirty-three percent of a seven-day week working or commuting to work. This means that sixty-seven percent of the time, you are the boss and get to decide what you do or don't do.

I have found that most people don't create problems for themselves during the fifty-five hours they are doing work-related activities. During this period of time, most people get to work on time, follow company procedures, and produce work at a level that meets expectations.

It is the sixty-seven percent of the time when people are their own boss that they create major problems for themselves that can affect their attitude about their job and just about everything else in their lives.

It doesn't matter whether you are single or married, because an awful lot of people manage to make poor decisions in their personal lives that cause them a constant state of anxiety.

<u>Poor Decisions Single People and Married People Make When:</u>

a. Deciding how to manage their relationships.
b. Deciding how to manage their money.
c. Deciding what to do in their spare time.
d. Deciding how to manage their career.

The main reasons married people get divorced are that they are unhappy with their sex lives and/or because they have money problems.

The main reason single people break up is because they are unhappy with their sex life, or in the case of some females, they are unhappy with their sex lives and/or because they don't think their mate will provide them with a lifestyle that they want for themselves (potential to make money).

In future chapters, I will describe some of the stories NDJ experienced during his "I'm the boss" time and the life lessons he learned.

Chapter 25

Public Service Company of Colorado In-House Training Class:
Sections 5—7 and Beyond

My fear of failure kicked into high gear on day one of the class and every day after that for six months.

After we completed Sections 3 and 4, each student was given an assignment to develop three types of computer programs using IBM assembler language and CICS. The first program was an inquiry program that allowed the user to enter a file key on a screen, retrieve the file record associated with that key, and display the file on the screen.

The second program was an add transaction that allowed a user to enter a new key record into the system and all of the data fields associated with the key. This program was much more complicated than the first because it required edits, which enforced the rules for data content for each individual field type associated with the key, before the program added the new record to the file.

The third program was the most complex because it combined the functionality of programs one and two and added an additional function that allowed existing data fields to be displayed as did program one. However, it then allowed certain fields to be modified to replace previous values. Editing was required for the new values to replace an existing field as well as associated editing, which required that certain values be acceptable as long as the value of some other related field was within some pre-established range of values.

The interesting thing about the three programs was that they were a part of a huge project development effort that would result in the development of hundreds of programs to be used by real users to support a PSCCO business function. Each student would contact the project manager for the development effort to get their assignments, and they would be given a complete set of program design documentation that described the purpose of the program, the file layout information, a set of JCLs to assemble a program and make it ready for testing, and a schedule for completion of the task, indicating the hours estimated to design and code the program.

This was a real-world exercise, and it was the first time that I realized how expectations were defined and expressed. It was a little bit scary because when I was a part of the survey team, we all had an understanding of how long things were expected to take, but I never felt the pressure that would have broken up my job duties as a transit operator into tasks measured by hours or half-hours. All I could do was work as fast as I could, maintain the highest level of accuracy possible, and then see how I measured up to the task estimates I was given. It was just another curve ball that I had no way of anticipating, and I had no way of changing what people expected.

Finally, after six very intense and long months, I experienced my second graduation ten years after my North High class of '64 graduation. I was told that I had the second-highest score on the aptitude test, and once again I was ranked second in my class with guess who ranked number one? Yes, Neil Terry was ranked number one. In this case, it really didn't matter because the entire class managed to pass the course successfully, and all twelve of us were given the new job title of junior programmer. For me this meant another pay raise.

I was assigned an office on the eighth floor of the PSCCO building. Each office housed four people with huge desks, CRTs that were mounted on an arm attached to the desk, and there was a tray that housed the keyboard attached to the CRT. There were tons of little cubicles on the wall near the desk that were used to keep punched cards for commonly used JCL needed to add and execute programs on the IBM mainframe computer.

I went to work wearing a sport coat and tie every day. I worked in a beautiful building in downtown Denver on 15th Street. I ended up carpooling with Fred Medrano to save money on parking. I can tell you for sure, I was the happiest, proudest guy on the planet. My memories of Samsonite seemed almost like a bad dream, but I knew it wasn't a dream at all. I could not even imagine it possible that there was anyone in the PSCCO building more determined to become a valuable employee. My memories of the factory would never leave me, and I would always strive to be the best at my job so I would never have to return.

I had always imagined that the top-notch people in society were likely to participate in two to four graduation events in their lifetime. First high school, second college, third a graduate degree like an MBA, and fourth a graduation for a doctorate degree. So, when I was handed a Certificate of Successful Completion of the In-House PSCCO Computer Training Program, I wondered if I was looking at the word "graduation" in its most narrow context. I had never thought of myself as a person with a big vocabulary, so I often went to the dictionary to look up words whose meaning I thought I already knew. When I looked up "graduation," I noticed another meaning: a division or interval, as on a graduated scale.

Letting my imagination run with this newfound knowledge, I imagined that we are a kind of vessel with small lines that represent the liquid intake of knowledge or ability. If we were hollow with no body organs to confuse my meaning, we would notice how we add small amounts of liquid every time we grasp some area of knowledge. In my imaginary hollow person, there might be some darker graduation lines that represent key milestones relating to age. Saying "dada," standing upright, taking some baby steps, and so on could be a collective set of knowledge for children from ages one to three. Imagining that every new language we learn, such as when we become a little league baseball player, represents milestones with a variety of skill requirements. On and on the process goes.

When I started to think that way, I realized that even if my second graduation wasn't from college, it was uniquely worth more to me than a four-year degree from any major university. How could this be true? For one, there were no major colleges that offered a degree in computer science. Also, there was no field of knowledge that was in more demand, and at this point in history, the computer technology boom was in its infancy. In general, we still used punched cards and paper tape as mainstream sources of input for early-day computers. Therefore, I found myself at the cusp of a major movement that was going to change every person's life forever. My potential upside was limitless.

Another thing that dawned on me was that I had managed to get myself promoted at both Samsonite (increasing my paycheck from minimum wage to three and a half times minimum wage doing piecework) and Public Service Company of Colorado multiple times (receiving a twenty-eight percent increase in pay at first and further increasing this by thirty-six percent in a period of just over five years).

In my current situation, I was transferred from the Transmission Engineering Department, where I was a transit operator, to the Information Systems Department where I started as a programmer trainee at the same pay grade and was then promoted to junior programmer with an eighteen percent increase in pay. In the ISD, there were so many promotion opportunities I almost could not believe the possible career paths that lay ahead. People were expected to advance from junior programmer to programmer to senior programmer to programmer analyst to senior programmer analyst to team leader to project leader to section manager. It was at the senior programmer analyst and system programmer levels that the career paths diverged. The system programmers were the tip-top of the food chain for all technical personnel. There were only two system programmer positions in the entire department and about fifteen to twenty team leaders and project managers. The two system programmers were Jim Peachinelli and Marko Mistoffi. One good thing for me was that system programmers seemed to have a lot of vowels in their names.

I spent the next year working as a junior programmer, and then I qualified for a raise and promotion to programmer. A little more than two years after graduating from my training class, I was still completely in love with my job. Then, out of the blue, my good friend Fred Sommers called me and asked me to meet him for lunch on Saturday. He told me he and his wife bought a house in the foothills west of Denver and that there was a pool table in the basement. He gave me his new address and phone number, and I told him I would see him soon.

I was very happy to hear from Fred because he had decided to leave PSCCO about eighteen months prior to take a job with a high-tech company at the Denver Technology Center (Tech Center). The Tech Center was a new real estate development on the south side of town where the cream-of-the-crop technology companies had congregated. They built state-of-the-art facilities to house their staff and produced products that were in some way related to computer technology hardware or software.

When I met with Fred for lunch, he looked great and was upbeat about the company he worked for. I just couldn't believe how big and how neat his new house was. It was a ranch-style home with a walk-out basement. They had been living there for a little over a year. It was immediately obvious that Fred was hitting them straight, and I couldn't be happier for him. Fred was the guy I called after Dean Miller told me I didn't pass the aptitude test.

Fred went to work for a company called Information Technology Services, Inc. because they promised to provide him with the training necessary to become a system programmer. Fred was on track to be another Peaches, and I couldn't have been happier for him. He was very bright, had an outgoing personality, and was one of those high-energy guys that are just fun to be around. When his wife, Jeannie, came downstairs with a tray of sandwiches, chips, pickles, and condiments, it was just like being in a restaurant. Everything was organized, and there were two kinds of chips in bowls. The pickles were on one plate, and on another were cold cuts with three kinds of cheese. There were two types of mustard along with mayonnaise and horseradish sauce. And best of all, there were cloth napkins. Jeannie asked me what I wanted to drink—naturally she had root beer—and then she left Fred and I alone. It may seem surprising that I can recall the details of my lunch as my story unfolds, but what I later realized that it was just this type of circumstance that made a lasting impression on me. In the future, if I would ever invite someone to my house for lunch, I would make sure to provide all of the ambiance and accoutrements that

Fred's wife did. First of all, it made me feel very special, and secondly, it made Fred and Jeannie appear successful.

As my journey continued, I took note of what seemed to be normal life experiences or lifestyles of successful people. Over time, I developed a mental list of things that people did that impressed me and how small, subtle things set people apart from one another. Eventually, I enjoyed bringing my observations into my own life, and just like everything else, I added things to my list that were unique to me and what I was trying to project. All the while, I realized that ninety percent of the people I invited to my home would never even notice the things that had made a lasting impression on me.

At that point, I was pretty sure that Fred had something important to say to me, and I was kind of anxious to hear what it was. Fred was a straight arrow. He told me he really liked his job and the company he was working for. He said that he had been doing the system programmer (SP) job right from the start. They sent him to Los Angeles for training, and he had a great IBM system engineer (SE) assigned to support his account. He went on to tell me who the key players were: Clem Gibson, Director of Operations; Fenton Miller, Manager of Operations; and Ralph Opgonorth, Manager of Programming. He reported to Fenton Miller. Apparently, Clem didn't like Ralph and wanted to replace him. Even better, Fred said that Clem wanted him to take Ralph's job. Then we got to the nitty-gritty: Fred tells me that he wants me to come on board to take his job as a SP.

I said, "Are you kidding me? I don't know the first thing about being a system programmer."

"Neither did I when they hired me," said Fred, "but we will send you to Los Angeles for training. I know you can do this."

You talk about a bombshell lunch announcement. I sort of imagined that Fred was going to talk to me about a job as an application programmer, but never in a million years did I imagine that an SP job was going to be on the table.

I told Fred that I would have to think about it, but off the top of my head I told him that I would feel bad telling Dwayne Gilbert I was going to quit after working for him for only a couple of years. I felt that PSCCO had made a big investment in me, and I felt obligated to pay it back by continuing to do a good job as a programmer. Fred knew me well and anticipated my reaction. He told me that this was business, and when he gave his two weeks' notice, Dwayne understood the terrific opportunity Fred had ahead of him. Fred said Dwayne would more likely be mad at him for trying to steal me away and not be mad at me at all.

That all sounded good, but it still didn't feel right to me.

"What do you think your chances are of becoming an SP at PSCCO?" Fred asked. Without waiting for me to answer, he continued. "They probably have a dozen people that are in line for the next SP position, not to mention that I would most likely need to move up through all of the levels, which can take eight to ten years, even if you're a superstar."

He was right about that. But still, up until now I had never made a job move unless I was in a bad situation looking to improve things. In my current job, I honestly still loved what I was doing, and in my mind, my future continued to look very bright.

Finally, Fred got to the essence of what he wanted to convey, and he didn't sugar-coat it. He knew I had a great deal of respect for Fred Eastom, the mechanical engineer in charge of the Cabin Creek hydroelectric project, so he started his final argument by saying, "I remember you telling me that Fred Eastom thought I was the best draftsman in the Mechanical Engineering Department, right?"

"Yes, that's what he said."

"Well, would it surprise you to know that I was the second to the lowest paid draftsman in the department? And I had absolutely no chance to move up in pay and gain ground on my peers until they all topped out and hit the top of their pay grade. John, the problem with PSCCO is that there is very little opportunity to advance for people like you and me. Yes, I realize you started as a clerk, got promoted to Transmission Engineering, and then got promoted two more times in ISD, but what I want you to think about is where you are now and what your realistic prospects for advancement are. That's what I did, and that's why I jumped at the opportunity to leave and go to Information Handling. John, I think you are a potential star, but what you have no awareness of is the fact that PSCCO does not have a single manager that doesn't have a degree. At this point, you might think that you don't have any desire to be in management, but even if that's true, you will most likely never get a shot at becoming a systems programmer at PSCCO. If that's true, then think about this: You're thirty years old now, and in about ten years from now you will be maxed out as a programmer analyst. At that point, you still have to work for twenty-five more years before you can retire. Do you really think you will still love your job when you find yourself in that situation? I know I wouldn't, and I don't think you will either.

"What we are talking about here is an opportunity for you to be trained as an SP on an IBM 370 VM1 state-of-the-art computer. Just so you know, the training I'm talking about here is a five-day class for thirty-five hundred dollars, and when you add airfare, per diems, and hotel stay, the total cost is close to five thousand dollars. Another thing I want to make you aware of is the fact that PSCCO's 370 155 is seven times more powerful than IHS's VM1, but the VM1 utilizes IBM's state-of-the-art virtual machine architecture that allows more programs to run simultaneously than the physical memory in the box can support. It does this by swapping programs executing in real memory in and out of virtual memory located on high-speed disk drives. I think that you would have to be crazy to pass up this opportunity.

"Something else that I want you to know is that the top people at IHS are in their thirties and forties. Can you name a single department manager at PSCCO that is under fifty? There aren't any. For me, once I started working at IHS, I felt like my possibilities for advancement were limitless. Why? Because I could clearly see that I would rather be a big fish in a small pond than a small fish in a big pond. Even if opportunities at IHS eventually reach some upper limit, the people at IHS are getting paid a hell of a lot more than the people at PSCCO. I'll use Fred Eastom again as an example. When I get promoted to programming manager, I will be making more than him, and as good as Fred is, there are dozens of mechanical engineers that could step in and take his place. In my situation, I have proven myself as an SP, and I will be given responsibility to manage a twenty-person programmer team. The key difference here is that I am an integral part of a profit center, not a cost center like Fred Eastom. Since all utilities are regulated, even though Fred's work to build Cabin Creek will generate revenue for PSCCO, his work does not cause the company to make more money—maybe even less money for every watt of electricity generated by Cabin Creek—whereas my job as programming manager will directly impact the company's bottom line since our products are all generated by the software my group maintains or develops. Big, big difference, and for me I see a very bright future for Information Handling Services."

I told Fred that I really appreciated him coming to me with this opportunity and that I needed a little time to think things over. I thanked him and Jeannie for lunch, walked down the steep sidewalk to my gorgeous 409 Chevy, turned the key, listened to that great sound coming from my engine and exhaust pipes, put it in first gear, slowly pulled away from the curb, and circled to the left to get back to the entry/exit point of the cul-de-sac.

I thought, "Wow, what a day today is. This may be the biggest career decision I've ever made in my life." Actually, it was the only career decision I had ever made, because up until now, I made *job* decisions. I hadn't really thought of my work as a career before, and to be honest, I was a little bit afraid that I might make the wrong choice.

When I pulled my car into my off-street parking spot at home, I went to my half of the duplex my parents now owned and lay down on my waterbed. I knew everything Fred said about the job at IHS and my long-range future at PSCCO was true. The key differentiator between the two companies was risk. If I stayed at PSCCO, it was much safer and secure; electric utility companies don't go out of business. While Fred was upbeat about IHS and their prospects, how could I possibly gauge how stable it was going to be down the road? I couldn't. But, even if they went out of business the next year, I would have gotten the training I needed to be an SP, and there certainly must be other companies that would want to hire me in the future, right?

I knew I was right. Why, then, was I not just happy and excited about my bright future? When I thought about this for a few minutes, I realized that my problem was that I had never imagined leaving PSCCO. The last time I had feelings similar to this was when I contemplated what I was going to do after I graduated from North High School. I solved that problem by joining the Navy. Now I somehow needed to muster the courage to leave the nest.

I can still remember reporting to work at the Holly Service Center when I was hired as a clerk—driving there in my 409, parking in a fenced parking lot, wearing clean clothes to work with the knowledge that they would still be clean at the end of the day, entering a spotlessly clean office environment without the awful sounds that emanated from the Samsonite foundry, and being introduced to dozens of very smart, accomplished professionals who I provided support to will forever be in my memory. I remember opening the door to walk into the building as an employee for the first time, saying a prayer that went something like this: "Dear God, thank you for answering my prayers and helping me find this job. I love you."

Later that Saturday, I called Fred and told him I wanted to pursue the job at IHS. He told me he would make arrangements for me to interview with Ralph Opgonorth, who would be looking to hire the senior programmer. Fred told me they were going to wait until I was on-board before giving Ralph his walking papers. He told me just go along with program, meaning that Ralph would be asking questions and giving me his perspective about what he was looking for, and then Fred would contact the IBM SE to make arrangements to get me into the next available VM operating system class in Los Angeles. When I hung up the phone, my life went from cruising speed to warp drive. And there was one thing that I knew for sure: I had better come up with a game plan for my new, unpredictable, and very exciting future.

NDJ Life Lesson:

Leaving the PSCCO nest where I'd spent my ninety-five percent of my career was one of the most exciting and scary decisions that I had ever made in my life.

There were two ways to approach this situation: I could think of every possible reason to not leave or I could think of every possible reason I should leave.

If I combined the two approaches, I would be undermining my ability to make a good decision. If I thought about all of the reasons I should stay, I also would be undermining my ability to make a good decision.

It became apparent that if I thought exclusively about the reasons to leave, I would be able to evaluate the upside in leaving.

The lesson here is that you must focus on the positive aspects of your important decision in order to make the best possible choice. If there doesn't appear to be enough pluses, the case is closed, right?

Chapter 26

Goodbye to Public Service Company of Colorado

After nearly ten years, I found myself saying goodbye to PSCCO.

I remember writing my first resignation letter and then walking down to Dwayne Gilbert's office to give it to him. I remember thinking, "I hope he's not in his office so I can just leave it in his inbox." But then I realized that that wouldn't do me any good because sooner or later I would have to meet him face to face and tell him I decided to leave. One thing that made this so difficult was that I knew Dwayne would quickly conclude that my old friend, Fred Sommers, was the likely culprit behind my wanting to leave in the first place. Also, I knew that Fred had talked to Dwayne on my behalf when Dean Miller tried to sabotage my move to ISD. And on top of everything else, I couldn't help but feel guilty about leaving PSCCO only two years after I completed the training program that made me so marketable in the first place.

Fred assured me that Dwayne Gilbert would not try to make me feel bad about leaving and that he would totally understand my motives. I knew Fred was right about this because Dwayne was a very experienced manager and a really good guy. Fred encouraged me to let Dwayne know that Information Handling Services had offered to send me to Los Angeles for training as a system programmer and that this was the main reason I felt I had to leave. The carrot that IHS had given me was too powerful to ignore, especially since I had always shown a strong preference for assembler language programming versus PL1 and had told Dwayne that I wanted to be an SP someday.

When I got to Dwayne's office, he was there and looked up to acknowledge me. He said, "Hey John, what's up?"

I handed him my letter of resignation. He unfolded it and asked me to have a seat. He was totally professional. He did not say or do anything to make me feel uncomfortable, and he asked me one question: "Would I be wrong if I guessed that you will be going to work with Fred Sommers?"

I replied, "No, you wouldn't be wrong. I am going to work at Information Handling Services," and then I went on to tell him how I was being given an opportunity that I just couldn't refuse. I was somewhat surprised that Dwayne didn't say something about the fact that I had only a couple years of experience and that it might be a huge jump for me to try to take on an SP job at this point in my career. But he didn't say anything to discourage me or question my decision to leave. He stood up and extended his hand. I shook it and thanked him for everything he had done for me.

I left his office, realizing that what was done was done. I still remember how afraid I was as I walked back to my office. I realized that I turned in my letter of resignation before I had received my offer letter from IHS. What if something went wrong and they postponed my job offer? Oh, man what on earth had I just done? I picked up my pace, and when I got back to my office, I dialed Fred's number at his, praying he was at his desk.

"Hello. I'm not here to take your call. Please leave a message at the tone," is what I heard after three rings. Yikes, what had I done? I was so anxious to write my resignation letter and give it to Dwayne that I totally forgot to think everything through. This was an enormous wake-up call for me. It reminded me a little of the time when I was playing Izadore at nine-ball at Fisher's pool hall. What happened was that Izzie put me in a position where I was playing over my speed limit, and when that happened, I lost all the money I had with me. Now, once again, I found myself playing over my speed limit, but this time I put myself and my job at risk. What an idiot move I just made.

In the end, things worked out okay for me. I got my offer letter from IHS, and it included the salary I had been promised. Fred told me not to worry about the SP training in L.A. because Ralph wasn't aware of that aspect of my employment agreement. I was so anxious to be able to brag about my new job, I almost screwed the pooch, as they say in some places. I knew I needed to get my mind in the game and avoid creating problems for myself to have any hope of taking advantage of this great opportunity.

On my last day at PSCCO, the guys in my cubicle and Fred Medrano, my carpooling buddy, took me to lunch at my favorite deli located a few blocks from the office. They all chipped in to buy me a really nice basketball because I had told them I still liked to go to a gym near my house to shoot hoops or play pick-up games. I loved shooting hoops and hearing the sound of a "swoosh" when you made a perfect shot without touching the backboard or rim. The ball was made of leather, not rubber. It was really, really neat. I remember leaving the building on my last day, and no matter how hard I tried, I just couldn't shake this sense of fear I had. I couldn't help but wonder what on earth I would do if something went wrong for me at IHS.

At the end of that very eventful day, I found myself walking out of the PSCCO building for the last time as an employee with an awful feeling in the pit of my stomach. No matter how many times I had thought this through and came up with the same conclusion, which was to resign and make the move, I still couldn't keep myself from being worried. Being afraid or worried isn't a problem unless you allow those emotions to impact your ability to make the right decision or you are unable to function at your best.

The most important thing to remember at times like these is that nobody knows you're afraid besides you. So, whatever you do, don't tell anyone. Talking to someone about something like this does absolutely no good and can in fact damage your image in the eyes of the person you tell. Some people will disagree with my statement and say that it is okay to be totally honest with your spouse or significant other. I say to those people that there is nothing to be gained by sharing your concerns with another person; however, there is the potential for loss. Why give your partner any reason not to believe you are a hero or a star?

And if you're paying attention here, you may recall the life lesson I learned in Chapter 3: Most of the things that you are afraid of never actually happen, unless of course you let someone know you're afraid.

NDJ Life Lesson:

Sometimes people become heroes or stars because of how their actions are viewed by others. Why would you want to change their perception of you by telling them that right before you were heroic you were afraid?

Chapter 27

The Big 3-0, a Key Life Event for North Denver Johnnie

Most people look at certain birthdays as key points in time when their future needs to be reevaluated and they feel a need to define some goals that they want to achieve. For me, sixteen and twenty-one were two obvious points in time, and with the impending arrival of my thirtieth birthday, I felt compelled to review my current circumstances and determine if was time to make some changes.

My new job opportunity at Information Handling Services catapulted me into a huge career-oriented change, and now I needed to decide if additional changes were also needed. At that moment, I couldn't help thinking back to when I was a sophomore at North High School when I had three areas of focus (survival, girls, and cars) and a single purpose (to get laid). To accomplish my objectives, I decided to adopt a new image, acquire a cool car, and develop a strategy to meet girls. Now at age thirty, I needed to determine what my goals were going forward and come up with a plan/strategy to make them happen.

The first thing that came to mind was my image. At PSCCO, the work dress code required a coat and tie for men every day. Fred told me that nobody, including the president of the company, wore ties, except on those occasions where he was going to visit a customer who had a coat-and-tie dress code for their own employees. Fred said the dress code and IHS did not allow for jeans, but dress slacks, khakis, or docker-type pants were okay. No ties required and no athletic shoes or sweatshirts allowed. So, right off the bat, I needed to shop for an entirely new wardrobe for work.

Next, as much as I loved my 409, it did not represent the professional image I wanted to represent. I needed an adult car with class, not a classy hot rod. The first adult car that came to mind was a 1966 Thunderbird. This car was the first adult non-hot-rod car that I ever liked. It was much smaller than most of the other luxury cars and had great styling. All of the overtime I had accumulated over the past two years enabled me to stash some cash away in my savings account. With a decent down payment and with the big raise I would be getting at his, I could afford the monthly payments for a great-looking Thunderbird. This was my first huge step toward projecting an image of a successful professional.

I needed to reevaluate my strategy for meeting girls. For the past several years, during the height of the Disco Revolution, I would go to one of the most popular D-bars on the west side of town, La Pichette (meaning "the pitcher" as in a pitcher of beer). Thursday nights were ladies' nights, and you could pretty much count on the place being packed. Over the years, I made a few friends at that bar, which meant that whenever I decided to go, there was likely somebody to talk to.

My best disco buddy was a guy named Jimmy Romero. He was all about two things: girls and cars. He was the only guy besides myself that had two cars: a 1962 fuel-injected 327 Corvette convertible, white with red interior, and a 1962 Chevrolet Impala SS 327, white with red interior. My two cars were my 1959 metallic green dented Opel and my 1964 metallic green Chevrolet Impala SS 409. We would park next to each other in a location just to the west of the bar that was big enough for both of our cars and had some built-in protection to the left and right to help shield our cars from door dings that can happen when careless drivers park too close to your car. Our parking spots were always available because they were located at least a block away from the disco's front door, and Jimmy and I got there as close to nine o'clock as possible.

One particular ladies' night, I had a great deal of news to talk to Jimmy about—first, my new job at the Tech Center, and second, my decision to get my first adult car, a 1966 Thunderbird. Going full-out adult in my car choice was really an earth-shaking announcement, especially from a guy that had been driving a 409. Jimmy was a really cool guy to hang out with. He wasn't particularly good looking for a Latino guy, but he had such a big personality that people just liked being around him, including attractive girls.

After talking about my pending car decision, I told him about my new job and how big of a deal it was for me. I told him I would be going to California soon for training and that my new company was located at the Denver Tech Center. Jimmy worked for the water department; it was kind of a family thing. His dad and his dad's dad had worked there, and he had cousins that worked there. Jimmy liked his job. He hated wearing a tie and loved being able to wear jeans and cowboy boots to work with a belt that had a big-deal, cool belt buckle. He didn't like country and Western music like most of the rednecks at the water department, but he loved cowboy boots. I think he had six to eight pairs.

We both showed up at the disco bar on Thursdays, Fridays, and Saturdays, unless one of us got lucky and met someone to ask out on a date. I told him that my new job was going to require me to work a lot more hours and more days each week because I would be on call 24/7 to provide computer support in my new job. This meant I would plan on going out to the disco bar on Thursdays only.

This news for Jimmy was tantamount to the breakup of Sonny and Cher, or Dean Martin and Jerry Lewis. We both knew that one of us was going to have to grow up someday, but I think we always hoped it would be the other guy. The shock of Jimmy, my cousins, or one of my North High alumni seeing me drive a gorgeous Thunderbird down the streets in North Denver would without a doubt be upsetting, or at a minimum, surprising. A Thunderbird would suggest that I somehow managed to start my own business of some kind. Maybe I discovered an old secret family recipe for sausage, or better yet, I was accepted into the mob. My car would have to have been a Cadillac, Chrysler, or Lincoln and would have to be black for the later possibility. For the secret sausage situation to have happened, all of the little old ladies would have to have been talking about me at the dinner table. Since that didn't happen, no one in North Denver would ever be able to imagine that the guy who started his career at Samsonite Luggage just ten years ago could have become this successful this fast by just working hard, could they?

NDJ Life Lesson:

Ten years is a long time unless you are very, very old or have spent that time doing things that are very, very fun.

How you spend the years you have been given will determine how much fun you have getting old.

Chapter 28

Information Handling Service
IBM 370 VM1

After spending a week in Los Angeles attending system programmer training class, I remember thinking to myself on the flight back to Denver, "I have acquired the knowledge and skills that will ensure my future success as long as I deliver the results my manager expects."

For the first time in my life, I felt like I would have if I had gone to Regis High School, had somehow gotten a scholarship to Regis College, and graduated with a 3.5 or above GPA. A split second later, I thought to myself that if had I gone to Regis and graduated with top marks, what on earth would I have studied? Since there were no opportunities to major in computer science, what would I have chosen to study and what kind of job would I have now? There was no way for me to answer that question, but at the same time I think it is fair for me to say that I cannot think of any other job that would have provided me with the challenges and unlimited possibilities I had. And, I had this great situation because I didn't go to Regis, because I somehow knew that I needed to get away from the parochial school system and the priests and nuns that were in charge. For the first time in my life, on my flight back to Denver, I realized that none of my current reality would have been possible had I not walked away from St. Catherine's. And, had Peter Schavinski not started the fight with me in eighth grade, I would have never left. Could it be possible that just one small change in events would have changed my entire life forever, and that event was my first fistfight?

In 1959, when I left St. Catherine's never to return, I started down a new life path, and I could never imagine where it would lead me. My situation, as improbable as it was, was real, wonderful, promising, exciting, and offered a world of amazing opportunities. Could it be possible for me to be where I was if I had chosen to go to Regis High School and then Regis College? Of course it could, and here's why: While attending Regis High School, I would have undoubtedly been exposed to science courses and higher-level mathematics that may have led me to major in math or science in college. The PSCCO in-house training program had twelve students—three PSCCO employees and nine college graduates with majors in math or science. Maybe, just maybe, I would have been one of the nine graduates if I went to Regis in ninth grade. This possibility isn't any less probable than the path that I chose to follow. I'd like to believe I somehow would have found a way to be where I ended up regardless of the path I took.

On my first day of work at Information Handling Service, Fred Sommers met me in the lobby, escorted me to my new office adjacent to the computer room, and introduced me to my new boss, Fenton Miller. Fenton was about forty years old with prematurely graying hair, a reasonably fit physique, and a Texas accent that I enjoyed hearing. He was completely competent in his job as computer operations manager and had a well-trained staff of computer operators, scheduler, and a rocket-speed keypunch operator. Now he had me, a well-trained system programmer with zero experience.

My office was more like a cave than anything else. It was only five feet wide and twelve feet deep. I had adequate furniture, including a desk, table, and a hanging program listing folders containing every single line of code currently being utilized by the IBM 370 VM1 mainframe computer. Being a visual person, I added a four-foot by eight-foot magnetic board to the wall behind my desk and used metal squares, rectangles, and circles to represent every piece of hardware inside and outside the computer room. Using a label maker, I provided a description for each magnetic piece on the board. I color-coded certain connections and locations to make it easier to identify each piece of hardware. This schematic would prove invaluable when it was time for me to perform my first sysgen. Sysgen is short for system generation, and it refers to the specific level of the virtual machine's operating system. Periodically, IBM would release a new VM operating system that contained fixes for known problems, software to support new features, or new hardware. When IBM released a sysgen, its customers had ninety days to upgrade their machines to the latest version. If the customers didn't comply, IBM had the right to refuse to support a customer's system.

Fortunately for me, the next IBM release was seven months away, so I had a good amount of time to get up to speed on the current system and ample time to prepare for my first sysgen. My job was to keep our computer up and running at least ninety-eight percent of the time. Having more than two percent downtime was simply unacceptable, and this was a key metric that Fenton would use to evaluate my performance. Our shop was a 24/7 operation, meaning we had people working three shifts with staggered workweeks, which meant that people would be using the computer seven days each week. All of that boils down to making sure the computer is operational 164.64 hours out of the 168 hours available.

There were literally thousands of things that could happen to cause the computer to shut down. A hardware malfunction with a disk drive was one possibility. When programs are running and they utilize data on a disk drive that all of a sudden stops working properly, the program will have an abnormal ending (ABEND). The computer operator will look at the printout that the ABEND produces and locates the ABEND code. Next, the operator will call the on-call system programmer and explain what happened. The SP will need to determine if it is a problem with the disk drive or the disk itself. If the disk is good but the drive is bad, then the computer operator will stop the unit, unscrew the disk, relocate it to another drive, and change the JCL so that the physical location of the disk is overridden from its normal address to its new temporary address where the disk now resides. If it is this type of issue and the system programmer is at home watching TV or sleeping, the issue can be resolved over the phone. However, if the disk itself is bad, then the system programmer will have to leave home, go to the office, locate the back-up version of the file on tape, restore it to a new disk, and run any prerequisite updates necessary to get the new version of the file in sync with the file as it was on the disk when the program was first run earlier that evening.

The picture I'm trying to paint here is that being the lone SP in a facility that operates 24/7 is a tremendously challenging job. It took me about three months to get to the point where I felt comfortable enough to handle my responsibilities effectively. After that, I needed to begin preparing for my first sysgen. One of the things I liked about my new job was that I was always busy doing something. We had twenty application programmers on the first floor writing code, and when they ran into some problems or issues with their program, they called me, just like I used to call Peaches. I have always enjoyed debugging programs and trying to figure out what you needed to do to get things to work.

One thing that was very different between PSCCO and this was that at PSCCO I was an hourly employee and at IHS I was a salaried employee. That meant goodbye to overtime. I thought the sixteen-percent salary increase I got to come to IHS would cover the loss of overtime income at PSCCO, but what I didn't realize was that I would be working a lot more hours at IHS than I did at PSCCO. Another thing I liked about my job was that when there were no programmers calling for help and the system was running smoothly, I was free to read IBM manuals and sysgen listings in order to better understand my environment. I know these activities sound like a nerdy, odd sort of pastime, but I always felt that the time I spent doing this was just like adding a few dollars to my savings account every month, and over time, my investment in the search for information would reap big dividends someday. Besides, what else could I do with my discretionary time? I guess I could have read car magazines, flirt with some of the attractive girls that worked there, or just zone out, but that obviously would have been a waste of valuable time for a person still on a mission to find ways to excel. And of course, it is so easy for me to remember the life lesson about how successful people always seem to be reading something.

NDJ Life Lesson:

Learning lessons in life can be very meaningful unless you fail to use the information you learned when the opportunity presents itself.

To do this, you have to pay attention to what is going on in your life when it's going on and not simply realize after it's too late that you could have been doing something when you actually see what you should have been doing. But guess what? It's too late.

Stay alert. After all, it's your life that's going on here!

Chapter 29

Information Handling Service
NDJ and Dale Carnegie

After working at IHS for six months, I managed to meet all of the key players. I really liked working for Fenton Miller, and he really liked working for his boss, Clem Gibson. Fenton and Clem went way back to their college days at Texas A&M and remained good friends and working companions. Clem was the second-in-command as director of operations, reporting to the President Tom Waters. Clem was forty-one years old and Tom was forty-five. Clem was extraordinarily competent with high energy, a big smile, strong handshake, and sharp image. He had both feet in the IHS boat with total loyalty to Tom and an undeniable desire to make IH*HIS* a world-class player in the high-tech industry.

Meanwhile, my good friend Fred Sommers took over responsibility for the twenty programmers that provided maintenance support for the existing in-house applications and worked on a new set of software that was being developed in order to add and expand the services IHS could offer its customers. The new services were also expected to attract many new customers. As part of Clem's skill set, he canvassed all one hundred thirty of the current customers to learn about what they wanted in terms of enhancements, but he also asked them to speculate about new services they thought would complement our product line. Clem was a dynamo, and he was determined to do everything possible to grow the company.

What I didn't know was that my friend Fred was having some kind of personal problem, and the problem was beginning to have significant negative impact on the projects he oversaw. Another thing that happened a couple of months after I was hired was that Fred recruited Fred Medrano and Bob Richards, both from PSCCO. Fred really had a hard-on for PSCCO for some reason and went out of his way to steal their people. It just wasn't like Fred to be this inconsiderate, and when I ran into Fred, I always thought that something was wrong but had no idea what. I certainly remember being at his house for lunch, and he seemed very happy, motivated, and anxious to have me come on board to be part of a really great company. Now he seemed moody; he simply did not act like the guy I had known for more than five years.

As a part of Clem's plan to roll out the company's new, enhanced services, he came up with an idea that would make it possible for all IHS employees to be aware of the rollout and have each department develop a strategy to support the company's efforts. To that end, each employee received a letter from Tom Waters asking them to develop a two-minute presentation to specifically describe what their department would do to make the rollout a success. The best presentation from each department would be selected, and the author of the presentation would be invited to present their idea at the company's annual employee meeting in December. The company rollout was scheduled for January, just four months out.

I came up with an idea for the Computer Operations Department, and my idea was accepted, which meant I would be expected to present the information at the meeting. Fenton was happy with my idea and told me that Tom was meeting with all of the presenters in his office before the annual meeting. I asked Fenton why he wanted to meet with me. He said he didn't know, but in a kidding kind of way told me not to be late. The next day, at ten a.m. sharp, I walked into Tom Waters' office. It was the first time that I'd ever been in there, and it was unbelievably impressive. A beautiful desk, executive chair, guest chairs, coffee table, small couch, a couple of matching chairs, and really cool contemporary art paintings and sculptures. I was totally impressed. Tom stood up and extended his hand to greet me, and he put me at ease.

Tom began by saying he liked my idea for the rollout and felt that I really grasped the importance of having all employees be a part of it. My idea essentially was to keep all employees apprised of the status of the rollout throughout the course of the year. So, instead of this one-time event being the focus at the annual meeting, we would provide monthly progress updates by developing a simple CISC program that every person could access to get a progress report. People that didn't have access to CRT would be able to find a report version of the status on the bulletin board in the cafeteria.

"Great," I said as I stood up to leave when Tom stopped me.

"I've invited you here today so that you can make your presentation to me, an audience of one. Okay?" In that moment, I sat back down, pulled out my written presentation, and started to read it to him. Tom said that he wanted me to stop, start over, and he wanted me to stand up when I read my presentation. When I did that, I totally froze. I immediately had trouble breathing. I could hardly get the words out of my mouth. I just could not believe how afraid I was to make a presentation to one person while I was standing. I was sure I could have done it if I remained seated.

Tom could immediately see my discomfort and asked me to take a seat. I was so embarrassed that I wanted to just get out of there. My career was over in the blink of an eye. I would never be able to look Tom in the eye knowing he knew just how afraid I was to stand up and say something. What kind of future would someone like that have? Tom told me not to worry and that he would get back to me about what we could do to fix the problem.

I was so embarrassed beyond anything I'd ever experienced, and I could not even think of anything that could be done to save me from this tragedy. I had to walk past Fenton's office to get to mine, so when I returned, Fenton asked me how it went. I stepped into his office and told him the whole story and how embarrassed I was. He told me not to worry and said that things have a way of working out. Fenton told me not to be too hard on myself.

Then his phone rang, and he picked up the receiver. "Fenton Miller. Yes sir, right away," he said and hung up the phone. Fenton stood. Then I stood, and I went back to my office.

Fifteen minutes later, Fenton came into my office and said that Tom still wanted to use my idea, but we were going to have Dave, our scheduler, read my presentation. "And there is something else that Tom has asked me to do for you," Fenton said.

"What's that?" I asked.

"Tom wants me to get you scheduled to take a Dale Carnegie training course."

"What's a Dale Carnegie training course? I don't understand."

Fenton told me that Dale Carnegie training is made up of several things, but first and foremost, it is about teaching people how to be effective public speakers. My head was spinning. I had just embarrassed myself in front of the president of the company, who now wanted to enroll me in a public speaking course. I still vividly remember the fear I experienced when I stood up in front of Tom and tried to read my presentation, and he wanted me to go to a place where my fear would be magnified a hundred times when I tried to speak in front of the strangers in my class.

"Please tell Tom thanks," I said to Fenton, "but I really don't want to go to this class. I don't really think I'll need this type of training because I want to remain a system programmer, and I have no interest in doing any job that requires me to make speeches."

For the entire time that I worked for Fenton Miller, I had never seen him get mad, but that was about to change.

Fenton didn't raise his voice, but he did make direct eye contact with me and said, "John I really like you, but I think you don't understand what is going on here. The president of the company called me to his office and directed me to enroll you in a Dale Carnegie training course. I am telling you about what Tom told me to do, and somehow you have the idea that you can ignore me. I want to be clear about this. I am going to find out when the next Dale Carnegie course is scheduled to start, and then I'm going to tell you. It is my understanding that the course lasts twelve weeks and has meetings on Tuesdays and Thursdays. I know this because Tom is a Dale Carnegie graduate and a graduate assistant who is still involved with the program and occasionally volunteers his time to support the D.C. instructors. John, if you want to continue working for me at IHS, then you will do what I am telling you to do. I am not asking. This is a direct order. Do you understand?"

I was totally mortified by the way Fenton was strong-arming me, but I knew for sure that he was not bluffing, or if he was, I knew I was going to fold my hand. I would never know for sure. Maybe that's why Texas hold 'em is the Cadillac of poker where the best players are from Texas, like Fenton and Clem.

I said, "Yes, Fenton. I understand, and I will attend the class after you get me enrolled."

At the end of the day, I left the building, got in my 409, turned the key, and listened to the motor rumble. Then I just thought about what was arguably the worst day of my professional life. I had embarrassed myself in front of Tom, I found a way to piss off Fenton because of my total lack of professionalism in the way I responded to him, and I was going to be put into a situation with the Dale Carnegie training that I just might not be able to handle. The more I thought about it, the more fearful I became. What was going to happen if I attended the Dale Carnegie training and failed? I couldn't go to the downtown bookstore on 14th Street to bail me out of this one, right? Wait a minute, why not go to the bookstore and try to find out as much as I could about Dale Carnegie or the DC training course? I just might find out something that would help prepare me for a training program that was an inevitable and unavoidable part of my future. If I went to the bookstore, I would be doing something that just might stop my out-of-control paranoia that I felt thinking about Dale Carnegie.

A few days went by, and I got a call from Fenton to come to his office. He told me that I was enrolled in the next DC class that was scheduled to start in three weeks. He then handed me an envelope with some DC literature and a three-page form entitled "Student Biography." The form was to be completed and turned in to the DC instructor during the first evening session.

Then Fenton told me another thing that really surprised me. "John, I know you're apprehensive about this course, but I want you to know that Tom wants you to take it because he sees a lot of potential in you. And another thing I want you to know is that this course is costing the company four thousand dollars."

"I want to apologize for my behavior," I said and then explained just how afraid I was to go to the class. "I am honestly petrified to be in this situation, and that's why I behaved so poorly."

What Fenton said to me next was something I could have never imagined. "Almost every person on the planet is afraid of speaking in public," he explained. "I used to be afraid too. That is why the Dale Carnegie class is so successful and is always booked to the max. They teach you techniques and methods to overcome your fear, and they will teach you much more than just that."

Fenton explained that all professionals had two types of skills: hard skills like mine (using assembler language programming, CICS, JCL, and so on), and they had soft skills (relationship building, leadership, team building, making presentations, and so on). In order to advance in any company, every person has to be evaluated on both their hard and soft skills.

"So far in your career," Fenton said, "you have received training in your hard skill set. Soft skills are more difficult to develop because most people never realize how valuable they are, or they simply don't see themselves as someone who can actually advance in any significant way. Let's talk about Clem for a minute. He is what I would describe as a generalist. He really doesn't excel in any hard skill area; however, he has a strong understanding of many different hard-skill topics. He is a strong marketing person with very good accounting and budgeting skills and is excellent at team building and creating a focus within an organization that causes people to buy-in to his initiatives. And his soft skills are off the chart. He can get in front of five hundred people and make a presentation ending in a standing ovation. That's why Clem is the number-two guy in the company, and I'm sure someday he will be the number-one guy somewhere. John, you just have to suck it up, show up for the class, and do what you do every day here. Do the best you can. I'm certain you will benefit greatly from this course because just like Tom, I see a lot of potential in you."

NDJ Life Lesson:

Once again, our old nemesis Fear shows up and tries to cause havoc.

Fear seems to always be lurking around us, just waiting for a reason to whisper in our ear, "Watch out, be careful, it could be bad if..."

Fear never sleeps, never goes on vacation, and loves to whisper.

It's okay to listen because then you can take steps to avoid his warnings. Just understand that this guy will never go away.

When you really know you're hitting 'em straight is when you think about potential problems, so take steps to avoid them before Fear starts whispering.

Chapter 30

Information Handling Service
IBM 370 VM1 Sys Gen

I had been working at Information Handling Services for about nine months and was only a couple weeks away from performing my very first sysgen.

I spent nearly three months planning and doing the preparation necessary to upgrade the operating system of our IBM 370 VM1 machine. Chuck Wilhoite, our IBM system engineer (SE) reviewed my plan and gave me his blessing. Once the sysgen began, it would take eighteen to twenty hours to complete, assuming there were no major glitches like some kind of hardware failure. This was such a big deal because we were running three shifts twenty-four hours a day, which meant that all of the people who use the computer to do their job would be shut out of the system. To minimize the impact, I would begin the sysgen one hour after the end of the business day on Friday. This meant that the only people shut out were approximately twenty-five data collection and entry personnel at our Broadway facility.

I had produced a visual aid on the magnetic board on the wall behind my desk. I had trays of punched computer cards that I would submit to the card reader to initiate a sequence of jobs that were predefined by IBM to allow the existing operating system to run jobs to produce a new operating system. Because the IBM predefined jobs and sequences contained code for every single possible piece of hardware that could be plugged into the mainframe, there were certain processes that I didn't want to execute because we didn't have a particular kind of hardware.

At the same time, IBM provided code to support all non-IBM systems that were considered compatible to work on the mainframe computer. This was an area that caused the most concern for me because all of our disk drives and tape units were made by BSX, a competitor of IBM. We chose BSX drives, tapes, and disks because they were so much cheaper than the IBM equivalents.

The name of our company gave away our reason for using generic storage devices: Information Handling Services. We stored vast amounts of our customers' data, making disk and tape storage a huge expense for us. We were required by IBM to have at least three IBM disk drives and two IBM tape units. IBM wanted us to locate the operating system software on an IBM disk drive and use the other two IBM disk drives as the units to extend the 370's memory. Doing this allowed us to expand the capability of our mainframe by swapping code executing in real memory on the 370 with executable code that temporarily resided on the virtual memory located on one of the two IBM disks. Similarly, IBM wanted us to have at least two IBM tape units so we could perform reel-to-reel updates.

Having three IBM disk drives and two IBM tape units allowed us to determine, as an example, if a disk problem occurred on both the IBM and BSX disks, we could eliminate hardware as the cause and focus on the more likely scenario that an operating system was the problem. Being able to quickly diagnose where the problem was helped me isolate the issue more quickly and reduce the amount of downtime our user community experienced, which was a key measurement that defined how well I was doing my job.

Because IHS was using IBM's newest mainframe architecture, virtual machine (VM), we received exceptional support from IBM. Chuck, our IBM SE, was one of IBM's best and brightest. When I called Chuck with a question about my upcoming sysgen or a problem with our 370, he elevated my problem to the VM support team and got back to me as if IHS was as big of a player as PSCCO, whose monthly expenses for IBM hardware, software, and services were probably ten times more than what we spent. But because IBM had spent so much money on the research and development of the VM architecture, it was in their best interest to have maximum focus and support for its clients, who were the early users of the new gear.

The weekend of the big event, Fenton stopped by my office to wish me well before leaving work to go home to his family. He said he had a lot of confidence in me and was sure I would get the job done. Fenton had assigned Dave Hightower, our scheduler, and our best two computer operators to work with me over the weekend to complete the job. I was grateful to Fenton for his vote of confidence. I looked at the clock and told him we were starting at six p.m., just thirty-three minutes from now. I told him I, too, was confident but that if something unforeseen should come up that I would call him no matter what time it was. He turned away and headed out of the building.

I got up from my desk carrying a tray of punched computer cards, walked out of my office, turned left to see Dave, Donna White, and Cherrie Martin waiting for me. I handed Dave the tray of cards and asked him to put them in our card reader at six p.m. to get this party started. We all raised our arms and touched each other's hands. I loudly shouted, "Go team!" The team echoed my kick-off motto, only much louder.

I can't remember being in a situation with more pressure and stress than this one. Yet, I was not the least bit worried or afraid. I was focused and confident. Once the card reader accepted the job control language (JCL) I had put together to start the sysgen, it was a matter of monitoring which jobs or programs were being executed and waiting for each to complete successfully. When that happened, our high-speed printer immediately spewed out the first page of a printout with the job name and number in a size so large that it amounted to a font size of at least fifty, making the name and number readable from eight to ten feet away. On the second page of the printout was a completion code. Success looked like this: *Completion Code: 0000*. While the first job's results were being printed, a second and third job were either running concurrently or sequentially depending on how I had coded the JCL.

It had begun. We were at the four-minute mark of a twenty-hour ballgame following the high-four of my little team. A couple of hours into the sysgen, the team noticed that—with the exception of the cleaning crew upstairs—we were the only people in the building. Also, the fact that it grew dark outside created a completely different kind of atmosphere for all of us to work in. For me, it was the first time that I had stayed at work more than a couple hours after the end of the business day. I had on many occasions left work to go home and then returned after sunset when called in by one of the computer operators. What was going on now was an entirely different kind of after-work working experience. Another thing we all understood was that we were going to be there for a very long time, and it was going to be interesting to see how this one-off event was going to play out.

As nine p.m. approached, we agreed that we would order some food and the two computer operators would go and get it. This was a nice little change of pace from the planned monotony associated with successful sysgen. We had a minipowwow in the computer room with the sound of the printer printing in the background. Dave, our scheduler, who was more than a little overweight, assumed his leadership role as the person with the most experience and knowledge when it came to eating. He quickly gave the team three choices: burgers, pizza, or chicken. There was an immediate positive reaction to choice number two, so Dave quickly announced that we would order three pizzas with breadsticks and garlic butter. He then suggested the toppings be sausage, pepperoni, and supreme. The supreme was the be-all-and-end-all of pizza selections available to pizza lovers. In a New York second, everyone unanimously approved Dave's suggestions, and with a speed dial selection that Dave had obviously used many times before, we were only forty-five minutes away from having our first sysgen meal.

Our terrific pizza dinner ended about ten thirty p.m., just four and half hours after we started the sysgen. We began to realize the monotony of our task to generate a new operating system and install it to replace our current version, and the only thing for us to do was to not let the printer run out of paper and check that the completion code was 0000.

The next major milestone was up for discussion at five a.m., and once again the team looked to Dave to show us the way to a great breakfast. Dave came through when he sent Donna and Cherrie to a nearby International House of Pancakes. Their menu proudly stated, "At IHOP we proudly serve award-winning pancakes." When reading their menu, I always wanted to find out whom the sponsors of the Pancake Playoffs were and how often the awards were up for grabs. I never got around to asking those questions at IHOP because I thought it would delay me from getting my pancakes. But when I did give the server my order, I would always say, "I would like some of your award-winning blueberry pancakes."

The server would look at me as if I had come from Mars and then say, "Yes sir, right away." Apparently, IHOP management had failed to convey the award concept to their staff, and the staff didn't spend much time looking at the marketing-related information contained in the menu. If I were the manager of IHOP, I would explain to every employee the importance of reinforcing the fact that our pancakes were special, that in fact they were "award-winning pancakes." I think it would be a way of showing continuity amongst the staff and provide a vehicle to elevate each person's role in the delivery of great pancakes.

Leadership begins by setting a high standard for personal performance and finding ways to bring staff members together as members of a team with the sole purpose of providing each customer the highest quality food and service every single day. To accomplish this objective, each employee needs to understand why it is important to inform the customer about their special pancakes understand how IHOP is able to accomplish this feat. You have to be able to answer the question if asked, "Who gives out awards for pancakes?" or "How often do they have these pancake competitions?"

You need to give each server the answers, and when you do, that each person will gladly hype the pancakes with the knowledge that they won't look foolish if someone asks them a question whose sole purpose is to make them look foolish. Now that is what management and leadership are all about. It's about coming up with a way to promote your product, getting everyone on board to help make it happen, giving each person an explanation as to why what you're asking them to do is important, and lastly, giving the staff the knowledge about award-winning pancakes so that they can have credibility when a customer asks a question and not look like a parrot that is saying something just because he was told to say it.

The best managers look for ways to achieve success, exceed the corporation's expectations, and to create a work environment where employees have the knowledge and tools to perform their job responsibilities at the highest level possible. Everybody likes to work for a boss who thinks and behaves consistently and does not over react when an employee makes a mistake.

After breakfast, we were twelve hours into our eighteen to twenty-hour sysgen. I had established a chart with estimated run times for each job that was going to be executed from start to finish. It looked like we were at least one hour ahead of where I thought we would be, and if that were correct, we would wrap it up by eleven a.m. The printer kept pace with the relentless demands of the sysgen, and hour after hour produced scores of *Completion Code: 0000.*

Finally, at eleven twenty-two a.m., seventeen hours and twenty-two minutes after Friday's start time, the newest version of IBM's 370 VM1 operating system had been successfully installed on the IHS mainframe computer.

What a wonderful feeling I experienced at that moment in time. I thanked Dave, Donna, and Cherrie for the great job they did supporting me and kiddingly told them to take tomorrow (Sunday) off. Next, I called Fenton Miller to give him the good news, and I told him that I had contacted the manager at the Broadway facility to make sure they could access the programs and data on their terminals. The Broadway facility manager, Susan Sprigs, told me that everything there seemed to be operational and that she would be calling her people to come into work. Fenton was ecstatic and congratulated me. He said he would call Clem, whom he said would be really happy, and that he realized just how much pressure I was under to make it happen. After thanking Fenton for having confidence in me and not paying an exorbitant amount of money to have Chuck, our IBM SE, babysit me during the sysgen.

I said goodbye, left the building, and started to walk to my trusty 409 in the parking lot. When I first accepted the job at IHS, I thought about getting a new car to help me project a more professional image. But I decided to postpone making such a major financial decision until I felt secure enough in my job to make that move. When I got in my car, turned the key, heard the rumble of the motor, and felt the vibration of the cam shaft lopping along at idle speed, I started to think about which Ford dealership I should go to. I should have been exhausted, but I was still on an adrenaline after completing the most difficult project of my professional career. What a great feeling. I couldn't believe that all of this had happened to me. My last thought after I put my car in first and let out the clutch to start my commute back to North Denver was, "Thank you, dear God, for all of my blessings."

NDJ Life Lesson:

Unless you're an astronaut that goes to the moon or a member of a Super Bowl Championship football team, you will never be in a parade.

It is the journey, not the destination, that you remember.

Let me boil both of these observations down for you: No matter how significant your personal accomplishment is when you accomplish it, the gratification you enjoy from others or even yourself is so fleeting that if you blink, you will have missed it.

After completing the most complex, high-risk achievement of my life, I couldn't help but notice that after it was over, I felt like something was missing.

Yes, I received a compliment from my boss. Yes, I acknowledged to myself that I had done a tremendous job planning and preparing for the sysgen, so why did I feel a little bit down when it was all over?

I will tell you what I figured out, and I'm really glad I did.

If you are a guy like Jim "Peaches" Peachinelli, everyone expects you to be a star every day you come to work.

As I strived to be a top system programmer and eventually, when I consistently performed at that level, I realized that the best part of being a star is when you look in the mirror and think to yourself, "I'm proud of you, John. You did a hell of a job on the sysgen."

And that, my friends, is as good as it gets.
No parades for us!

Chapter 31

Information Handling Service
Dale Carnegie Training

Finally, the day arrived that I had dreaded for almost a month: the first Tuesday night Dale Carnegie training class at seven p.m. I tried to remember what Fenton told me about most people's fear of public speaking, but what really motivated me to be there was when he said he had given me a direct order to attend, and I told him that I would.

There were twenty-four students, one Dale Carnegie instructor (DCI), and one Dale Carnegie graduate assistant (GA). The GA was a former student who graduated from a prior D.C. class with high honors. Usually, high honors meant that the individual won the Impromptu Speaking Championship, or the Prepared Speech Championship. The DCI introduced himself as Jay Manning and asked that everyone address him as Jay, and then he introduced Margret Shepard as his graduate assistant. Margret was a former DC graduate and the winner of the Prepared Speech Championship that took place when she was a student.

And then Jay repeated a page out of the DC playbook: "Look around at successful businesspeople. You'll find that they are confident in their work, enthusiastic about getting things done, they are inspiring, and they empower others around them to succeed. They are engaged in all aspects of their work and life. This effective communication training course will help you master the human relations skills demanded in today's tough business environment. You'll learn to improve human relations skills, increase communication effectiveness, strengthen interpersonal relationships, manage stress, and handle fast-changing workplace conditions. You'll develop more effective communication skills and be better equipped to perform as a persuasive communicator, problem-solver and focused leader. What's more, you develop a take-charge attitude to initiate with confidence and poise."

Next, Jay, with the use of an overhead projector, displayed the outline of the Dale Carnegie course and gave a brief explanation for each item, adding that every item represented each week's topic of study.

"Every week for the next twelve weeks there will be 2 two-hour sessions. There are twelve topics that I will discuss during the Tuesday night session, and then during the Thursday night session, each student will make a two-minute presentation about that topic. After each presentation, the students will write the name of that evening's best presentation on a piece of paper that I will collect, and I will announce who the winner is. At the end of week six, I will also ask the class to vote for the person that they feel is the most improved speaker.

"Weeks eleven and twelve will deviate from this format. The Thursday night speakers will be asked to develop a spontaneous presentation. That evening, I will put slips of paper with twenty-four topics into a bowl. There will be a second bowl with the names of each student. I will pick out two names. The first name I pick will select a topic from the topic bowl, then he or she will have two minutes to develop a two-minute presentation about the topic they selected. The second person whose name was drawn will pick a topic slip, and while the first speaker is making their presentation, they will prepare a presentation for the topic they chose. We repeat those steps until all twenty-four students have completed their impromptu presentations. At the end of the evening, each of you will vote for the Impromptu Speech Champion.

"Week twelve, the final week of our course, each person will prepare a three-minute speech on any topic of their choosing. At the end of the presentations, you will vote for the winner of the Prepared Speech Championship. The winners of weeks eleven and twelve will also be entitled to become graduate assistants."

We then reviewed the outline of the course:

- Build a foundation for success
- Recall and use names
- Build on memory skills
- Increase self-confidence
- Put stress in perspective
- Enhance relationships and motivate others
- Clearly present ideas
- Energize communication
- Disagree agreeably

- Gain willing cooperation and influence others
- Manage stress
- Develop more flexibility
- Demonstrate leadership
- Celebrate achievements and renew your vision

Then the moment I was dreading arrived. Jay asked that each student stand up and introduce themselves. "Tell us your name, where you work, and what kind of job you perform. We'll begin here and go down each row and back to the beginning of the next row, okay?"

Standing in front of the person at the first desk, Jay nodded, and the introductions began. I was sitting in the second desk of the second row. Seven introductions later, I stood up and literally could not talk. When I tried, I began to hyperventilate.

As my breathing problem became more pronounced and apparent, Jay immediately recognized my discomfort and walked over to me. "John, it's okay," he said. He asked me to sit down. I immediately started to apologize, but Jay stopped me. "John, let me ask you a couple of questions, okay?" I nodded. "What's your last name?" he asked. Then he continued. "Where do you work? What do you do at Information Handling Services?" I answered all of his questions while seated, and then Jay said, "Thank you." He looked at the person seated behind me and nodded. After all of the introductions were completed, Jay thanked everyone and came over to where I was seated.

Jay looked at me and started to tell the class a story. He said that just a couple of years ago he developed an interest in cooking. He told us that every time he learned how to make a different dish, there always seemed to be some little secret involved in the recipe. Sometimes it was a special type of ingredient like sea salt instead of ordinary salt, some special type of pan or utensil that made a huge difference in the outcome of the dish.

Then he looked at me and said, "There are many little secrets that I will share with all of you about making introductions or remembering someone's name. John, let give you a secret I learned to use when someone asks me to introduce myself, okay? When you were seated, you didn't have any problem answering my questions, and now I'd like you to stand for a minute. What's your name?"

"John Santone," I answered.

"Where do you work?"

"Information Handling Services."

"What do you do at work?"

"I am a system programmer," I answered.

Okay, now here's the secret," he said. "When you stand to introduce yourself, you silently ask yourself the question and then answer it out loud. It is so amazingly easy to do once you learn this very simple secret."

From that moment on, I was never afraid of introducing myself, no matter how many people I was addressing. Now I realized how fortunate I was to be enrolled in this class, and I was looking forward to learning more secrets from Jay. Totally amazing.

As the class progressed, Jay kept his promise. He taught us very useful and practical lessons about how to project ourselves in the best possible way, how to remember people's names and why that was so important. By week six, the halfway mark, I won the Most Improved Speaker Award, voted on by all of the students in the class. When I think back to my very first mini-presentation when I stood to introduce myself and how each week I managed to deliver two-minute presentations that had merit, I can see why the class wanted to acknowledge my progress, and it really did mean a great deal to me.

When week eleven came around, all of the students were fairly apprehensive because all of our presentations up until now were prepared. No one really knew how they would perform when they had to come up with an almost spontaneous presentation on a topic that they selected. One thing for sure was going to happen: Thanks to Jay, every student had become very good at making presentations, and the smart money was betting that the students who had won "best presentation" during the prior ten weeks were the favorites to win tonight and the following week in the Prepared Speech Championships.

"Tonight, and a week from tonight," Jay started, "are a little bit like the Dale Carnegie Super Bowl. Speaking for myself and Margret, we are both excited to see how each of you deal with the spontaneous format of this evening's competition, and we are anxious to see who will be our next graduate assistant."

Next, Jay asked Margret to select a person from the bowl that contained every student's name and then select a topic from the other bowl. Then he asked her to do it again. Jay announced that Beverly Martinez would be the first presenter and handed her a slip of paper with a topic on it. Jay told Beverly that she would have two minutes to prepare a two-minute presentation. Next, Jay read the name of the second presenter, James Martin. Jay told James he would give him his topic when Beverly started her presentation. Margret performed the role of the timekeeper, starting and stopping a digital clock to help the students pace their remarks to conform with the rules stating that each presentation should last approximately two minutes. Each student was expected to end their presentations within ten seconds before or after the two-minute mark.

Unbelievable. Not only did we have to come up with a presentation in two minutes, but we were also supposed to talk about the subject for two minutes, which was a very long time when you were the only person speaking. A two-minute conversation is altogether a different kind of matter because you are able to develop your comments using the other person's comments, or if you initiate the discussion, you can do it to advance dialogue about something you feel well prepared to discuss. But in this situation, the other person only gives you a topic, and it is up to you to make a meaningful, and ideally a thoughtful or entertaining, presentation without any interaction. Not easy.

Finally, about midway through the program, my name was drawn, and I was handed a topic slip with a single word on it: advertising. I looked at the topic and immediately thought about my recent experiences and how watching advertisements on TV had made a big impact on my decision to purchase a new car. I remembered seeing a Thunderbird commercial that sealed the deal for me. My 409 just did not project the kind of professional image I wanted, and in keeping with the "Dress for Success" image strategy, not only your wardrobe needed to reflect an image of a successful person, but your car, your wristwatch, where you lived, and so on needed to reflect this as well. I knew I needed to make a change. The 1966 Thunderbird was the car that I knew I wanted. But how was I going to be able to make that happen? One night, in the middle of a pretty big snowstorm, I was heading west on Colfax Avenue toward my Thursday night disco hangout, La Pichette, when out of the corner of my eye I thought I saw a car parked in the used car lot of the Ford/Lincoln/Mercury Dealership. I was sure it was a '66 because of the distinctive rear panel and roof line. I made an immediate U-turn and pulled into the dealership. Because of the storm, there were no other customers, and because it was about eight thirty p.m., only a hour from closing time, even the salespeople that were there were not jumping through hoops to come out and greet me as I exited my car. Finally, one brave soul came out to meet me just before I was going to open the front door and come in. I asked him if that 1966 Thunderbird was for sale.

He said, "Yes sir, it is. She's a beauty, don't you think?"

I said, "I'm not sure. There's six inches of snow on it right now. Can you get a broom so I can take a look at this car?"

"Yes sir, right away!"

It was obvious to me that my sales guy was thinking that they would erect a statue of him in the dealership lobby if he could sell me a car that was covered with snow in under thirty minutes. We swept off the snow, and there it was: a beautiful, pewter-color '66 Thunderbird with maroon leather interior, chrome wire-wheel hubcaps, and whitewall tires. Only a little over six thousand miles on the odometer. Apparently, a wealthy doctor that loved cars bought the car and then decided he was really a Lincoln guy after all and traded it in after having it for six years. The salesman said the prior owner barely drove it because he had another car he liked more.

I thought, "Thank God there are rich car guys that can buy new cars, and because he didn't like it he didn't drive it!"

I never went back to the Lincoln Dealership to see if there was a statue in the lobby, but I found a great car at a great price. It was that Thunderbird advertisement that sealed the deal for me.

When the previous speaker's presentation ended, I was up. I informed the class that my topic was advertising. "I would like to tell you a story about how a commercial I saw on TV had a huge impact on me." I went on to tell the class about the snowstorm and how I managed to spot this car I wanted covered with snow on a used car lot. I remember adding a lot of humor to my presentation, and the class all laughed when I told them about the statue.

You have probably guessed by now that I unanimously won the Impromptu Speech Championship. Jay told us that he had never seen this happen before where one person got all of the votes. When I won the Most Improved Speaker Award, the award was a red Dale Carnegie ever-sharp pencil with raised letters that read "First Place for Most

Improvement—Dale Carnegie Course." The Impromptu Speech Championship award was a black Dale Carnegie ever-sharp pencil with raised letters that read "Outstanding Performance Award—Dale Carnegie Course." I was also given a certificate that said I had qualified to perform the role of graduate assistant at some future date.

NDJ Life Lesson:

At this point, you are probably expecting me to say something about how NDJ overcame his fear and then went on to accomplish an incredible feat by winning the Impromptu Speech Championship. And the life lesson would be something about overcoming his fear, which allowed him to succeed in the end. Right? No, that is not the lesson to be discussed here.

Instead, let's be honest about what the real life lesson should be in this circumstance.

This was the single worst episode in NDJ's career. He totally allowed his fear to control his behavior and was incredibly rude, almost insubordinate, initially ungrateful, and ignorant as he explained why he didn't need Dale Carnegie training.

In this case, the successful outcome is completely overshadowed by the immature and ignorant behavior of NDJ every step of the way as he railed against attending this class, almost like a child who tells his mother that he doesn't need to take his medicine.

The real life lesson that NDJ eventually learned from this experience was that when he was looking in the mirror and patting himself on the back because of the successful sysgen, he was also seeing himself as a star—a star like Peaches.

Eventually, NDJ remembered Peaches standing up in front of the class at PSCCO and delivering a dynamic, well-planned, and impressively effective presentation on the subjects of assembler language programming, CJCS telecommunications software, and job control language.

Then and there, NDJ realized he wasn't even close to being a star in the ilk of Jim Peachanelli because he was so totally lacking in many of the soft-skill abilities that Fenton Miller talked to him about in his office.

The bottom line here is that when you don't know what you are talking about and your reasons for explaining why you believe what you do have been formulated because you are afraid, you simply have to stop talking and start listening, because no matter what you say when you know you're afraid, you will definitely regret it later.

When you are in this type of circumstance, listen and do not talk. Then it is time to pretend again. Tell your boss "thank you" and then go back to your office and think things through before you respond with any comments. After careful thought, if you believe complaining is in order, then go back and think a hell of a lot more, because complaining about someone's generosity makes you look like an idiot. And after more contemplation, if you have developed a cohesive argument, then guess what?

You are an idiot.

Chapter 32

Information Handling Service
Fred #1 out, Fred #2 in, NDJ on his way out

At the annual staff meeting, Dick Hightower did a great job presenting the idea I came up with to support the new product rollout. The rest of the presenters also did a nice job explaining their roll-out initiatives. Even though I smoked the Dale Carnegie class with my win in the Impromptu Speech Championship, Tom and Fenton decided to stick with the game plan to have Dick remain the presenter because he had put a lot of work in preparing for his two minutes of fame and deserved to have the spotlight on him.

After all the department presenters conveyed their ideas, Clem took center stage to give everyone a status report describing the implementation of the new products and enhanced features that were planned for a January release. To everyone's surprise, Clem began by saying that the rollout was being delayed for three to four months. He went on to say that the system-level testing that had begun in mid-November was unsatisfactory in terms of the design for new features and had far too many errors in the code to be able to give it to existing customers. He was very disappointed but tried to emphasize the pluses that the company would realize after the problems were corrected. With that piece of very bad news, Clem thanked everyone for all of their hard work and dedication throughout the year.

After the meeting, I ended up in Fenton's office. "What the heck happened here?" I asked. "I can't believe my buddy Fred blew it, but he must have, right?"

"Yes, John, he blew it, and as to what happened, what happened is that Fred had some personal problems that made him to lose focus. Clem released him from the company yesterday when he had a complete understanding of how bad things were with the software."

"What's going to happen now?" I asked. "Who is going to take Fred's place?"

Fenton answered, "Right now I think Fred Medrano is being considered for the job."

"What? Why hasn't Clem talked to me about it?"

"John, I don't know for sure, but it might be that there's nobody to do your job."

I said, "Would you have a problem if I asked Clem about it?"

"No, but I'm not sure if it's going to do you any good."

"Okay, then. Thanks, I'll keep you posted," I replied as I left Fenton's office, hotter than a pistol. "I just can't believe Fred Medrano will be getting a promotion and start getting paid more than me," I thought. I remembered helping Fred in the PSCCO training class, a class in which he was ranked twelfth of twelve people. Crap, double crap. Fred's got a good personality, but that's it. This isn't really happening, is it?

A few hours later, I was in Clem's office. My worst fears were confirmed: Fred Medrano was going to be the manager of application development. Case closed. I told Clem that I was disappointed that I hadn't been considered for the job along with Fred, but I knew enough to limit my comments and to mask my displeasure as best I could.

Walking back to my office, I passed Fenton's. I looked in and said, "It's a done deal. Fred Medrano is going to be taking Sommers' old job." I kept moving to reduce any chance for further discussion.

When I sat down at my desk, for the first time in my skyrocketing career, my energy level was at an incredible low. I realized that for more than two years I had worked more hours than any other employee in the computer department. I realized that if I would take my total income and divide by the hours worked that I had taken about a ten-percent cut in pay from my previous job, and there was nothing I could do about it. I further realized that there weren't any more opportunities for me at Information Handling Services.

This was the first time that I had ever thought about my future at his, and it didn't look very promising. The biggest problem for me was the fact that I was getting burned out. The never-ending after-hours pages I received week in and week out had drained my energy level and my enthusiasm for my job. But now with the departure of Sommers and promotion of Medrano, I was forced to confront my reality for the first time ever.

One thing that really concerned me was the fact that if I appeared to be too upset about the personnel changes, I would be putting myself at risk big time. Between Clem and Fenton, they would not hesitate to search for a replacement system programmer. And once that happened, it would only be a matter of time until they found an acceptable replacement. Most likely, they would tell me that they realized how many hours I had been working and that they wanted to add someone that could share the workload. They would come to that realization because when I talked to Clem about being considered as someone that could replace Sommers, I told him how many hours I had been working.

Now, I would say that I managed to cook my own goose unless I could shake off this setback and get back to the high-energy, upbeat guy everyone was used to. Further, it had become crystal clear in my mind that I needed to begin looking for another job.

In Chapter 1, I said, "There are defining moments in everyone's life," and this moment was an extremely important one for me. At times like this there was no time to waste feeling sorry for yourself or waste time doing anything except being productive in a manner that could change things and improve your career outlook. That evening, I pulled out my old resume to update it and looked for the sources that were available in the Denver job market to find companies looking to hire high-level computer software developers. By the next morning, I managed to find three prospective employers, and I produced an up-to-date resume, a list of references, three envelopes, three stamps, and one mailbox. My job search had officially begun. By taking steps to address the problems I identified with my current job and future prospects, I was automatically energized and able to reestablish myself as a positive employee trying to do the best job possible. Also, by taking the steps that I had taken, I was able to feel empowered instead of a victim of an unfair decision.

I sent my resume to Johns Manville Corporation (JM), a huge company whose headquarters had been in Manville, New Jersey, but the company had built an absolutely beautiful building on Ken Caryll Ranch, a working cattle ranch in the foothills about twenty-five miles southwest of Denver. The building was so stunning that it had been featured in *Architectural Digest*.

One morning at work, I received a call from a person named Gilbert Samson telling me that had received my resume and wanted to meet with me to talk about a job opening at JM. He invited me to lunch that very day, and I agreed to meet with him. The lunch went fantastically well, and he said that he was going to recommend me as a qualified applicant for the open position. "Great," I said and told him that I would wait to hear from him.

About three p.m. that same day, I got a call from my lunch companion, who told me that they wanted me to come to the headquarters building for another interview two days hence. "Perfect," I said, and we set a time for my next meeting.

Driving up this enormous hill that was the entrance to the Ken Caryll Ranch provided a breathtaking vista of huge red rocks, patches of green pastures, and a sleek, silver, futuristic building that looked as though it had been built on the side of a cliff. When I got to the building, the road led me to the back of the facility and an enormous semicircle parking lot with multiple levels, creating the appearance of an amphitheater with cars taking the place of people convened to watch some great performance. The signs directed me to the non-employee parking area and once parked, I walked to a center building entrance that housed a huge stainless-steel receptionist desk. I was so impressed with this high-tech facility that it created a very strong impression that only the very best people worked here and that only the very best people would be hired to work here in the future. End of story.

I was escorted to the northernmost area of the facility, which was located one floor above the receptionist area. Once there, I was taken to the office of Jake Reager. Jake and I seemed to have so much in common in terms of our technical background. Jake had also moved up in the ranks to become a systems programmer and was an extremely impressive individual who I really enjoyed talking to.

I asked Jake if he could tell me more about the position he was interviewing me for, and he provided me with a very thorough description of the job duties. He told me that JM, like most large companies, had developed a centralized systems architecture whereby all application software resided on a large IBM mainframe computer, and with the use of CICS, they made a variety of software applications available to remote plant sites throughout the country. However, JM's strategic plans called for the introduction of a distributed processing architecture to allow for the availability of certain functions using small computers. These functions would run in a stand-alone mode, thereby off-loading processing requirements from the mainframe computer and creating the opportunity to make available to individual plant sites the ability to have custom reports created separately and apart from the standardized reporting provided to all users of the application. Because of this shift, they were looking to add people with strong technical backgrounds to help facilitate the new decentralized strategy.

"John, I think your job duties initially will involve helping us establish Datapoint mini-computers into a variety of locations with a focus on the order entry application that is currently in use throughout the company," Jake said. "This means you will be provided training on the Datapoint hardware and software and be assigned to the Application Development & Support Group, which is responsible for the order entry software. How does that sound to you?"

"That sounds exciting. I love new challenges," I replied. At the end of the interview, Jake told me that someone from the Personnel Department would be in touch and thanked me for my interest in Johns Manville Corporation.

All of my instincts told me that I would be getting a job offer from JM, but I wasn't sure about the salary they would offer and if they were planning on interviewing more candidates before making a decision. My apprehension about salary and timing were quickly erased when I received a call from Gilbert Samson two days after my interview with Jake Reager. Gilbert told me that I had been selected for the opening and that the salary I had asked for was agreed to. Something didn't line up, but I couldn't put my finger on it.

"What's next?" I asked Gilbert.

"Well, when can you start work at JM?"

"I will need to give two weeks' notice," I told him. It was Thursday, so I told him I would turn in my resignation letter tomorrow and gave him a start date of two weeks from the upcoming Monday. I asked him when I would be able to get my offer letter, and he told me he would meet me for lunch the next day and have all the paperwork with him.

I met Gilbert at the same restaurant where we had our initial meeting. With paperwork in hand, Gilbert proceeded to give me an offer letter with the salary and start date. Good, right? But now, the thing that I couldn't put my finger on had shown up front and center. My offer letter was not from JM; it was from GS Enterprises, a staffing company JM uses to provide temporary contract help. Yikes!

"I thought I was getting a job offer from JM, not GS Enterprises," I told him.

"JM won't hire any computer-related personnel directly," he explained. "They want to see if you are going to be a good fit. To do this, they use companies like mine to find people and make them available for interviews. They provide the prospective employee a six-month contract, at which time they decide if they want to extend the person a job offer to become a JM employee with all of the benefits. This is the only way to become a JM employee. What do you want to do?"

At that point, I was emotionally committed to leaving Information Handling Services and becoming a JM employee, but one thing was for sure here: This was about to be one of the riskiest moves I had ever made.

Naturally I said, "I would be happy to join GS Enterprises because I really want the opportunity to become a full-time JM employee, and I'm confident I can make that happen."

The next day, I gave Fenton Miller my resignation letter. I told him I liked working for him and that he had been a good boss but that I just couldn't continue in my role as an SP because of the amount of overtime that I had been required to work for more than two years. I told him I hoped he would understand. Fenton, being the classy guy he was, stood up and extended his hand to me and wished me well. Because there was almost zero discussion about replacing me, I am pretty sure that he and Clem saw this coming and had already found my replacement. They were doing what they needed to do to make sure IHS had the necessary resources to support the business, and I was doing what I needed to do to manage my career, and at the same time, try to have a personal life.

NDJ Life Lesson:

There are times when it's time to say goodbye, even though you didn't plan on leaving and you didn't really want to leave.

The hundreds of hours of overtime that I worked and didn't get paid for are hours I spent without any chance of getting anything in return.

In reality, those overtime hours were spent learning and doing things that made me valuable to Johns Manville Corporation, and unless I cashed in the value of the time I spent becoming marketable to JM, I would have totally lost the chance for any tangible benefits to come my way.

That's why they say in the stock market, "Buy low and sell high," and when your managing your career, they say, "Leave when you want and not when they tell you you're not wanted."

Chapter 33

Johns Manville Corporation
Welcome to the Big Leagues

Johns Manville Corporation was like night and day compared to Information Handling Services. It was a Fortune 500 company with thousands of employees and billions of dollars in assets. IHS was a company with about one hundred people and sales of about 120 million dollars.

The JM facility, furnishings, artwork, space-age design, and unbelievably impressive executives and senior management were so incredibly intimidating it is hard to explain. The casual dress code at IHS didn't compare to the high-end suits senior management wore and the very nice suits worn by every white-collar employee in the building, both men and women. This was definitely the big leagues, and I really had the sense that they were not going to hire computer people into their high-end, super high-tech environment unless they looked like superstars looking for a place to do super things.

This feeling was almost palpable, because from the moment I arrived in the building, the people that greeted me at the reception area knew I would be there, and when I introduced myself, Person 1 immediately knew who to call, what to say. A few minutes later, Person 2 was introducing themselves to me, asking me to follow them to my work area. Once at the work area, I was taken to Person 3, who told me that Jake Reager wanted to say hello but was out of town on an assignment. He said he would talk to me when he got back. Then Person 3 took me to my cubicle and along the way pointed out nice-to-know-about things like the location of the restrooms, the supply cabinet where I could find paper, Post-its, paper clips, and so on. I was told that I would receive a desk template, stapler, three-hole-punch, and a wastepaper basket, as well as a complete set of Datapoint (DP) technical manuals that would be delivered to my office sometime that afternoon. Person 3 showed me where her cubicle was and told me to let her know if I didn't receive the manuals by two p.m. I had everything I could imagine to help me feel welcome, and most importantly, to help me become productive as soon as possible. It was overwhelming just how professional everyone was and how well they understood exactly what they needed to do.

Person 3 left and told me Person 4 would be coming to give me a sign-on procedure so I would have access to the mainframe computer from the 3270 terminal in my cubicle. Ten minutes went by, and Person 4 greeted me. He took me to an area where there were eight DP mini-computers. He explained that these were community computers and that people who needed to use them for their work would always be able to find one or more of them available since there were only five people assigned to work on the DP mini-computers.

"However, with the addition of you," Person 4 explained, "there are now six people. The DP is a key part of the department's strategy to decentralize our application systems architecture."

I explained that Jake had talked to me a little bit about the decentralized strategy when he interviewed me. I then asked Person 4 if he was part of the DP team and what his role was within the department.

By this point in our conversation, I realized I hadn't used my Dale Carnegie training; I couldn't remember his name. I made a mental note to not let that happen again. It would be a huge plus if I could remember people's names, which was something most people don't make a priority.

Before anything else was discussed, I apologized for not remembering his name. He promptly said, "Not a problem," and he extended his hand to me, saying, "I'm Ted Minor."

I grabbed his hand and said, "John Santone. I really appreciate you helping me get on board." I then asked him for the name of Person 3, and he said, "That's Stephanie Sanders. She is one in a pool of administrative assistants assigned to support the first-level managers in the department." To help me understand a little bit more about the chain of command, Travis explained that I would report to Jake Reager, the team leader in charge of the DP integration project. Jake reported to Ron Walsh, a first-level manager who had three team Leaders: Jake, John Eck, and Bob Shoup. John Eck's team was made up of application support analysts supporting the order entry and inventory applications. Bob Shoup was the team leader responsible for supporting the current order entry and inventory mainframe applications. Stephanie Sanders was one of three administrative assistants, the other two being Becky Shepard and Suzie Hernandez. I asked Ted if there was an org chart I could get a copy of. He said he would get me one.

I was beginning to realize how huge the computer department was, how incredibly well-defined things like roles and responsibilities were, and how much structure existed to make sure things were not only done, but done in a way that management determined they wanted them done.

In that moment, several realities hit me right between the eyes. First, I did not know a single thing about a DP computer. Second, I had better get my hands on the technical manuals that Stephanie Sanders told me would arrive in my cubicle later that day. Third, I better find out if there were restrictions about taking technical manuals out of the office, if I needed to get permission to stay at my cubicle beyond normal working hours, and if I would need some kind of approval if I left the office and came back later that same day.

Fortunately I thought of those things ahead of time. Ted explained that manuals were not to be taken from the building without written approval. If I intended to stay late, I didn't need prior approval, no matter how late I stayed. However, if I left the building and then came back later that evening, I would need written approval. So, it looked like I was going to need to bring something to eat for dinner when I wanted to work some casual overtime reading manuals and getting up to speed.

There was one question that I had about working extra hours that Ted didn't know the answer to, and that had to do with badging in and badging out. Working for GS Enterprises meant that I was an hourly employee. I would get paid for the hours worked, which could be calculated by subtracting the badge-out time of day from the badge-in time of day. Naturally, GS Enterprises charged JM more than what they were paying me, and that delta represented their profit. I needed to get permission to work more hours than I was getting paid for, and if I badged-out before I actually left, how could I reenter? Well, this problem had to be elevated pronto because I knew I needed to do a hell of a lot of reading and working on the DP equipment if I was going to be able to be productive, and I needed to do it very, very quickly. Being willing to outwork the competition was one of my secret weapons, and more than ever I needed it now.

I talked to Gilbert Samson and explained to him that I was planning on working some non-billing hours on my own so I could get up to speed on the DP hardware as soon as possible, and he had no problem with that. One down, one to go. With Jake Reager out of the office, I located Ron Walsh, introduced myself, and explained to him that I was planning on staying a few hours each day after quitting time. I told him I had already run this by Gilbert Samson but wanted to get his approval to work some unpaid overtime to get up to speed as soon as possible. Ron appeared delighted to have someone show this kind of initiative on his first day at work.

"No problem," he said. "Let us know if you need anything to help."

I felt pretty good about what I had been able to accomplish thus far, and I just needed to feel that way every day for the next six months so I could receive a full-time job offer from my boss.

By the time I made it back to my cubicle, there were nine DP technical reference manuals on my desk. I looked at the titles of each manual and decided to first look at the reference material that described the hardware and how to use it. I quickly ascertained that the DP computer was an octal machine compared to the IBM 370 VM1, which was a hexadecimal machine. On the IBM computer, there were sixteen bits in a byte of data, and in a data point there were only eight bits in a byte of data. Another way to think of it is that when people do arithmetic, they use a base of ten. Zero to nine is ten digits, and you have to add another digit to represent ten to nineteen. In hex arithmetic, zero to fifteen can be represented with one digit, and you have to add another digit to express sixteen to thirty-one. In octal arithmetic, zero to seven can be represented with one digit, and you have to add a second digit to express nine to sixteen.

This may not seem like a big deal to most programmers who have used higher-level languages like COBOL or PL1 because neither of those languages allows the programmer to access anything smaller than a single byte. As an assembler language and systems programmer, I had been working with hexadecimal machines exclusively. The change from hex to octal was almost like having to learn a new language. People writing application programs using Datapoint proprietary programming language, which was a hybrid version of basic, would never know or care about octal arithmetic. However, a person that was going to want to interface with data coming from an octal machine and send it to a hex machine would need to be able to understand this difference and develop a program to bridge the two separate ways of describing data. I figured that I was just such a person because Jake didn't hire me to write programs in basic, and it was a lot more likely that he would expect me to figure out how to write lower-level programs in the DP environment. In that instant, I looked at all of the other manuals to see if there was something akin to assembler language in world of Datapoint. Turns out that I didn't have an assembler language-like manual in the books I had received.

Before panicking, I thought about it for a little bit and realized that there may be a group of utility programs that came with the machine to perform this type of function. As I scanned the rest of the manuals, I noticed a distinctive feature that DP incorporated into their system architecture. It was possible to establish a DP computer as an application processing (AP) computer or a data processing (DP) computer. This meant that the programs would run on the AP device, and all of the data used by those programs would be located on the DP device. This feature would speed up performance big time because every read/write instruction would execute on the DP device, and only processing instructions like "display a screen" would execute on the AP device. Not only that, but if you added a third processor to the configuration as a DP device, you could speed up performance even more while creating redundancy in the overall configuration in the event that if one of the three computers stopped working for some reason, you could reconfigure the devices so that there was one AP and one DP to rearrange the disks. In this way, the data that was spread across two DPs was available on one DP and the programs were executing on the remaining AP.

Having a hardware configuration that allowed you to have redundancy was a big plus since most computers did not support this type of architecture. And when there was a severe enough hardware problem with a computer to cause it to not work, the time it took to get a repair person to the site, diagnose the problem, and get a replacement part can be significant. As people became more and more dependent on computers to do their day-to-day work, a severe hardware malfunction could cause huge problems in lost productivity and lost revenue when orders can't be written and inventory can't be sold. Now, I understood why Datapoint was selected to support JM's distributed system architecture.

I managed to get up to speed on the Datapoint hardware and software fairly quickly and was given the responsibility of providing support to application programmers writing code for the DP. I would also be learning how to install DP computers at JM plant sites when needed. When I was assigned to go to a Manville plant located in St. Augustine, Florida, it was the first time I had ever seen the Atlantic Ocean. It was my first ever business trip, and I didn't even have a credit card. Fortunately, JM provided an American Express card to employees that traveled as a part of their job. Turns out that you can't rent a car without a credit card.

Who knew this kind of stuff? Not a guy that showed up at the pool hall with eight hundred to one thousand dollars in his jeans pocket, which was exactly fifty percent of his net worth at any given point in time. Yes, JM was the biggies as far as NDJ was concerned, and his knowledge of how businesses operated, planned, and developed far-reaching strategies was doubling just about every three months. Up until then, NDJ believed his technical abilities held the key to future success. Now, however, Manville has expanded his horizons in the same way that Christopher Columbus's journey created unforeseen possibilities for his life forevermore.

North Denver realized that if he were truly going to succeed beyond the level of a top technician, he would have to develop a strong set of soft skills and utilize everything he learned in Dale Carnegie training and more. Further, he would have to develop some new skills in the area of project management, project planning, system-level design, and somehow find a way to stay abreast of the latest trends in technology. And, if all that weren't enough, he would have to compete with some of the very brightest people in the computer department who wanted what he wanted.

I remember thinking about all of this shortly after my six-month probation period ended and I was hired by JM as a full-time employee. It was great to get that monkey off my back, but I knew then and there that I was going to have to find a new set of goals. More than that, I had to find a way to get the kind of visibility among my peers as a strong player that could, and has always, delivered results. I needed to be thought of as the guy everybody wanted to fly the plane when the pilot and copilot became incapacitated. At the same time, I did not want to develop the reputation of a person that would do anything and everything to get ahead. I remember going to the Saturday matinees and watching the cowboy movies. All of the good cowboys wore a white hat, even the Cisco Kid, one of my favorites. I remember thinking that in the real world, most of the people I was competing with had black hats; they were willing to bend the rules, fudge when they described their results, and put other people down to make themselves look better. I always saw myself as a guy with a white hat and would always do the right thing. Knowing that my approach could put me at a disadvantage at times, I never for a second thought about changing hats. I knew it was still possible to win when you wear a white hat.

NDJ Life Lesson:

The first rung on a ladder does not expand your horizon very much, and the second rung provides you with a somewhat better view.

The interesting thing about people's ideas about moving up on their career ladder is that they may actually believe that when they are on the top rung of their ladder, they have the same view you have on the top rung of your ladder.

It's an easy mistake to make, because when you reach that highest viewpoint, there is no way for you to get higher to see more.

But what if you went to a place with a different ladder? When you arrive at this new place, you ascend to your rightful rung on the ladder and notice something new. You notice more rungs on this new ladder—a lot more rungs.

It is only when you change ladders that the possibility of new horizons exists. Unless your ladder is in a dynamic company with a top-tier management team, you will never see what is possible.

If you're willing to do all you can to reach your potential, don't settle by working for a company that offers you only the ability to earn a living!

Chapter 34

Johns Manville Corporation
NDJ Expands Leadership Skills

As time progressed, I continued to expand my skills. During my second year working at JM, they introduced something called SDM 70. SDM stood for system development methodology, and it represented all of the steps needed to take place in order to develop a successful software application. Every single task was defined over a set of five manuals, and a deliverable was defined. Estimating guidelines were provided as well as example deliverables.

JM adopted this methodology so that all new project development would be consistent and so everyone would have a clear understanding of what they would be expected to do for every single task for the entire life of the project. This was another groundbreaking development and another example of how JM management was doing all they could to provide its staff with the very best tools and work environment. This was truly revolutionary for its time, and for me it was a tremendous boon insofar as my need to enhance my project management abilities. I honestly could not believe how fortunate it was for me to have been given this material to use. In addition, all project managers, team leaders, and senior system level programmers were provided training by representatives from SDM 70.

Shortly after receiving my SDM 70 training, I was given a small project to manage. My boss, Ron Walsh, wanted to see if I could manage a small team and deliver a good result. Originally I had reported to Jack Reager, but he left to become chief technical fellow at Colorado UTE. Ron asked me to use the SDM 70 project life cycle and gave me two people to manage, a senior programmer named Stan Ackerman and a relatively inexperienced programmer named Donna McCann. I told Ron I knew Stan but didn't know Donna and asked him to give me some background information if he could. He said essentially what I already knew—not a lot of experience, but he hadn't worked with her before. She was a fairly new hire, so I guess we would see what there was to see when I got together with both of them to kick off the project.

The first thing you have to realize when you are going to manage people is that they expect you to know more than they do about the project you are managing. That only seems reasonable, right? Of course it's right, and for that to become a reality for my team, I needed to review the user requirements that were broadly stated on their request for programming services. This little project was very straightforward. The users wanted four new report programs coded, which would help them manage their budget for expenditures associated with part-time people that they utilized throughout the year, and they wanted to have a small database by vendor that listed their personnel, job description, hourly rate, and so on.

Up until that point, they had put together a number of Lotus spreadsheets on a project-by-project basis. There was no way to easily figure out which company did what the previous year and how many people they provided. Okay, this was straightforward. I came up with some numbers to run by Ron that reflected the time needed to do the analysis of the user requirements, look into the possibility of converting the spreadsheets into the new database format, and define the format and content of all four reports. I came up with a timeline of four and a half months, soup to nuts, and Ron approved my plan. Now I could schedule a meeting with Stan and Donna because I actually knew more than they did about the project.

In my meeting with Stan and Donna, I introduced myself and asked that they tell me a little bit about themselves. I gave them an overview of the project using the white board. Because I am a visual person, I like to draw pictures of things to help explain my words, and I find that putting things up on the board makes it easier for people to interact and collaborate with the discussion. By the end of the meeting, I gave Stan and Donna their initial assignment, which was to meet with the two users and begin defining the end products—the four reports. Doing this would allow us to back into the design of the database and determine if any of the data they wanted in the reports currently existed somewhere in a database.

I asked them to schedule a meeting, or meetings, to get the definition of the reports completed. I gave them a form from the SDM 70 manual that defined the format they were expected to follow and then return it to me when the task was completed. In the meantime, I told them I would be contacting the Database Group to give them a heads up that we would be coming to them to establish a new database and that we would need their support to make it happen. I told them the time frames I had in mind in order to complete the project on schedule, and I asked that they let me know if they would be able to give me the support I needed in the time frame I defined. Naturally, there was an SDM 70 form precisely for this purpose, and I would have it partially completed by the time of our initial meeting and complete the remainder of the form when Stan and Donna buttoned down the data requirements.

At the end of the meeting, I told Stan and Donna that we were a team and that I was expecting all of us to do our best work possible. "I don't have a problem with either of you questioning a decision I make about the project," I explained, "as long as you also provide a different solution to the approach I have made. I will listen to your suggestions. However, if I believe my original approach is best, I will expect you to totally support it. I will not tolerate people who say they will support me and then go around complaining to others about what I did. Once I say no to your idea and reaffirm my original directive, that's it! Do you guys both understand what I'm saying here?"

Stan and Donna nodded in affirmation.

"Okay. Then let's all do our best to represent our department and make our users happy with the outcome of this project. On three, go team. One, two, three, go team!"

Donna got up to leave the conference room while Stan said that he would like to have a minute of my time.

"Okay, Stan. What can I do for you?"

"This project is critical for me because I believe Ron Walsh is going to use it to evaluate me as a potential team leader, and I will do everything I can to make it successful. I respect you as someone who can be an effective leader."

"Thanks for saying that, Stan, and I appreciate your support of me as a leader."

Then Stan told me he was also concerned about Donna's skill level, but he didn't have anything concrete to substantiate his statement.

I said, "Let's all just try to do our best and see what happens, okay?"

Stan nodded and got up to leave the conference room. So far so good.

Stan and Donna did a great job getting all of the data requirements nailed down, and it was clear that this was going to be a stand-alone database since almost none of the data were currently available in existing files. I love it when a plan comes together. Next, we rolled through the tasks needed to define the program processing requirements. We needed one data entry program, one file conversion program (to take the historical data from the Lotus spreadsheets and populate the database), and four report programs. Following the coding and unit testing of each of the six programs, we needed to develop a test plan to ensure that all of our programs worked properly. After that, we had to decide where to meet after work to have a drink and a mini-celebration for the success of our mini-project.

So, if that is how the project was going to go, then why did I bother to add this little story in my book? If this were a movie, there would be some land-shark music playing in the background, because we both know something bad is about to happen, right? Of course something bad is going to happen, and I'm going to tell you.

We were rolling along on schedule until it was time to start coding the first two programs. Approximately four weeks into a fourteen-week project, I conducted our weekly Friday morning status meeting. Stan was expected to report the progress of his program design and initial coding of the data entry program, and Donna was expected to do the same for the first report program she was assigned. There were eight hundred man-hours of work left to complete the project. Stan had worked twenty-four hours on his program, and it was estimated that it would take sixty hours to complete the design, coding, and unit testing. Stan said he was ahead of schedule and believed he could complete the task in the next sixteen to eighteen hours. If Stan's estimate was accurate he would complete a sixty-hour task in forty-two hours.

Next, Donna reported her status on her first report program. She said that she had not yet completed the program design part of her task, and that was all she said.

"Okay," I said. "How do you stand in terms of hours? There are fifty hours allocated to complete design, coding, and unit testing. How many hours have you spent on the design part, and how many hours do you think it will take to complete the program design?"

Donna said that she really hadn't started the design part and wasn't sure how long it was going to take. As I listened to this I started to get dizzy. It was as though Donna managed to get amnesia and simply wasn't able to remember what her job was. Moreover, she didn't seem able to acknowledge the seriousness of what she stated and for some unknown reason didn't seem to want to resolve the issue. When the dizziness stopped, I realized that I could not get to the bottom of this problem by badgering Donna to "wake up" or say something else that would not resolve whatever issue that caused this complete disconnect. I told Stan that he could leave since I wanted to talk to Donna in private.

"What's the matter?" I asked Donna when she and I were alone.

She looked at me with tears in her eyes and said, "I just can't work with Stan." I was silent. She went on to tell me that while Stan was an excellent programmer, he was definitely not a team player.

"How so?"

"Listen, John, I'm new to the department. I haven't had any SDM 70 training, I haven't coded a single program yet, and when I asked Stan about something about SDM 70, he just points me to the bookshelf where the five manuals are and tells me everything I need to know is there. I know you said we're a team, but Stan hasn't done one thing to help me get my bearings. I think he wants me to fail so he can come in at the last minute to save the day."

"I'm sorry for what's going on," I said. "Hang in there. I'm going to get to the bottom of this, and if what you're telling me is true, then I'm going to fix this problem. Go back to your desk and start working on the program design, but first, come with me back to my cubicle so I can show you where the information about program design is in my set of SDM 70 manuals. You can make a Xerox of the forms that represent how the program design documentation should look."

I reserved the conference room for another hour and went to find Stan and ask him to come with me back to the meeting room. When we got there, he shut the door and immediately offered to code all of Donna's programs himself. He said that having me be successful as a team leader was the most important thing as far as he was concerned because most of the other TLs didn't have a strong technical background and were basically incompetent. I thanked him for his vote of confidence and asked him to sit down.

I began by saying that having one of the best programmers in the department code all of the programs was probably the worst idea he could come up with. "If I'm going to be an effective team leader," I explained, "I need to find a way to work well with strong senior people like yourself, less experienced people like Donna, and everyone in between. This project is not about me demonstrating to Ron Walsh that I can lead a team of two people to produce six programs. This project is about me being able to get the best possible work from the people assigned to me so that we can deliver a high-quality system to our users, and while we're doing that, we need to represent our department as competent professionals who understand our role in the company. That is what we are here to do. Do you remember our first meeting when I met with you and Donna and said we need to be a team? Guess what, Stan? You're not being a team player insofar as

Donna is concerned. She hasn't been at JM very long, doesn't know anybody but you and me, and how much have you done to try to help her be successful?"

Stan looked at me, puzzled.

"Let me answer that," I continued. "Zero point zero. That's how much help you've been to her. And I will not have that kind of behavior continue with anyone who works for me. Do you understand? Now, here's what I want you to do. First, I'm correct in saying that you have the input and output sections of your data entry program completely defined?"

Stan nodded.

"So, your I/O definitions should be able to be used in all four of the report programs, correct?"

Stan nodded again.

"So, what I want you to do is give Donna the code you came up with and tell her I want all of the programs to have common code whenever possible because it will make maintenance a lot easier when people try to modify our work in the future. Now, this is the kind of thing I think a senior programmer who is also a team player would have done already, you know what I mean?"

Any guesses about what Stan does? All of you that voted for "Stan nodded" win.

"Stan, I think you're a top-notch guy, but my job is to help you reach your potential, which is superstar. That's what I want for you, and doing things like I just described and running a team this way is what a superstar does. Got it?"

"Yes," Stan replied.

I extended my right hand to him and said, "Are we good?" Stan shakes my hand and says, "Absolutely."

After that meeting, we completed the project one week ahead of schedule. Afterward, Stan and Donna were frequently seen having lunch together, showing each other pictures of their children. Ron Walsh also gained confidence in my ability to be a team leader.

NDJ Life Lesson:

When I saw our project start to go down the drain and Stan offered to bail me out by writing all of the programs himself, I realized that being a good leader involves a great deal more than just knowing about what needs to be done.

On my very first project as a team leader, my image as an effective project manager was on the line four weeks into the project. I remember thinking, "Why is this happening, and what am I going to do to fix this problem?"

An experienced project manager would have done exactly what I did. However, I literally had no experience managing other people, and a simple speed bump like the one that happened on my first project seemed like a life or death decision.

Unfortunately, when most new managers face this kind of adversity, they panic because they know if the project fails that it is over for them as a leader. So, what they do is try to strong-arm a person like Donna because she's not doing her job.

Then, to make matters worse, they suck up to Stan and tell him that they are going to give Donna one more chance, but if she doesn't deliver, then they're going to need him to come through for them. Naturally, Stan nods in agreement.

I can still remember the fear I had when I confronted Stan in the conference room, because I knew if he told me that it wasn't his job to help bail out Donna, I wasn't sure what I would have said to him or what I would have done going forward.

It is precisely this kind of thinking that paralyzes so many managers, experienced or not, and keeps them from doing the right thing.

While it was true that I didn't know what I would do if Stan failed to cooperate, I wasn't going to let a hypothetical possibility keep me from doing the "right" thing and calling Stan out for his bad behavior.

Please do not aspire to be a supervisor, team leader, or manager if you do not have the strength of character to do the right thing for all of the people who work for you and count on you to have their back.

Chapter 35

Johns Manville Corporation
The Fiberglass Project

I had worked at JM for a little over three years. During that time, I couldn't help but notice how incredibly stable the company's senior management appeared to be and, to be honest, how incredibly competent. If you were a vice president, director, or second-level manager, you pretty much didn't have to worry about getting canned unless you did something like sexually harass someone or commit some kind of crime like embezzlement.

The one group of senior managers that didn't fit that mold was the executive-level managers in the Information Systems Department. Why was that the case? Well, for one thing, the ISD was a cost center, which meant that they did not do anything to directly generate revenue for the company. Instead, they had a huge budget that was spent on performing a function that, for the most part, could not be seen as something that gave the company a competitive advantage over their competition.

The biggest fear the senior managers of ISD had was being tasked with the development of a major new computer application with the purpose of giving JM a competitive edge in the marketplace. Then, in 1978, ISD senior management's worse fear came knocking on their door when the top money-making division at Manville decided to invest 200 million dollars to expand its capacity by enhancing existing plants and adding a new production facility. In addition to expanding its ability to produce more product, the division insisted that they have a state-of-the-art computer system to give them a competitive edge. The division I'm talking about is the Fiberglass Division.

It had been rumored for quite a while that the Fiberglass Division was going to ask ISD to develop a new computer system. The management at ISD had been working closely with IBM for the past few months after the announcement of a new distributed processing computer (DPC) — the IBM 8100. I was one of several senior technicians sent to Los Angeles to attend an IBM 8100 programming class. Having spent quite a bit time working on the Datapoint mini-computers, I immediately recognized how much more sophisticated IBM's new computer was. It was clear to me that the 8100 was going to be the answer to the Fiberglass Division's request for a state-of-the-art computer system, and it would support the strategic plan that ISD management had in place to establish a decentralized system architecture by establishing distributed processing capabilities at the user location.

While in L.A. attending the 8100 class, one of my peers, Ernie Tolvo, came over to me to have a chat. He was one of those poster-boy figures of a tough guy from Boston (or "Bah-sten" as he pronounced it), right down to his bullying posture and take-no-prisoners attitude.

Ernie came over to me and said, "I hope you know you've got no chance to be the team leader on the Fiberglass project." He continued by telling me that he had been at JM for nearly ten years, and there was no way in hell that management was going to put a guy like me in this kind of position. "It'll never happen," he said.

I didn't respond and just let him unload, because I was pretty sure he had more to say. He explained that when he was named team leader that he was not going to ask for me to be on his team, and that it was doubtful that I would ever have a need to use the training I was receiving there. After that comment, he stopped talking and with his body language said, "What do you think of that?"

It was times like this that I was almost glad I was the smallest guy and subjected to bullies of all shapes and sizes. The thing was that they all had the same modus operandi — that is, to say they want you to be afraid. They want you to fear them from a physical standpoint, and even more importantly, they want you to fear their words, their threats. Ernie had been an accomplished bully in his younger days, and in times of stress or worry, he couldn't help himself from bringing intimidation to the forefront.

It was my turn to respond, so I said, "Ernie, it's obvious you've given this team leader opportunity a great deal of thought, but I'm not really sure why you've decided to tell me all of this. I'm thinking that you don't want me to get my hopes up for the team leader job, and you're just trying to help me understand why I've got no chance. Or, there might be another reason. You might be hoping to get me to throw in the towel, and when we get back to work, tell Ron Walsh I'm simply outmatched by Ernie and no longer want to be considered for the job." I ended the conversation by telling Ernie that I was confident that they would pick the best person for the job, and I added one more piece of information for Ernie to think about. "Ernie, I have never been passed over for a promotion in my entire career, and I honestly can't think of a single reason why this situation is going to be any different."

Of course, all of you reading this book know that what I told Ernie about never being passed over for a promotion was a big fat lie, because that's exactly what happened to me at Information Handling Services. Nonetheless, my untruth was the perfect thing to say in this particular situation. At St. Catherine's, while attending every First Friday Mass and taking Communion, I would have gotten two Our Father's and one Hail Mary as my penance, and after saying the last prayer, my soul would have instantly become brand-new, just like it was when I was baptized.

However, in that moment I really didn't think I sinned. Funny how things that I once was absolutely positive about, like mortal and venial sins, can be disintegrated when, as an adult, you get to decide what makes sense and what doesn't.

After returning from the 8100 training class, it was clear that there was going to be a green light given to ISD by the Fiberglass Division to get started with the development project. The word on the street was that they wanted the project to be completed in the next nine to ten months, and that meant that the project manager and team leaders needed to be named, along with the initial technical staff, programmers, and analysts pronto. Everyone in the department, knew that Bob Shoup would be the team leader for the new inventory system and that Greg Pruitt would be the team leader for the systems group responsible for CICS and telecommunications support. The only question was who was going to be named team leader for the application development work on the IBM 8100.

It was a Friday afternoon, and we were told that the team leader decision would be made before the end of the day. At about two p.m., Ron Walsh called me to his office and told me that I was going to be the team leader. I cannot tell you how happy I was to receive the news. I came out of Ron's office, and the people who had been trained on the 8100, minus Ernie, were waiting there. When I opened the door to exit, six people waiting for me to say something or do something greeted me. I gave a thumbs-up, and honestly was congratulated by each and every member of my newly formed team.

When I was in Ron's office, he told me I was getting a promotion, some more money, and my very first private office. While it was technically true that I had an office at IHS—it more than a little resembled a cave—I thought, "This is my very first beautiful and big office."

The first thing I did was have my crew follow me to my new digs and then have them help me relocate my things from my cubicle. By three p.m., all of the hoopla was over. I found myself sitting in my new office looking around, and out of the blue, it hit me. I realized that it was totally up to me now, and what in the hell was I going to do next?

Wow, only a little more than an hour after my big-deal promotion and I was alone in my office and alone with my thoughts. I became incredibly worried thinking about what was going to happen on Monday morning when I came into work and had six people looking to me to tell them what I wanted them to do. I mean, it was not acceptable for me to say, "Hey, I just got promoted last Friday afternoon. How on earth can you expect me to be able to be ready to tell all of you what to do on Monday morning?"

At that very moment, I became overwhelmed with fear and realized that I was already behind schedule in terms of my ability to hand out assignments to my new team. I immediately started looking for a couple of 3-ring binders, some graph paper (16-inch by 32-inch), a computer symbols template, pencils, pens, a 12-inch ruler, a three-hole punch, and several pads of white paper with half-inch lines. Once I had assembled all of my supplies, I headed for the parking lot where my car was waiting for me on the third tier of the parking lot, the farthest away from a possible door ding as physically possible. There was silence as I turned over the engine of the Thunderbird, but the T-Bird's 8-track tape player ended that reality with the strong beat of Fleetwood Mac and Stevie Nicks singing "Rhiannon."

"Man oh man, it doesn't get any better than this," I thought, because at that moment in time, I could not be any happier. I was the team leader on the Fiberglass Project. "Thank you, dear God. Thank you!"

Friday nights were usually reserved for the disco or the pool hall. It was a pretty binary decision, A or B. But this

Friday wasn't like any other Friday. I had so much anxiety about what I was going to do on Monday I just could not let it go. I had to start doing something to solve this problem.

After dinner with my mom and dad, who were also my next-door neighbors since I moved into the other side of the duplex from where I lived since I was a kid, I went home and took out the graph paper I brought from work. I remember how helpful the magnetic board had been for me when I was preparing for my first sysgen at IHS, so the first thing I did was begin developing a schematic for the new Fiberglass system. I needed to draw a picture that showed all of the major functions that would be required by the users and another picture that depicted all of the major computer hardware that needed to be in place to support the development effort and ultimately the end user's environment. Once again, I was reminded of Danny Martin in the Structural Engineering Department saying, "Before anything can be built, at a minimum you need to be able to visually understand the front elevation of the building." In this case, I needed to create the picture before I could build the system.

I worked until a little after midnight and ended up with a pretty good representation of a system diagram for the software, both application and system-level software, and a decent schematic that described all of the hardware at the plant location and JM Data Center. Now I had a good chance of falling asleep.

The next day, Saturday, I knew exactly what I wanted to start working on. Because I had a great deal of knowledge about the order entry functions performed on the Datapoint computers located at the plant and because I had been a system programmer in my previous job, which gave me an in-depth understanding of CICS (the system that would be the interface between the IBM 8100 and the IBM 370 mainframe computer), I could begin to see the functions that my team needed to develop on the 8100 and that they also had to develop a new CICS application that would determined which CICS application program to execute when a transaction was sent from the 8100 to the mainframe computer.

I began to envision a non-standard method for initiating a CICS program. Ordinarily, every CICS program was associated with a four-digit command code so that when a user performed a function like entering an order, the command code followed by a predefined sequence of data was sent to the mainframe. The command code caused the order entry program to start running, and the data associated with the command was read and processed. In the new system, the 8100 would not send a standard CICS command code; instead, it would send the same CICS command code followed by a packet of header information that would direct each transaction to the appropriate CISC application, which would then read the data that followed the header information. This was the only way that the 8100 would be able to interface with CICS and not be required to tie up the resources, both telecommunications and processing, while waiting for all aspects of the data entry function to be totally complete and error free. Once I came up with this design concept, I was unbelievably relieved. While I had been aware of this issue, I never really had any reason to try to figure out how to reconcile it.

By the end of Sunday afternoon, I had put together two 3-ring binders with key Fiberglass 8100 design information. I had come up with detailed program function diagrams for about twenty separate programs. This was not as hard as it sounds because most of the functions existed on the Datapoint-based software, so it was a matter of duplicating the functionality on the 8100. It didn't take into account any new data fields or functionality that the users may want added to the new system, but it was a significant start, and I felt like I could roll into work on Monday with a pretty decent game plan.

On Monday, I was informed that four members of my six-person team would be attending an 8100 programming class in Los Angeles. The team was leaving Tuesday to attend the three-day class Wednesday through Friday. My team consisted of Jill Tisdale, a person that talked fast, worked fast, brought a positive energy to her work, and whom I viewed as an incredibly impressive young woman with a great deal of potential; Ellen Faverty, a person I had recently interviewed and recommended for hiring; Beth Gresh, the daughter of the director of systems software, though I had no experience working with her before; and Ken Jurak, a fairly recent hire with a strong work ethic who was well-liked by all. There was one more person on my team, Jan Donovan, who was an IBM SE assigned to support all 8100 hardware and software-related issues. I had met Jan before and found her to be extremely bright, almost the prototype of a woman that would break through the glass ceiling—which was real and a significant impediment that has led to so many inequities in the way women in the workforce are treated.

Two of my team members were IBM employees, both experienced 8100 programmers. An important issue I had to address as soon as possible involved getting two IBM 8100 computers that were the exact same configuration to be established in the Savanna, Georgia Fiberglass Plant. Additionally, I needed to have a computer room constructed adjacent to my office and near the cubicles assigned to my team members. I went to my boss and gave him my requirements. He said, "No problem," and less than three weeks hence—walla-bingo-bango-bongo—all done.

I had a gorgeous computer room and two beautiful new IBM 8100 computers with eight disk drives and two high-speed printers. One of the 8100s would be used as the development machine where all new programs were created and unit tested. The second 8100 would be the system test/production machine where all testing to simulate the future production environment would take place. We established stringent rules for program-naming conventions and a procedure to adhere to so that the unit-tested version of a program could be moved to the system test machine, complete with programmer sign-offs that required SDM 70 documentation, along with all SDM 70 tasks required to design, program, and thoroughly unit test every program before it was allowed to be moved to the 8100, which would become the future production version of the Fiberglass System.

On the first Monday following my naming as team leader, I met with the two IBM employees assigned to my team, Bud Anderson and Larry Wheeler. I cannot tell you how fortunate I was to have Bud on my team. Larry seemed to be a solid asset, but Bud was one of those once-in-a-lifetime kind of people that I can honestly say I've never again met the likes of.

During my initial meeting with them, I reviewed the system-level schematic I produced over the weekend and then focused on what I believed to be the key program function of the entire system. I explained how orders were entered into the current Datapoint environment, whereby an entered order that does not pass all of the editing criteria of the order entry application on the mainframe must be totally reentered and resubmitted. This was the Achilles' heel of the current system, not to mention the total lack of user-friendly screen definitions throughout the Datapoint front-end processes. I showed Bud the functional schematic I developed, explaining that it was incomplete in terms of defining all edits. However, it represented a design concept that established an order entry staging area that would reside on the 8100 after the order was transmitted to the mainframe.

Further, I showed Bud and Larry the protocol I came up with that would allow the CICS software to recognize which CICS function/command code would be used to respond to the user's requirements. Even though my schematic was incomplete, I could tell that Bud totally got what I was trying to say to him. There were some 8,100 functions built into the 8100's operating system that would support the CICS interface I defined as well as the ability to remember which completion codes went with which orders now residing on the staging area.

I told Bud that I wanted him to write this key program, and he immediately and enthusiastically said, "Yes sir. I'd be happy to do that." I instantly asked Bud to call me John and not sir, and we were off to the races. I asked Larry to develop a program-naming convention procedure for programs and files and to let me see it as soon as it was done; I wanted to distribute it to the team the following Monday when everyone was back from training.

"Okay, John," Larry responded. "No problem."

Monday was a big success from my standpoint. We were moving in the right direction on all fronts thus far; however, I still needed to meet with Bob Shoup, TL for the order entry and inventory mainframe applications, and Greg Pruitt, TL for the systems group. Then, my phone rang, and I thought, "I wonder how many people know my phone number in my new office?"

I answered the phone, and on the other end was a friend of mine who I had worked with for the past few years, Steve Bratek. Steve was working in the Fiberglass Division, reporting to Mike Sieden, the director responsible for seeing to it that ISD produced a new computer system that would meet the end user's requirements and provide the Division a competitive advantage in the marketplace. Steve told me that Mike Sieden would like me to come down and meet with them on Tuesday to give Mike a status update on the project and to establish an ongoing method to keep him up to speed regarding progress of the development effort.

"Okay," I told Steve, "but I think it would be a good move for Mike to call Ron, or I'll ask Ron to call Mike, because I can only provide status on the 8100 development effort."

Steve didn't respond right away. Then he said, "How about ten a.m. in Mike's office tomorrow?"

"Okay, see you tomorrow," I said. I hung up, called Ron, and suggested he call Sieden. Ron agreed, and that was that.

Tuesday, I showed up at Mike Sieden's office, see Bratek, and introduce myself to Mike. He said that Steve told him a lot of good things about me and that he was looking forward to working with me on the project. Then I presented my system schematics. First I showed him the software diagram depicting all major components in the system, and then I showed the hardware schematic with all the major components. As I explained each diagram, I provided him an overview of how I saw the system working, and I was able to explain my role and my team's roles in developing somewhere in the neighborhood of seventy to one hundred programs. The exact number would be determined as I continued defining the functional schematics for each and every program.

I explained that at this point in time, I was not aware of any new data requirements for the initial phase of the development effort, but if there were going to be some new functions and/or data added to the order entry function, that I would need those defined ASAP.

I gave Mike and Steve the SDM 70 forms that I wanted them to review for any changes or additions to the order entry system so that I could incorporate them into the programming effort. I gave Mike an approximate date for by which I would complete a detailed project plan depicting all tasks, start and end dates, and persons responsible for the work. I let him know that I had already given Ron my hardware and software requirements to support the development effort along with a diagram for the construction of a computer room near my office that would be a mirror image of the computer room at the plant location, except that our room would house two computers so the footprint was twice as big as what would be needed in Winder.

Mike seemed very pleased with my presentation and said he was surprised that I had made so much progress given that I had been selected as the TL on Friday afternoon. Working all weekend not only gave me peace of mind to be able to roll in on Monday literally on a mission, but it was also great to have taken the initiative instead of acting unsure about what I could and could not do.

Later on Tuesday, I met with Bob and Greg together to save time, stopped by Ron's office to let him know how it went with Sieden, and asked him if he had talked to Mike.

"Not yet, will do," he said.

"Okay, over and out," I replied.

This was day two, and I was loving every minute of it... so far. I was not naïve believing that every day was going to be like the last two, but you might as well enjoy the good days and keep the memory of what happened in your mind so when the rainy days showed up you could remember they too will pass. When I was in charge and able to operate with little or no supervision, I was definitely at my best. I was super energized and super aware of what I was being allowed to do.

When people place that much trust in me, I will climb Mount Everest in tennis shoes if that's what is required to complete my responsibilities at the highest level possible. I never take that kind of trust for granted, and I take time out to tell my boss that I appreciate the confidence he has in me.

Day three. I called Bratek and asked him if he could come down to my office because I wanted to talk to him about screen layouts for the 8100 programs. Steve was aware of the Datapoint terminals and had used the less-than-wonderful user interface that was in place for the order entry functions. When I met with Steve and Mike, they told me that Steve would be doing the screen design for the new system. I was very happy with that decision because this kind of work was definitely in Steve's wheelhouse. He had high standards when it came to the appearance of whatever he was involved with, whether it was his image, his office, car, or anything that reflected personal taste. I knew he would that use that mentality when he designed the user screens on the 8100. The reason I wanted to meet with him was because the 8100 offered a much more robust set of options available to the developer or analyst. One example was that the 8100 supported terminals with twelve function keys that could be programmed and utilized as a part of the screen design in order to provide enhanced ergonomics for the user. I wanted to show Steve all of the various options he could take advantage of when he designed his screen. Naturally, if he decided to utilize the function keys, he would need to define their usage as a part of the SDM 70 documentation he would produce for our programmers, which would allow them to incorporate using function keys when they produced program design documents. Steve was genuinely happy with the information I had given him. I was certain he would come up with some great screen designs and that he would find innovative ways to use the ergonomic features embedded in the hardware and software of the 8100.

The Fiberglass project became the most widely talked about event for sure during the time I had been there, but some of the—old-timers—the guys that had 10-plus years' experience and moved from the original corporate headquarters in New Jersey, acknowledged that something special was going on. The twenty or so team members on the overall project were given the best cubicles, the newest terminals, and shared an esprit de corps that made everyone stand a little straighter, move a little faster, work a little harder, and still manage to enjoy themselves. For my part, I was totally immersed in my element because I had managed to gain all of the skills I needed precisely when I needed them the most. The momentum I experienced on days one and two never dissipated. In fact, I realized just how much my energy level could be transferred to the staff and how their unique personalities could in turn influence their peers. We managed to keep the project on schedule, and there was an overwhelming sense of optimism as we reached the 65%-complete milestone.

At this point in the project, there was one more huge milestone—developing a comprehensive system test plan.

We would need to test not just every program, but within every program we needed to execute every line of code present. To do that, we needed access to people who, in the real world, understand how every function works, why it is required, and when something is performed, if there are indirect consequences that cannot possibly be understood by a programmer with mostly vertical knowledge of his/her code and no understanding of downstream consequences. It was exactly this kind of possibility that made this task so incredibly complex and virtually impossible to accurately estimate how long it was going to take. Adding to the risk was the understanding that our team of 8100 programmers could not complete more that forty percent of the work that comprised a complete test plan. We need strong user involvement.

Early on in the project, I had made Bratek and Sieden aware of this issue and just how critical it was, but that was nearly seven months ago. Now I was recommending that we have the order entry clerks—two from the Winder plant, two from the second site installation location, and one from the third sit—come to Colorado and spend two weeks with us so we could develop comprehensive test scripts.

Preceding this event, the project development team, working in conjunction with Bob Shoup's order entry/inventory team, developed programs to populate our system testing database on the IBM mainframe computer and uploaded some valid data to our test system 8100. All of this coordination and our ability to recognize what we believed to be at least ninety percent of the possible outcomes was the single most important task that remained on our project plan. Even if the code on the 8100 was in pretty good shape, meaning on a scale from one to ten with ten being the best, if we didn't score at least an 8.8, that would mean that there were far too many errors embedded in the code and it couldn't be put into production. Even if the screens were gorgeous, the ease of use was spectacular, and the time savings over the old system was out of this world, no one would care because our system is unreliable.

After a nearly three-hour meeting with Fiberglass Director Mike Sieden, Computer Operations Manager Steve Bratek, ISD Director Ray Southard, ISD Applications Development Manager Ron Walsh, and Team Leaders Bob Shoup, Greg Pruitt and myself came to an agreement that we would get everything we were asking for in terms of people and the duration we needed them. We decided that if we could provide the order entry people with printouts of all screen displays, they would be able to come to Colorado for only one week and then complete the remainder of the test scripts using the screen facsimiles brought back to their locations.

We also reached an agreement about bringing the same people back to Colorado to execute all of the test scripts and work with our technical team to resolve issues as they were discovered. The actual execution of the test plan was expected to take about thirty hours. However, as problems were found, programs were fixed, units were tested, and then the test script executed for the second time, we thought the thirty hours would turn into fifty to sixty during the first iteration, and hopefully the second attempt to execute all of the test scripts would be completed in twenty-four hours tops.

During the project's final week, the system test plan was executed and completed. John Matosek, the IDS vice president, wrote a letter to his Fiberglass counterpart and copied all project participants, stating the Fiberglass Division's request to have ISD develop a new computer system had been successfully completed on time and within budget. Mr. Matosek, a really terrific and truly nice man, personally thanked all ISD and Fiberglass personnel that worked on the project. He described the effort as an exceptional accomplishment and that he greatly appreciated the confidence that Fiberglass's senior management demonstrated by having all of the work performed by JM employees.

I had known that the last four weeks of the project was the most critical time of all, and I was totally focused on every aspect of work required to bring our project across the finish line as a winner. At least one other individual recognized how important the last four weeks were besides me, and that person was Steve Bratek. Steve did all the right things while I did all the right things for the project. Sounds confusing, right? I will explain what I mean by stating a simple fact: Steve knew what was going to happen in his future, and I didn't.

Once Steve realized what I realized, that the project was going to be an enormous success, he talked to his boss about his future in the Fiberglass Division. When I realized the project was going to be a big success, I buckled down and worked even harder to keep anything from falling through the cracks, to make sure everyone knew what I needed them to do.

It never dawned on me for a minute that I had better talk to Ron Walsh about my future in ISD. Why would I need to? Surely Ron knew I had done an outstanding job as a team leader. I hoped he realized that I had been much more than just a team leader; I had actually performed the role of system architect by developing the protocol used to direct all of the transactions generated by the 8100 to flow into the correct application transaction, allowing the most effective use of computer resources possible and at the same time creating a methodology for future expansion for new functionality on all 8100 computers deployed at JM.

During the course of the project, I had met with Ron Walsh's boss only once during the first week. Ron told me, "Ray Southard wants you to stop by his office." When I went to Ray's office, he stood, extended his hand, and congratulated me on my promotion to team leader. Then he sat down in his huge executive chair, leaned back, put his hands behind his neck, and stared at the ceiling while he talked to me. He kept rocking back and forth in his chair, leaning back as far as he could, and looked at the ceiling tiles as though there were hieroglyphics written on them that only he could see. It was the most peculiar thing to see because he kept talking and talking without any possible chance for me to join this odd conversation. I wanted to flip him the bird, but I thought that he probably had a camera filming me and would look at the movie when I left.

NDJ Life Lesson:

I had never been so proud of my team and myself. I could never have imagined what it would be like to work on something for ten months straight and make hundreds, maybe even thousands, of decisions all directed at one precise outcome.

In a way, at least for me, it was like Camelot, where we found ourselves in a place that we never really knew could be real, and not even in our imaginations would we have been able to project a circumstance that was our reality for close to a year.

One lesson that I learned through this experience is that you cannot begin to estimate the power that a group of people can bring to bear toward a common goal when they believe in each other and the company they work for.

I also learned that you must always take responsibility for managing your career. You can never assume that your good work, or even excellent work, will have any impact on your future opportunities as an employee.

Most employees live in the present and the past. They believe the work they have done over the years for a company is similar to a 401K and that all of their good work from the past still has value for the company.

In contrast, management lives in the present and the future. They believe all employees that have worked for the company have been fairly compensated and that each employee received their check and cashed it, so there really isn't any more to say about it.

I have learned that you must get in sync with management and live in the present and the future. Doing this will cause every employee to place much more focus on how they carry out their job duties in this moment in time in the present.

This in turn will allow each employee to compartmentalize every day of their employment with the company they work for. When you believe that your value to the company can only be represented by what you do today, then it's clear that your performance that day will represent you in the best possible light.

Tomorrow's performance is only twenty-four hours away, so it's really no big deal for you to motivate yourself and do your best again.

When you get in sync with management, things get a lot easier immediately. You realize that yesterday is over, so there is no sense in holding onto that memory, thinking that the company will use your past performance as an important component in deciding how they see you today, just twenty-four hours later, right?

When you get in sync with management, it's hard to complain about not getting the proper recognition you deserve, because at the end of the week when you get your paycheck, you will receive exactly what you really do deserve.

When you're in sync every day for a month, you know you did the very best job you could because that is always what you do.

Now, the next thing I'm going to tell you is extremely important. Earlier, I said that management thinks about the present and the future. I have explained to you how focusing on the present, insofar as your daily performance in the workplace is concerned, is essential if you ever really want to advance your career.

I also said that management thinks about the future and that you should too. Now, I want to explain what I mean by that. Let's just say you are one of five salespeople at your company and currently ranked number three. When I say you need to think about your future, in this example you have to find a way to increase your productivity. Period.

There are likely several reasons why you're not number two, and you need to figure out what they are. Maybe numbers one and two simply work more hours, make more phone calls, or have more in-person visits with their customers. Maybe it's something else, but if you truly want to succeed, you must find a way to win! Don't just try to be number two, but place a tremendous focus on improving. This effort to invest your time in your future will eventually pay dividends if you are committed to succeed and do it wearing a white hat.

Now, here is the punch line to all of this: When you strive to get ahead, move up in the chain of command, or get a bigger paycheck, you have to decide what it is that you're going to do to make it happen. You have to have a specific goal in mind that you can describe to your boss. If your goal is to work somewhere else and pursue a specific goal, you have to be able to describe what you want to your spouse, friend, or family member.

Once you have a conversation with your boss about the goal you want to achieve and evaluate the feedback you get, then and only then can you decide what to do. Remember, ever since you got in sync with management, they have seen you at your best each and every day. You are dealing from a position of strength and credibility.

This is what it takes to manage your career. It takes a lot more effort than just showing up at work with your shoes polished!

Chapter 36

Johns Manville Corporation
Go West Young Man

Following the completion of the Fiberglass Project, I found myself literally exhausted. I participated in the work associated with installing the new IBM 8100-based system at the Winder, Georgia plant and the McPherson, Kansas plant. After the first installation, the users could simply not have been happier with the new order entry and inventory systems. We hit the ball out of the park.

While the working on the installs was the obvious goal of the Fiberglass Division, it turned out that ISD didn't have any goal insofar as technology was concerned. Yes, ISD had developed a strategic plan that called for the implementation of distributed processing and decentralization of functions. They didn't actually know what that meant in real-world terms. When the Fiberglass Division decided to invest 200 million dollars to increase production and build a new computer system, they were amenable to purchase all IBM equipment, and because of that, we built the new systems. However, a couple of months after the successful installation of an IBM 8100 in Winder, GA, the Pipe Division asked ISD to build them a new order entry and inventory system, but they did not want to use IBM equipment. For some crazy reason, ISD senior management said okay.

I am not sure if our vice resident, John Matosek, or director, Ray Southard, ever consulted with anyone about the Pipe Division's request, but I do know that nobody asked me. The next thing I know, Ron Walsh called me into his office to tell me that I was going to be the team leader on the Pipe project and that it had to be done using Datapoint equipment. Having worked with DP equipment for nearly two years and having firsthand knowledge of the IBM 8100, I told Ron it couldn't be done. I told him if the Pipe Division wanted all of the functionality that the Fiberglass Division had in its system, it just could not be done on a Datapoint. The DP hardware, for one thing, did not support an interface to CICS, which was required to make it all work.

I asked, "Why would the company want to spend more money building a new system when they just paid for a state-of-the-art hardware and software system that uses IBM equipment?" I did not get an answer to any of my questions or concerns. I was simply directed to call Hank Petrosyan, the director of the Pipe Division. I told Ron that this was going to be a disaster. Just a little less than three months after the Fiberglass project, my career went from *Star Trek* to *Train Wreck!*

I met with Hank Petrosyan. He was an Armenian and wanted to make sure you knew that five seconds after you met him. I, however, did not know anything about what being an Armenian was supposed to portray. If I was going to take a stab at it, it would be that "Petrosyan" was Armenian for "asshole." Hank had absolutely the thickest mustache I had ever seen, and the part of his face that was shaved looked like he still needed to shave. Yikes, this guy looked like a gorilla. Then I stopped the thoughts I had in my head about Hank when I wondered what he would look like wearing a short-sleeved shirt!

He began by saying that he had heard good things about me from Mike. I looked kind of blankly him, and he clarified by saying "Sieden."

"Oh, yes!" I said, acknowledging that I knew who he meant.

"John, I am going to cut to the chase," he continued. "We are not going to want an IBM solution. We want a Datapoint solution."

"My boss, Ron Walsh, let me know that before I got here, but I will have to be honest and say I'm not sure how we could duplicate the functionality we have on the Fiberglass system using Datapoint equipment," I said.

"Well, that's what you're going to have to figure out, right?" asked Hank rhetorically.

"Yes," I replied. "I'm going to look into it right away." Then I got up and left.

I went and talked to Ron. I told him what happened and that I needed to talk to the Datapoint rep to see if we could get them to develop some special communications software, and Ron nodded.

Then, out of the blue, I got a phone call from a friend of mine that used to work at JM. His name was Monroe Hyatt, and when he worked there he was the top Datapoint guy in the department. Monroe and I went way back to when I was first hired as a contract programmer at JM. We both shared a love of Las Vegas, and at least three or four times he and I got in his beat-up old Thunderbird on a Friday afternoon and drove for twelve hours nonstop to get there. We took turns driving, split the cost of gas and the hotel room, stayed there for about twenty-four hours, and drove home Sunday with another set of stories of wins and losses.

Monroe was married to a gal named Judy, and they had a three-year-old son. When we pulled one of our Vegas trips, Monroe drove Judy to the train station so that she and her son could visit her parents in Salt Lake City, Utah. We never considered having them come with us in the car because it just wouldn't create the right kind of vibe with a child crying and preventing us from the "boys will be boys" kind of behavior we had perfected as we became friends.

So, I got this call, and I said, "What's up, Monroe?"

A little over a year ago, just before the Fiberglass project got started, Monroe resigned from JM to take a job at the Stardust Hotel in Las Vegas. He told me he saw an ad in the Vegas paper looking for someone to manage their Data Processing Department, and the ad stated the person must have strong Datapoint skills and experience. This was down the center for Monroe, so he applied and got the job. I really hadn't talked to him since he left.

Monroe told me that the owner, a guy by the name of Allan Glick, decided he wanted to expand the computer department considerably, including the establishment of an entire back office application, significant enhancements to the current reservation system, and a new time and attendance system. Further, Mr. Glick wanted the software to run on a hardware platform that could guarantee high-speed processing for all functions, and implement a highly reliable configuration with some levels of redundancy built into system hardware.

I told Monroe that that sounded out of this world. "How on earth did Mr. Glick get that level of understanding about what he wanted?" I asked.

Monroe told me that his boss, Bill Rivers, told him that Allan Glick was one of the smartest people he had ever met, and when he decided to do something, he really dived in and researched the subject thoroughly, also bringing in experts to help him understand what he didn't.

"Bill Rivers said that I didn't have the project management experience to head up this kind of effort," said Monroe, "but that I wouldn't have to worry about losing my job. He told me he was happy with my technical skills and that I would report to the new person, whoever it is. That's when I told my boss about you, John. I told him you were the best project manager and that you love coming to Las Vegas to visit. He told me to contact you and ask you to send him your resume. I know they are going to bring somebody in, and as far as I'm concerned, I think you would be great for this job, and I think you would love living here."

I told Monroe what had happened to me, and because the Fiberglass project was over, they wanted me to develop a new system for the Pipe Division. I told him that I had met the director from Pipe, and I thought he was the biggest jerk I'd ever met who was that high up in the organization. I said that I hated the thought of having to try to come up with a half-ass system simply because Hank Petrosyan was a Datapoint bigot and didn't know his ass from third base.

"I would need a couple of days to update my resume," I said, "and to come up with a cover letter. I'll fax you a copy then."

Monroe said, "No way. Forget the cover letter. Get your resume updated tonight and fax it to me tomorrow! Bill Rivers has hired an outside consultant to screen candidates and ended up with the best three for him and his right-hand man to interview. There's no time to waste, okay?"

"Yes, I got it. You'll have it first thing tomorrow. Talk to you soon, and thanks, Monroe, for thinking of me for this. Bye."

NDJ Life Lesson:

Once again, I find myself disappointed with my circumstances after having just completed an amazing accomplishment.

The next assignment I was given to work on, the Pipe project, was a no-win situation, and when I discussed it with my manager, I did not get the sense that he would elevate "our" predicament to his boss. I was fairly certain about this because I don't think he viewed Hank as a problem for both of us.

Meanwhile, Steve Bratek, who had done a great job designing the screens—the best I'd ever seen—was in good shape with his future assignments because he actively managed the outcome by discussing options with his boss.

No sour grapes from me. I learned that there was still an awful lot I needed to learn when it came to managing my career.

And finally, what happens next? Will North Denver Johnnie hear the long-ago call from Horace Greeley? Will NDJ believe there is a manifest destiny propelling him to reach higher, accomplish more, and influence people to strive for excellence?

The answer to those questions can be found in Part 2 of my journey.

Thank you for reading my book.

—North Denver Johnnie

Epilogue

As my journey progressed and I applied street-smarts knowledge and logic each day at work in an effort to reach my potential, I realized there was something more that added to my power and ability to advance my career. During my times of reflection and projection, I used a skill set that I acquired when I read a special book. Yes, once again, here I am talking to you about reading books, and for me it was a way of adding new knowledge that would help me create an enormous source of power in my life.

The book I'm referencing here is Richard Bach's *Illusions*. After reading this book, I became aware of something I will call spiritual power. This power is something that everyone can acquire if they want to. On the cover of Bach's book, there is a blue feather. The feather is emblematic of freedom — freedom from our terrestrial reality by virtue of the airplane giving us the ability to fly and freedom to determine our spiritual reality that we may never have realized was even possible.

In Bach's story, there are two biplane pilots, one highly evolved spiritually and the other hoping to find some better answers about his life after this life. After reading the book, I always kept a feather, usually in my jewelry box, to help remind me of my spiritual power. Right now, I have a 3-inch white feather. During my quest to become a poker champion, I looked at my white feather to remind myself of how powerful I could be when I believed I could achieve any goal. In Part 2 of *Journey*, I will describe a goal I established for myself when I was celebrating my seventieth birthday. Shortly thereafter, on September 18, 2016, I won the PPC Fall Classic poker championship.

Now my goal is to become a successful author and to complete Part 2 of *Journey*. With the firsthand knowledge of how difficult it was for me to complete Part 1, I am trying to improve my odds by staying aware of how amazing things can happen when you remember how powerful you are when you tap into your spiritual powers. Now you can understand the reason I have a blue feather on the front cover of my book. And, in keeping with my belief in staying focused and doing all I can to succeed, I went all-in when on August 17, 2017 I got a tattoo on my left forearm, exactly like the picture on the front cover of this book. It is very hard for me to lose sight of my goals and potential now that I have a 6-inch blue feather tattooed on my left arm.

All of this takes me back to Chapter 1 and my life lesson: "Never give up, especially when it's your turn." I believe it is my turn to share my knowledge and experiences with others who, like me, want to strive to reach their potential. And I don't intend on giving up on my efforts to make it happen.

I would be remiss if I didn't explain my reasons for writing this book in the first place. So, I am going to let you in on my motivation to write and publish *Journey, Part 1*.

I learned the hard way that it is essential to manage your career and not rely on just doing the best you can every day with the belief that your boss surely will see how valuable you are to the organization and that he/she will be your advocate when it comes to promotions, salary increases, and performance appraisals. This naïve, simplistic strategy produced the results I deserved, which is to say that none of my superiors ever came through for me. Yes, I did receive "atta-boys" and good reviews, but that was all. And yes, all of this frustrated me a great deal.

Finally, I realized I was only playing defense, not offense. If my career could be thought of as a football team, then you can see the point I'm trying to make here. I played defense by being an overachiever and always trying to exceed management's expectations. Why do I call this approach "defense"? Because, at its core, all I was accomplishing only kept me safe from layoffs, demotions, and getting my salary frozen at the top of whatever level my job description mandated. The funny thing is, all I was doing was improving my chances of not losing my job. And even then, none of my efforts guaranteed anything.

At some point, I realized that I needed to play offense *and* defense. It is essential to do things to market yourself within your organization. You must be able to communicate your accomplishments in a way that is not over the top, not always looking like the person saying, "Look at me, aren't I smart? I know you know how much more I know than the other people". Believe me, there are people that are only about promoting their worth to their managers, even when it is not based in reality. Be that as it may, you do not need to care what others do to promote themselves to management, but you do need to do some level of self-promotion or you will be only playing defense. This is the reason I believe that each and every day you must do the very best job possible, think about your future by investing time and effort to improve your current skill set, and acquire new skills that may prove as a "difference makers" when your name comes up during management meetings involving personnel and promotions.

In doing this, you will become empowered in the sense that you know you have a strategy and the desire to execute your plan. I believe that my book will become the basis for many people to take charge of their careers and eventually enjoy the empowerment that you will surely find.

We all have setbacks, get bad breaks, or even just plain get screwed by an incompetent, insecure boss at some point in each of our journeys. But it is how you handle that setback that defines who you are. For me, my biggest setback came in 1996 when I was diagnosed with multiple sclerosis (MS) and four years later was forced to resign my job for medical reasons. I will end my story by sharing a testimonial I received from my pain management specialist:

To say that North Denver Johnnie embodies what all is ideal in an individual would do him an injustice. Facing, overcoming, and continuing to tame both physical and emotional maladies, NDJ presses the resume/play button of life with both conviction and perseverance. I've had the singular privilege of knowing and walking alongside the genuine individual and have been graced with calling him my friend. They say enduring hardship builds character. NDJ takes the enormous leap from that understatement and restates it by using hardship as the embroidery and has crafted a life that is worthy of copy.
—Rudy Panganiban, M.D., FAAPMR

Lastly, I would like to thank my wife Gayle, who stuck with me through thick and thin, after I was diagnosed with MS in 1996. The unpredictable symptoms that inevitably arrive and affect people that have MS cause a great number of spouses to leave their mate in order to avoid seeing and living with a person suffering from this typically unrelenting disease. I was very fortunate when I entered a clinical trial for people with primary or secondary progressive MS which is the type of MS that I have. Montel Williams, the popular TV personality has the relapsing/remitting type of MS which is the most common form.

Nonetheless, when our total combined income was reduced by 80% following Gayle's company going out of business, and our plan to downsize was so drastic, and the possibility of losing our home was a real, Gayle double-downed in her efforts to help both of us survive this emotional and life changing catastrophe, by doing everything possible to keep our ship from sinking. To that end, this 52-year-old young lady, without the benefit of a college degree, attacked the job market in Tampa where the unemployment rate exceeded the national average, and landed a great job with Raytheon Corporation.

I have often told Gayle that her life story has been very similar to mine coming from a dysfunctional family. It was my good fortune that when she saw me at Johns Manville Corporation, she decided I had potential, and she decided to have someone introduce her to me, and then she decided she wanted to make me happy. The only thing I had to do was to pay attention to what she was doing, and to not for a moment try to understand why she was doing it. Lucky me.

Appendix 1:

North Denver Johnnie's Job Choices and Motives for Leaving Old Job

When I went to work at Samsonite Luggage as a hand fork operator, I knew I wouldn't love the job, but I took it because I knew I needed to make money. I needed to find a way to survive! Then, when I was promoted to punch press operator, I knew I wouldn't love that job, but I took it because I would make a lot more money than my old job.

When I left Samsonite Luggage to become a clerk, I was pretty sure I wouldn't love that job, but I took it because it was so much better than my job at Samsonite Luggage. My job as a punch press operator at Samsonite paid over four dollars per hour while my clerk job at the Public Service Company of Colorado paid $2.24 per hour, but I was sure that the PSCCO job would lead to better long-range job opportunities.

When I accepted the promotion to rear chainman in the Transmission Engineering Department, I knew I wouldn't love my new job, but I would be able to make more money and learn marketable skills for the future.

As I advanced from rear chainman on the survey crew to transit operator, I made more money and learned marketable skills that afforded me the ability to earn a salary that would allow me to enjoy a comfortable, middle-class lifestyle.

When I left the Transmission Engineering Department to become a junior programmer in the Information Systems Department, I believed I would be going into a job that had unlimited possibilities for advancement and that I wouldn't have to deal with the weather and other working conditions that could sometimes be brutal and dangerous.

When I left PSCCO, I loved my job but better loved the idea of learning how to become a system programmer at Information Handling Services, especially since reaching that level at PSCCO wasn't a cinch, even if I didn't mind waiting ten to fifteen years for it to happen. And, if that weren't bleak enough for me to contemplate, there would be no way that I could have been promoted into a management position without a degree.

The reason I left IHS initially was because I was passed over for a promotion. Then, because of my less-than-polished way of trying to find out if I was being considered for the programming manager position, I knew that my boss, Fenton, and his boss, Clem, would more than likely begin a "Replace John" initiative that would lead to my resignation.

I left Johns Manville Corporation because, after leading a monumental effort to produce a new, decentralized system architecture for order entry/inventory applications for the Fiberglass Division, I was given a no-win assignment to do the same for the Pipe Division using Datapoint computers. Besides being sent to Siberia for my efforts on the Fiberglass Project, I had to watch two other people that I had led just months earlier enjoy the fruits of my labor. No fun. I'm out of here!

Cast of Characters

(In order of appearance)

1. Johnnie Dane Santone – He is on his journey to becoming North Denver Johnnie
2. Peter Schavinski – Nice kid, duped by the bullies
3. Elizabeth Zarlingo – Brilliant student
4. Sister Mary Magdalene – Not so nice nun, looking to assert herself
5. Mother – Not so nice person
6. Father Lemieux, the monsignor – Not nice, shot burglar breaking into rectory
7. Tommy – My cousin, the son of my mother's youngest sister
8. John Marvin – Starting center on the basketball team at North High School
9. Frankie Valli- Starting singer of the Four Seasons
10. Don Wagner – My first fight victory at North High
11. Connie Thomas – Don Wagner's girlfriend before fight
12. Frank Garcio – Fifth or sixth toughest Pack Rat
13. Jimmy Spinelli – One of my best friends at North High
14. Don Evans, Dean of Boys – Very tough but fair man
15. Cheryl Piccoli – Second prettiest girl at North High and one of the nicest
16. Glenda Crumbaker – The prettiest girl at North High (a Doris Day look-alike)

17. James Dean – Cameo comment and reference to his car in *Rebel Without a Cause*
18. Forrest Fischer – Owner of Fischer's Billiards
19. Mrs. Fisher – Owner of Forrest Fischer
20. Harry Marks – Nighttime proprietor at Fischer's Billiards
21. Virgil Abernathy – Postal worker, champion snooker player, mentor to NDJ
22. Danny Polidori – Best friend, third best-looking guy at North, stand-up guy, never let you down
23. Mr. Polidori – Danny's father, very strict, saw only black or white, really good dad
24. Alice Garza – Eighth grade classmate
25. Carol Galasso – Eighth grade classmate
26. Karen Botero – Eighth grade classmate that I kind of liked (What's before first base?)
27. Piorina Ritola – Eighth grade classmate and as pretty as her name
28. Tony Yackavetta – Eight grade classmate, cool guy but never stood up for classmates against bullies
29. Johnny DeSalvo – Eighth grade classmate, "Mr. Brylcreem" (must have bought it by the case)
30. Joe Vichorelli – Eighth grade mate, his cousin picked me up when it snowed
31. Johnny Pollice – Eighth grade mate, his doctor dad gave him hormone shots so he grew taller than me
32. Larry Griffith – Eighth grade classmate and number-one bully
33. Pope – Popes are Italian; we played the pope card when others played the Mafia card
34. Frank Sinatra – Cameo comment
35. Dean Martin – Cameo comment
36. Eugene Smaldone – Joe Vichorelli's cousin
37. Checkers Smaldone – Joe Vichorelli's uncle
38. Clyde Smaldone – Joe Vichorelli's uncle
39. Joe Fazaro – Leader of the Pack Rats

40. Michael DeBaca – Second-best looking guy at North, all around really great guy
41. Johnny Romola – Best-looking guy at North (just ask Mrs. Romola)
42. Brad Pitt – A guy that most guys who believe in reincarnation want to be
43. Napoleon – We had something in common, the "short" thing
44. Jerry Gennadus – '63 midnight-blue, split-window coupe, fuel-injected corvette
45. Rich Ido – '62 gold with black landau top 426 Ford Victoria
46. Richie Falconi – '62 Chevrolet SS 409, white with red interior
47. Becky Wright – First real girlfriend, the cutest girl in the whole wide world
48. Jesse Montoya – Head of La Raza, Mexican gang
49. Robert Vigil a.k.a. Doberman – Second toughest Pack Rat
50. Freddie Villanueva – Classmate at North High School
51. Izadore – Pool player/aficionado
52. Johnny Archer – Co-owner of Family Fun Center, flashy, huge diamond ring
53. Tony Archer – Co-owner of Family Fun Center, regular guy, did the cooking
54. Cheryl Watson – Katharine Hepburn of North High
55. Julie – Daughter of pharmacist
56. Bob Casagrande – Varsity team wrestler at North High
57. Mr. Moles – Wrestling coach, first name Bob, had moles (good fit)
58. Dean Naismith – Junior varsity team member
59. Ronnie Lopez – Varsity team wrestler at North High (fictitious name)
60. Mike Miller – Classmate at North High
61. John Marseco – Friend of Danny Polidori, only guy I ever met without tear ducts
62. Gene Autry – Childhood hero, still have his lunch box with cowboy code on it
63. Jenny – Horseback rider who loves to hear herself talk

64. Russell Maxwell – Seaman recruit, one of the heaviest members of the U.S. Navy
65. Faye – Sweet girl, parents wouldn't let me date her because I wasn't Jewish
66. Uncle Tommy – My mother's oldest brother
67. Jesse Mason – Trained NDJ to be hand truck operator at Samsonite
68. Manuel Rodriguez – Shop foreman at Samsonite Luggage Foundry
69. John LaMotte – Best punch press operator in foundry
70. Wolfgang – Polish painter, worked with my dad
71. Barbara Busch – Friend and confidant who helped me get out of the foundry
72. Willis Bashore – Office manager at the Holly Service Center of PSCCO
73. Merlin Olsen – Assistant office manager at the Holly Service Center of PSCCO
74. Sid Barcelon – NDJ mentor, gave Johnnie his nickname, NDJ gave Sid his nickname "Colorado Sid"
75. Jimmy "Pic" Piccoli – Big-time bookie, pinkie ring with diamond the size of a dime
76. Ken Griffey – Clerk at Holly Service Center of PSCCO, great family man
77. Fred Eastom – Mechanical Engineer, boss of Cabin Creek Hydroelectric Plant
78. Uncle Nick – My dad's oldest brother
79. Uncle Tony – My dad's youngest brother and my favorite uncle by far
80. Aunt Sophie – Uncle Tony's wife, nice woman, always wore too much lipstick
81. Nicki Berry Santone – Uncle Nick's adopted son, first gay person I ever met
82. Sylvia Santone – Uncle Nick's adopted daughter, first lesbian I ever met
83. Dean Miller – Director of Transmission Engineering (PSCCO)

84. Bobby Green – Member of Transmission Engineering Department (TEG)
85. Larry Weave – Member of TEG, one of the smartest, nicest people I know
86. Arnold Schwarzenegger – Cameo comment
87. Neil Terry – Member of TEG and one of the smartest, nicest people I know
88. Ron Hall – Datapoint salesman and Fortran programming instructor
89. Fred Sommers – Good friend, very smart programmer at PSCCO
90. Dwayne Gilbert – Fred Sommers' boss
91. Jonas Markham – University of Colorado in-house instructor (fictitious name)
92. Fred Medrano – PSCCO in-house programmer, training class student
93. Jim "Peaches" Peachinelli – Senior system programming engineer
94. Marko Mistoffi – Senior system programmer (fictitious name)
95. Jeannie Sommers – Fred Sommers' wife
96. Ralph Opgonorth – Manager of Programming at Information Handling Services (IHS)
97. Fenton Miller – Operations Manager (IHS)
98. Clem Gibson – Chief Operating Officer (IHS)
99. Jimmy Romero – My disco buddy, cool guy making the most of his assets
100. Sonny and Cher – Cameo comment
101. Jerry Lewis – Cameo comment
102. Bob Richards – Recruited from PSCCO by Fred Sommers to IHS
103. Tom Waters – CEO at IHS, an exceptional, forward-thinking executive
104. Chuck Wilhoite – IBM System Engineer (fictitious name)
105. Dave Hightower – Computer Operations Scheduler (IHS)
106. Donna White – Computer Operator (IHS)
107. Cherrie Martin - Computer Operator at (IHS)
108. Jay Manning – Dale Carnegie Instructor (fictitious name)

109. Margret Shepard – Dale Carnegie Graduate Assistant (fictitious name)
110. Gilbert Samson – Owner of GS Enterprises that provided staff to Johns Manville Corporation (JM)
111. Jack Reager – Exceptional senior technician (JM)
112. Ted Minor – Technical resource (JM) (fictitious name)
113. Stephanie Sanders – Administrative Assistant (JM) (fictitious name)
114. Ron Walsh – First-Level Manager (JM)
115. John Eck – Application Support Analysts Team Leader (JM)
116. Bob Shoup – Team Leader for order entry/inventory systems
117. Becky Shepard – Administrative Assistant (fictitious name)
118. Suzie Hernandez – Administrative Assistant (fictitious name)
119. Cisco Kid – Cameo comment
120. Stan Ackerman – Senior Programmer (JM)
121. Donna McCann – Programmer (JM)
122. Fleetwood Mac – Cameo comment
123. Stevie Nicks – Sexist girl I didn't know
124. Jill Tisdale – Senior Programmer on 8100 development project
125. Ellen Faverty – Programmer on 8100 development project
126. Beth Gresh – Programmer on 8100 development project
127. Ken Jurak – Senior Programmer on 8100 development project
128. Jan Donovan – IBM System Engineer assigned to Fiberglass Project
129. Bud Anderson – IBM Senior Developer on 8100 development project
130. Larry Wheeler – IBM programmer 8100 team (fictitious name)
131. Greg Pruitt – Team Leader Systems Group (JM) (fictitious name)
132. Steve Bratek – Good-looking, New Jersey's version of Bruce Jenner
133. Mike Sieden – Director, Fiberglass Division, competent, hard charger
134. Ray Southard – Director, ISD Applications Development, read ceiling tiles

135. John Matosek – Vice President, ISD, a really nice man, good leader
136. Hank Petrosyan – Director, Pipe Division (fictitious name)
137. Monroe Hyatt – Former JM employee, relocated to Nevada
138. Judy Hyatt – Monroe's wife
139. Allen Glick – Owner of Stardust & Fremont in 1979, progressive manager
140. Bill Rivers – CFO at Argent Corporation (parent company of Stardust & Fremont)

Acknowledgements

I would like to thank the following people who provided me with unwavering support and encouragement throughout my efforts to write *Journey of North Denver Johnnie:* Gayle Santone, Dr. Rudy Pandanigan, Tom Ackerman, Jill Tisdale Deem, Jan Donovan, Dr. Walt Brewer, and Dr. Joseph Lanese.

I would also like to acknowledge David Sinai, Janice Wendt, and Christal Johnson at Picsera, who are responsible for image enhancement and initial book cover design.

Lastly, I want to acknowledge Halo Publishing for providing me with a dream team of talented and dedicated professionals that have made my dream come true, including Lisa Umina, Jodie Greenberg, Molly Nero, and Summer Abate.

About the Author

My friends that know me well know that I am North Denver Johnnie 24/7 and that I don't don my NDJ cape only in times of crisis.

As I began to achieve a level of success as a computer programmer, my fellow employees' impressions of me went from "different" to "eccentric." Believe me when I say that eccentric is much better.

In 1987, as the operations manager for a computer consulting company, it was only when I developed strong relationships with the staff and management that I cautiously allowed North Denver Johnnie to show up on the scene. To generate more revenue, the company sought out aggressive managers with the ability to see business opportunities. In this climate, North Denver Johnnie was at his best, and stepping forward with his credentials as a street-smart guy that loves to win was the right move for the right reasons.

From then on, North Denver Johnnie was a prominent aspect of my identity. At the same time, I would never talk about how I utilized my street smarts to reach decisions or navigate aspects of my professional life. When employees see the branch manager as a winner with strong technical skills who is willing to provide support for his staff to facilitate their success, then you have a branch office with limitless potential to support the corporation, the customers, and the employees.

In 1988, I was promoted to branch manager and relocated to Orlando to take over a branch acquired through one of our competitors. At my going-away party, the branch manager wrote me a poem, framed it, and gave it to me. The poem read:

Ode to North Denver Johnnie
From out of the West, "Go East!" they were told,
To America's Heartland for fortune and gold.
Hustling suckers at pool and golf without shame,
North Denver Johnnie—the man and his dame.
Alas, but the Heartland proved a little too tough;
In a few short years, they'd had more than enough.
Packing club & cue, table & tee,
They fled south to join forces with Minnie & Mickey.
Oh, North Denver Johnnie, we all hate to lose ya,
For two short years how we loved to abuse ya.
But if leave you must, then leave you shall;
We'll not soon forget you, not you or your gal.

John wants to convey his appreciation to all of the people that helped him during his career, and he wants his former employees to know that being their manager was one of the best experiences of his life.

CPSIA information can be obtained
at www.ICGtesting.com
Printed in the USA
BVOW09s0918271017
498801BV00004B/4/P